This book is due for return on or before the last date shown below.

The New Economics of
Sovereign Wealth Funds

The New Economics of Sovereign Wealth Funds

Massimiliano Castelli
Fabio Scacciavillani

A John Wiley and Sons, Ltd, Publication

This edition first published in 2012 by John Wiley & Sons Ltd
Copyright © 2012 Massimiliano Castelli and Fabio Scacciavillani

Registered office
John Wiley & Sons Ltd, The Atrium, Southern Gate, Chichester, West Sussex, PO19 8SQ, United Kingdom

For details of our global editorial offices, for customer services and for information about how to apply for permission to reuse the copyright material in this book please see our website at www. wiley.com.

Library of Congress Cataloging-in-Publication Data

Castelli, Massimiliano.
 The new economics of sovereign wealth funds / Massimiliano Castelli, Fabio Scacciavillani.
   p. cm.
 Includes bibliographical references and index.
 ISBN 978-1-119-97192-4 (cloth)
1. Sovereign wealth funds. I. Scacciavillani, Fabio. II. Title.
 HJ3801.C37 2012
 332.67'252—dc23

                                                                                    2012004085

A catalogue record for this book is available from the British Library.

ISBN 978-1-119-97192-4 (hardback)   ISBN 978-1-119-97344-7 (ebk)
ISBN 978-1-119-97345-4 (ebk)   ISBN 978-1-119-97346-1 (ebk)

Cover images reproduced by permission of Shutterstock.com
Typeset in 10/12pt Times by Sparks – www.sparkspublishing.com
Printed in Great Britain by TJ International Ltd, Padstow, Cornwall

I would like to dedicate this book to my wife Britta, my source of inspiration in life, and to my daughter Vivien who came to life while writing this book.
Massimiliano Castelli

This book is dedicated to the memory of my father Francesco, the birth of my daughter Vera and the eternal cycle of renewal they epitomize.
Fabio Scacciavillani

Contents

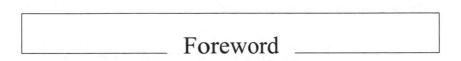

Foreword

This book on Sovereign Wealth Funds (SWFs) is both timely and provocative. It comes at a time when the role and nature of SWFs are developing rapidly. It captures a great deal of the history of that development and makes a number of pertinent observations about SWFs' future.

The book places the development of SWFs in both an economic and political context. In many ways, their development has mirrored the shifting balance in world economic power as China and other countries have emerged as major players.

The authors also address the very fundamental and ongoing questions about how the wealth being built up in SWFs should be used. Central to that consideration is the question of inter-temporal allocation of resources. This issue is not peculiar to SWFs but is one that confronts all governments as a crucial consideration in their decisions on the scope, nature and timing of infrastructure development.

The international political issues relating to SWFs are also discussed. In many ways, these are akin to the issues surrounding direct foreign investment policies in the 1960s, 1970s and 1980s. Then the debate centred on national sovereignty. Today the issues are more pointed, with SWFs being seen by some as foreign government bodies with ownership stakes in other countries' critical institutions.

From my own experience, both in the asset management industry and as the chairman of a public investment corporation, SWFs have played an important role in two other respects.

First, they have clearly put pressure on the industry to perform better by being part of the increasing sophistication of the industry's client base. This has often been reflected in the development by SWFs of in-house capabilities that compete directly with those provided by the industry. This has meant that providers of asset management services have often been keenly tested to deliver more.

Second, they have – and rightly so – placed pressure on fees. Not only in terms of the overall level of fees, but also in pushing the industry to be more aware of the role of performance fees.

The authors of this book have considerable experience from working in the public sector and in the asset management industry. They are to be commended for their energy in bringing a great deal of information together in a highly readable form. And they are also to be commended for having the courage to make some broader observations in an often provocative way.

John A. Fraser
Chairman and CEO, UBS Global Asset Management;
Chairman of the Victorian Funds Management Corporation, Australia

List of Tables and Figures

TABLES

FIGURES

List of Abbreviations

ADIA	Abu Dhabi Investment Authority
ADIC	Abu Dhabi Investment Corporation
AUM	Assets Under Management
BoP	Balance of Payments
BP	British Petroleum
BPM6	Balance of Payments Manual 6
CalPERS	California Public Employees Retirement System
CFIUS	Committee on Foreign Investment in the United States
CIC	China Investment Corporation
COFER	Currency Composition of Foreign Exchange Reserves
CPIS	Coordinated Portfolio Investment Survey
ECB	European Central Bank
FSA	UK Financial Services Authority
FWF	Future Wealth Fund
FX	Foreign Exchange
GCC	Gulf Cooperation Council (comprising Bahrain, Kuwait, Oman, Qatar, Saudi Arabia and UAE)
GDP	Gross Domestic Product
GFSR	Global Financial Stability Report
GIC	Singapore's Government Investment Corporation
GIMF5	Global Integrated Monetary Fiscal Model
GPFG	Norway's Government Pension Fund-Global
HFSB	Hedge Fund Standards Board
HKMA	Hong Kong Monetary Authority
IFSWF	International Forum of Sovereign Wealth Funds
IIP	International Investment Position
IMF	International Monetary Fund
IOSCO	International Organization of Securities Commissions
IWG	International Working Group of Sovereign Wealth Funds
KIA	Kuwait Investment Authority

KIC	Korea Investment Corporation
KSA	Kingdom of Saudi Arabia
LTCM	Long Term Capital Management
NBER	National Bureau of Economic Research (United States)
NYSE	New York Stock Exchange
OECD	Organization for Economic Cooperation and Development
PIH	Permanent Income Hypothesis
PIMCO	Pacific Investment Management Company
PWG	President's Working Group on Financial Markets
QIA	Qatar Investment Authority
RMB	Chinese Reminbi (or yuan)
SAA	Strategic Asset Allocation
SABIC	Saudi Arabian Basic Industry Corporation
SAMA	Saudi Arabian Monetary Authority
SWF	Sovereign Wealth Fund
SWFI	Sovereign Wealth Fund Institute
UAE	United Arab Emirates
UCITS	Undertakings for the Collective Investment of Transferable Securities
WEO	World Economic Outlook, a semi-annual publication of the International Monetary Fund
WTO	World Trade Organization

Acknowledgements

Fabio Scacciavillani wishes to thank Dr Nasser Saidi who has been deeply influential in shaping many of the ideas contained in this book and his former colleagues at the Dubai International Financial Center, Aathira Prasad and Fahad Ali' with whom he worked extensively on research focusing on the shift of the world's economic barycenter.

The authors would like to thank Simone Tagliapietra, currently a researcher at the Fondazione ENI Enrico Mattei for his research support in the preparation of the forecasts on the 2016 size of Sovereign Wealth Funds included in the Appendix to Chapter 2.

Introduction

Sovereign Wealth Funds (SWFs) have become one of the most closely scrutinized phenomena in financial markets over the past few years. Despite (or, some would say, due to) their tendency to maintain a low profile and discretion in their activities, they have been the object of political fears, virulent controversy, media indignation and public scourge. Nevertheless, they have been discreetly courted by capital-starved corporates and banks, governments seeking funding and finance professionals eager to manage their assets.

This ambivalent attitude has pervaded the policy debate and the public's attitude since the middle of the last decade when SWFs made waves in the exclusive world of international high finance.

The SWF phenomenon can be analysed at various degrees of granularity. Most books devoted to SWFs have focused on the undue influence they might exert through the acquisition of 'strategic' assets and on the political backlash that has resulted (for example, Quadrio Curzio and Miceli, 2010; Subacchi, 2008; Park, 2011). Others have analysed the implications for the balance of economic power, the links to financial protectionism, the threats to national security, the impact on financial markets. Lately an extensive literature has been devoted to the framework proposed by the international community to regulate their activity (among others, Das *et al.*, 2010; IMF, 2007; Park, 2011; Truman, 2010).

This book will focus on the big picture which has been lost in the noise of diatribes and the narrow visions of most analyses. Few seem to have realized that the rise of the SWF is driven by a tectonic movement: **the shift of economic centre of gravity from mature economies to large emerging markets (especially in Asia), and to commodity-exporting countries**, some of which (e.g. Australia, Canada, Norway) have been wealthy nations for a long time. The increasing prominence of SWFs is therefore a symptom of a rebalancing in economic weight and represents one of the channels through which the **secular shift to a multipolar global economy** is taking place.

Furthermore, given the current macro trends, the assets under management (AUM) by SWFs are destined to increase substantially (see the Appendix to Chapter 2). As China turns into the dominant economy on the planet (exerting a pull on other large Asian countries), its growing middle class will propel global growth and a super-cycle in commodities – i.e. a long period in which natural resources will be in high demand – is taking root.

In explaining these dynamics and their repercussions this book will follow three intertwined lines of analysis:

1   the shift in economic centre of gravity towards the East and the macro-economics of current account surplus management;
2   the choice of investment strategies and the fiscal policy options available to countries that run a structural current account surplus, thereby accumulating a considerable stock of foreign assets;
3   the political ramifications of acquisitions by state-owned entities of a controlling stake in large privately owned companies, the corporate governance issues they raise and the risk management tools they need to adopt.

Stated differently, instead of debating whether SWFs have gained too much power and whether measures to regulate their activities are warranted, we try to analyse the role of SWFs through the prism of the macroeconomic forces that are redefining consolidated global equilibria. Once these macro elements have been brought to the fore and put into context, it will be easier to lift the debate above the fray of politics, separating the specious arguments from the legitimate worries.

A FEW STYLIZED FACTS

SWFs are hardly a novel feature of global capital markets. The first SWFs managing sizeable resources were established during the oil price boom of the early 1970s[1] when Middle Eastern oil exporters, following the example of Kuwait,[2] started diversifying their current account surpluses purchasing

---

[1] The first example of a SWF was an investment vehicle created in 1956 in the Gilbert Islands to manage the proceeds from export of phosphates. For those with an inclination for details, we should point out that the Gilbert Islands at the time was a British colony, so the fund might not be dubbed as 'sovereign'. Nowadays, it is worth about half a billion dollars and in the meantime the Gilbert Islands had become a sovereign state, Kiribati. There is an even older example of a state-owned investment vehicle, the California Public Employees Retirement System, better known as CalPERS. CalPERS differs from the typical SWF because it is funded by the pension contributions paid by civil servants, not by revenues or reserves accumulated by the government.

[2] Kuwait in 1960 launched the General Reserve, followed in 1973 by the Future Generations Fund, endowed with 50% of the General Reserve and also 10% of the yearly budget surplus. In 1982, the Kuwaiti government decided to consolidate all the assets of the Ministry of Finance,

assets worldwide. During the 1980s and 1990s SWFs continued allocating their wealth mostly in advanced economies without attracting much attention, except for relatively small groups of professionals specialized in catering to their needs. They were characterized by a conservative investment style and minimal involvement in the management of companies where they held a stake.

Only occasionally had some deals attracted media attention due to the sheer size of the operation, for example the investment by Kuwait Investment Authority (KIA) in the German car maker Daimler in 1972 or by the Libyan Arab Foreign Investment Company (Lafico) in FIAT, the largest Italian automotive company, in 1976. The reaction of the public and politicians at the time did not go much beyond surprise and vague concerns about foreign influence, but the acquisitions were hardly a *casus belli*. Actually, at least for the FIAT–Lafico deal, Italian public opinion was generally in favour, given the need of FIAT for fresh capital after disastrous losses. High profile acquisitions remained rare. Probably the only exception took place in the early 1980s when the British government led by Margaret Thatcher reacted very strongly to the acquisition of a 20% share in the newly privatized British Petroleum by KIA. The motivation in that case was not completely gilded: in Europe at the time 'privatization' to most politicians and pundits was a bad word. It evoked all possible evils and spurred heated rhetoric. Just across the Channel the newly elected French President Mitterrand in that year enacted a massive wave of nationalization in all major sectors, including banks, technology and defence. If a landmark sale of a state-owned company had resulted in the transfer of a controlling stake to a foreign government, the privatization process would have been ridiculed. KIA was therefore pressured by the British government to halve its stake to less than 10%.

The picture has changed profoundly. After decades below the financial radar, the golden age of SWFs started at the turn of the millennium, with more than 20 funds created since 1998. The public has come to associate SWFs with China and the Arabian Gulf countries, a perception justified by the sheer size of entities such as the Abu Dhabi Investment Authority (ADIA) and the China Investment Corporation (CIC). In reality a number of other countries – e.g. South Korea, Singapore, Australia, Iran, Russia, Canada (the province of Alberta), Libya, Chile and even some US states (Alabama, Alaska, New Mexico and Wyoming) – have set up investment vehicles managing large resources.[3] The trend has been spreading to smaller countries endowed with natural resources, e.g. Botswana, Trinidad and Tobago, Papua New Guinea,

---

as well as the General Reserve and the Future Generations Fund, under the Kuwait Investment Authority. The Abu Dhabi Investment Authority (ADIA) and the Singaporean fund Temasek Holdings were both set up in the 1970s.

[3] The list is not exhaustive, as some countries do not fully disclose the assets managed by their investment vehicles.

Mauritania and East Timor whose funds are tiny if one considers their absolute size, but substantial relative to the GDP of those countries. More than 30 nations currently have an institution that can be categorized as a SWF. The majority is not even remotely linked to oil producing countries, as in the case of Singapore, South Korea, China, Ireland, Australia, Chile and Taiwan. In other words the emergence of SWFs is a global phenomenon not distinctive of a particular part of the world or of a specific group of countries.

According to the figures compiled by the SWF Institute and Prequin, the value of combined global assets held by SWFs – due to the strong expansion by commodity-backed SWFs – is estimated to have reached nearly US$5 trillion in December 2011 (see the Appendix to Chapter 2), US$1 trillion above the US$3.75 trillion recorded in September 2008 at the inception of the financial crisis. By comparison in December 2007 the total assets under management stood at US$3.2 trillion.

The balance of investing power has shifted from the Middle East to Asia: the Middle Eastern SWFs account for 40% of total assets.[4]

SWFs UNDER THE SPOTLIGHT

Although SWFs have been in existence for decades they have acquired a higher profile over the last five or six years for two main reasons: a spate of high-profile acquisitions which threw them under the limelight of international media and a relentless surge in their AUM. The latter factor – on which we will focus extensively in this book – stemmed from two interrelated developments:

1   a worldwide surge in raw materials and commodity prices (not only hydrocarbons), which has all the characteristics of a long-term cycle (some dub it a super-cycle);
2   the rise of emerging markets (in particular India and China) where the demographic wave, thanks to capital inflows, is no longer feeding a vicious circle of underdevelopment, but is propelling growth and an expansion of the middle class.

The acceleration of investment activity by SWFs has been staggering. A report by Monitor Group reviews more than 1100 publicly reported transactions by SWFs between 1975 and March 2008 for a combined value of US$250 billion, a mere subset of all the transactions by SWFs. In 2000 the SWFs included in the sample were involved in publicly reported operations totalling US$3 billion. In 2007 the analogous figure was US$92 billion. In the first quarter of 2008, before the acute phase of the financial crisis, the

---

[4] As a comparison the US$1.6 trillion attributed to the largest MENA funds is just over half the foreign official assets of China (over US$3.0 trillion).

operations had reached US$58 billion, exceeding the US$50 billion recorded in the whole period 2000–2005 (Monitor Group, 2008).

It is only natural that such a phenomenon would attract media coverage and, as a consequence, enter the political agenda. The hype and, in some cases, the hysteria, found fertile ground among the American public in the aftermath of 9/11. The concerns which the terrorist attacks fostered extended to immigration policy, technology transfers, trade agreements and inevitably impacted inward foreign investments.

Ironically, the first politically charged events which drew attention to SWFs, were related to government-owned companies, not SWFs. In late 2004 China National Offshore Oil Corp (CNOOC Ltd), a Chinese state enterprise[5] tried to acquire Unocal Corp., an oil company, for US$18.4 billion. US lawmakers argued that 'economic and national security interests' would be jeopardized if a company controlled by China's government were to buy a major US oil company holder of sensitive drilling technologies.

This political obstruction meant that CNOOC's bid would be subject to a rigorous – and obviously contentious – review, delaying the acquisition by at least two or three quarters. After that process hardly any assurance of successful completion could be envisaged. In February 2005 CNOOC withdrew the offer, issuing a blunt statement which stressed that had it not been for the political backlash, the management was ready to increase the offer. Eventually Unocal was acquired by Chevron that had made a competing, but arguably less attractive, bid.

A few months later, in winter 2005–2006, Dubai Port World, a company owned by the Government of Dubai, launched a bid for P&O, a British company which ran the ports of New York and Long Beach, key access points for merchandise into the US.[6] Opposition focused primarily on the supposedly negative consequences of having a foreign entity managing security in sensitive areas of access to US territory. The fact that P&O was British, and therefore a foreign company, did not seem to deter critics. Even the *New York Times* in an editorial[7] on the P&O deal, asserted that 'it is not irrational for the United States to resist putting port operators, perhaps the most vulnerable part of the security infrastructure, under [the] control [of an ally whose] record in the war on terror is mixed'. When the (US Treasury) Committee on Foreign Investment in the United States (CFIUS) approved the deal in February 2006 after a standard 30-day review, DP World agreed to an additional 45-day security review.

---

[5] CNOOC Ltd, based in Hong Kong, is part of the China National Offshore Oil Corporation, owned at 70% by China's government – an arrangement that helped secure favourable financing terms unavailable to Chevron.

[6] DP World is not even a SWF, but a state-owned company that runs a number of port facilities all over the world and has a reputation as one of the most efficient operators.

[7] The President and the Port, *New York Times*, 22 February 2006.

The fact that an Arab company was acquiring key logistic infrastructure in the US undoubtedly hit a raw nerve. No matter that the UAE government had close diplomatic ties and had been a staunch ally of the West for decades. Even a reputable paper like the *New York Times* seemed to miss the simple truth: in the United States, as everywhere else in the world, responsibility for security arrangements is assigned to law-enforcement and intelligence agencies, not to port facilities operators. In March, following a 62-to-2 vote in Congress forbidding the acquisition, DP World was forced to spin off the American assets of P&O.

Suspicion towards SWFs was exacerbated by the fact that other countries perceived as hostile to Western interests such as Russia, Venezuela, Libya and Iran, were also running SWFs. The emergence of China as an industrial powerhouse and therefore perceived in some countries as a threat to local industries added to concerns.

People in the US, who for their academic role, public service record and intellectual reputation would be expected to have a balanced view, expressed the same uncompromising views: 'The logic of the capitalist system depends on shareholders causing companies to act so as to maximize the value of their shares. It is far from obvious that this will over time be the only motivation of governments as shareholders. They may want to see their national companies compete effectively, or to extract technology or to achieve influence'.[8]

Let us pause for a moment on this remark because, coming from a former Secretary of Treasury and later a prominent figure in the Obama Administration, Mr Summers' point is that public institutions might have ulterior motives or pursue stealth agendas in their investment strategies. If this had been a genuine worry, during his tenure at the Treasury, Mr Summers could have raised this issue in regard to CalPERS or the Alaska Fund, or even Freddie Mac or Fannie Mae, which had indeed come under attack in Congress on several occasions.

In a similar vein, Hillary Clinton, who at the time was universally expected to win the Democratic nomination, was adamant: 'We need to have a lot more control over what they [SWFs] do and how they do it.' Once appointed Secretary of State, Ms Clinton has not taken any action or expressed similar qualms on SWFs.

Even the French President, Nicolas Sarkozy, vowed in 2007 to protect 'innocent' French managers from the 'extremely aggressive' SWFs (none of which had indicated any intention to invest in France). German senior government officials argued that SWF might be 'mischievous', which presumably meant that they could perturb the cosy relationships between trade unions, bureaucrats, banks and management which pervade the Deutschland GmBh.

---

[8] Larry Summers, quoted in the *Evening Standard* (London), page 27, 21 September 2007.

However this kind of view was not limited to developed economies. In 2006 Temasek caused issues in Thailand when it acquired the telecoms company owned by the then prime minister, Thaksin Shinawatra. In reality, Thai public opinion was against Mr Thaksin's use of a loophole to avoid paying tax on the US$2 billion his family raised in the sale. Although Temasek had nothing to do with it, it became guilty by association, and one of the arguments used against the operation was the fact that Temasek is a SWF. It also stirred opposition in Indonesia, over stakes bought in two telecoms companies through firms majority-owned by Temasek.

In short, instead of focusing on a thoughtful analysis of the role these new players could assume in financial markets, the opportunities they might create, the risks they might entail and the contribution to the solution of the global crisis they might make, the debate had often been deflected towards supposedly hidden agendas, influence peddling by foreign governments and even 'terrorism risk'.

The reactions to investments by SWFs, however, underwent a sharp U-turn as the economic barometer pointed decisively towards stormy conditions. As *The Economist* noted drily, 'There is a wise old proverb about beggars and choosers'.[9] When it became clear that the Western financial system was on the verge of a crisis (even though the extent of the meltdown was not yet even remotely envisaged) the attitude changed drastically. The emissaries of the same governments that were criticizing the acquisitions by SWFs, warning of obscure influences by foreign governments, started a courting game. US Treasury Secretary at the time, Hank Paulson, instigated the activism of the IMF on the Santiago Principles. As the cracks in the US banking system widened he travelled to Abu Dhabi in 2007 to solicit Arab SWFs to invest in US banks.

By the end of 2008 the aversion to SWFs had all but evaporated in the countries battered by the financial meltdown and the negative attitude to the support of foreign governments (not only from SWFs) had all but receded (for an overview see Enrich *et al.*, 2008).

In 2011 announcements by Chinese government officials to buy public debt from Greece or Portugal were positively received in recipient countries and marked by rebounds in bond markets. It did not spark outrage that the announcements came from a Prime Minister, whose motivations, almost by definition, would be eminently political. This sudden reversion to *pecunia non olet* attitude is compelling evidence that the rhetoric against lack of transparency constituted a sort of fig leaf covering economic nationalism.

Above all, none of the public figures who on both sides of the Atlantic expressed outrage at public entities interfering in private markets found anything to object to when the US and UK governments bailed out the entire

---

[9] *The Economist*, 17 January 2008.

financial system and a large chunk of the insurance sector, while the US Federal Reserve became the largest holders of US government bonds and the European Central Bank became the only purchaser of sovereign debt of distressed Euroland countries.

While the animosity towards SWFs subsided in government circles, a degree remained alive even during the acute phase. In March 2009, the US Treasury launched the Public–Private Investment Program (PPIP) to acquire residential and commercial mortgage-backed securities from financial institutions struggling to raise capital. Under this scheme the US Treasury matched the funds from any investors, then credited six times as much capital. So for each dollar of fresh capital, the US government put up another dollar, and then the PPIP allowed the purchase of US$24 billion of distressed assets in the open market. Additionally the Federal Deposit Insurance Corporation would guarantee the debt being issued by the PPIP. This scheme was open to any domestic or foreign investor. Nobody seemed much concerned over the generous terms until the CIC expressed an interest in participating in the scheme. The reaction? 'Taxpayer dollars are subsidizing Chinese purchases of U.S. assets at a discount. This is insanity', wrote Barry Ritholtz in The Big Picture, a prominent finance blog in the US. One can debate whether the PPIP is a sound subsidy scheme, but the argument should not be influenced by the nationality of the participants.

Furthermore not all countries are in need and therefore the reflex against 'foreigners' occasionally resurfaces. On 11 February 2011, Ontario Finance Minister Dwight Duncan voiced his concerns at the prospect of Sheikh Mohammed bin Rashid Al Maktoum, Ruler of Dubai, increasing its minority stake in the company resulting from the merger of the London and Toronto Stock Exchanges.

The merger created the world's biggest trading platform that would dominate the raw materials and energy sectors, spanning 20 trading markets and platforms across Europe and North America. Furthermore it would also comprise the world's largest exchange in terms of the number of companies traded, with a total of more than 6700 listings.

Mr Duncan raised the fear that Dubai International Capital (not exactly a SWF, but a vehicle managing the personal wealth of the Dubai Ruler), with a 11.3% stake in the combined entity, would become the largest single shareholder, taking control of a 'strategic asset'. Mr Duncan was reported saying that: 'We do business with the Middle East, I am just not sure I want them owning our stock exchange'. To justify his position he called the Toronto Stock Exchange 'a strategic asset in a strategic industry'.

In his statements, however, Mr Duncan made a pertinent observation: 'If you went to try to buy the Dubai stock exchange, do you think you'd be able to? If you tried to buy a resource-based industry in China do you think you'd be able to?' In other words he highlighted the reciprocity principle which should underpin international financial relationships and which is often side-lined in the policy debate.

DEFINING SWFs

Despite the concerns, and contrary to common conviction, SWFs are not a homogeneous group and they differ in objectives, investment style, openness, accountability and strategy. Often the lists of SWFs published in the media include a mixed bag of institutions encompassing central banks, pension funds, domestic development funds and private wealth funds. In this book we will concentrate primarily on publicly owned investment vehicles with a mandate to transfer wealth to future generations by investing in an international portfolio of securities and assets, including companies. With this distinction in mind we are inclined to use a more specific definition, which would put paid to most misconceptions: instead of using the generic SWFs when we wish to emphasize the intergenerational transfer function we will refer to Future Wealth Funds (FWFs). We exclude from this category those investment vehicles that are primarily geared towards domestic development such as Sagia in Saudi Arabia and State Owned Enterprises (SOEs) such as Gazprom in Russia, Sabic in Saudi Arabia, CNOOC in China, Qatar Telecom International and obviously all the national oil companies such as Petrobras, Aramco, Total, Oman Oil, ENI or PEMEX. We will also exclude pension funds controlled by governments such as CalpERS as their function is primarily that of providing retirement income to their members.

Another source of ambiguity and misunderstanding comes from the fact that in addition to SWFs, which operate under a broad mandate, some countries have launched other public entities which belong to the loosely defined category of SOEs managing activities and investments in specific sectors. For example, in Qatar, Barwa and Qatar Diar operate in real estate domestically and worldwide. Dubai Port World focuses on transport facilities and logistics. The distinction between the SWFs and SOEs is clear, but this does not exclude the possibility that they might operate jointly. A recent example highlights this development: Qatar Telecom (Qtel) formed a joint venture with the Qatar Investment Authority, which in turn owns a 55% stake in Qtel, according to Reuters data. Qtel's Chairman stated that the venture would invest in foreign telecoms and IT companies.

Realities blur any classification of government-owned investment vehicles. Probably the only meaningful differentiations pertain to SWFs and FWFs which draw their resources from commodities revenues and those entities financed primarily through transfers of central bank reserves (Subacchi, 2008). Accordingly, throughout the book we will often distinguish between commodity and non-commodity based SWFs.

In Chapter 2, where we discuss in detail the size and growth of SWFs, we will define SWF as special purpose investment funds owned by the general government whose primary purpose is to hold, manage or administer assets to achieve financial objectives.

MISPLACED FEARS

A main theme pervading the book maintains that SWFs, and especially FWFs, focus on a longer term horizon, rather than quarterly reports. And in fact if one observes their track record – apart from a handful cases – it would be difficult to argue that they have pursued hidden objectives. Even in those instances where some have detected an ambiguity, e.g. the acquisition of Rio Tinto by CIC, the case was built at best on circumstantial evidence and divination of intentions rather than facts or proofs.

The largest SWFs are primarily a tool for inter-generational transfer, conceptually not much different from a pension fund. In the particular case of small countries endowed with natural resources, SWFs represent the tool to transform underground wealth into overground wealth. The strategies of most SWFs or FWFs display a higher risk tolerance than those pursued by, say, central banks, that need to keep a liquid pool of foreign assets to stem a speculative attack on their currency. But their strategies are more conservative than those of most private equity funds and definitely would not be on any meaningful level of comparison with the strategies of most hedge funds, although it is well known that some SWFs have invested part of their endowment in large alternative assets funds. In other words SWFs, and even more so those best described as FWFs, follow a wide spectrum of strategies that cannot be characterized precisely.

As a rule, SWFs have preferred to avoid the limelight. All SWFs have shunned investments in sensitive industries that could have stirred reactions on national security grounds or political controversy over foreign ownership. Most often SWFs are passive investors. This attitude was underlined in January 2010 by Sheikh Ahmed Bin Zayed Al Nehayan, at the time President of ADIA, in an interview with the German daily *Handelsblatt*:[10]

> We have no expertise in managing businesses directly, and have made it clear that we have no interest in doing so. As a matter of policy, ADIA does not exercise its voting rights except on rare occasions to protect our financial interests or against motions that may be detrimental to shareholders as a whole. This approach reduces the need for us to buy large stakes in companies or to take board seats. ADIA's philosophy since its creation has been to build a broadly diversified portfolio of investments.

---

[10] *Handelsblatt*, 14 January 2010.

We have worked very hard over the past 30-plus years to build open and trusted relationships with governments and regulators around the world that are based on these simple principles.

We will continue to follow a highly-diversified investing strategy that is focused on long term trends in order to best serve the current and future interests of Abu Dhabi. But I think the latest downturn has also served as a powerful reminder to all investors of the importance of risk management, and of having controls that act as a brake on excessive risk taking during bull markets.

Another SWF always cited as a gorilla in the financial market block is the CIC, established in 2007 with an endowment of US$200 billion (later boosted to US$300 billion) transferred from the central bank foreign currency reserves. CIC is also trying to adopt a similarly uncontroversial course of action. It poured several billion dollars into highly publicized acquisitions of minority stakes in prominent financial players, e.g. Blackstone (US$3 billion in 2007), Morgan Stanley (US$5.6 billion also in 2007), J.C. Flowers (US$3 billion in 2008), BlackRock, the world's largest independent money manager (US$713.8 million at an unknown date), Apax Partners LLP, the UK private equity group (2.3% in 2010 for an undisclosed price) and in one Canadian commodity company Teck Resources (where it holds a 17.3% share).

According to figures posted by the CIC in its first ever 13-F filing, mandated by the American Securities and Exchange Commission for investors in US listed securities, CIC had invested just US$9.6 billion, at the end of 2009, and with few exceptions has acquired stakes worth less than 10%, presumably to avoid government investment reviews. The CIC's US investments as they emerge from the filing are definitely 'unremarkable', in the light of the US$300 billion it can deploy: it suffices to say that a quarter of its US investments are in exchange traded funds.

CIC deliberately tried to eschew politically controversial operations, preferring publicly traded securities over direct investments and limiting its involvement to non-controlling stakes, while avoiding sensitive industrial sectors such as infrastructure, airlines, telecommunications or technology. CIC in 2009 held a portfolio composed of 32% in cash, 36% in global equities, and 26% in fixed income securities (71% of which was in government securities). Of the amount in equities, 43.9% was in North America, 28.4% in Asia Pacific, and 20.5% in Europe.

Apart from anecdotal evidence and occasional public statements by SWFs' management, systematic research conducted to analyse the investments track record did not detect evidence of a particular bias in the SWFs allocation choices. For example, a paper by Avendaño and Santiso (2009) issued by the OECD – an institution highly attentive to the activity of SWFs – concludes that 'The fear that sovereigns with political motivations use their financial power to secure large stakes in Western companies is shown to be unfounded'. To reach this conclusion the authors used mutual funds' investments as a benchmark to evaluate whether SWFs' portfolios present unusual features. A more circumscribed study by Beck and Fidora (2008) show that when the Norwegian Pension Fund, following the recommendation from its Ethics Committee, divested from stocks which violated its ethical guidelines (e.g. defence companies and those violating labour rights), the impact on the stock prices was small and statistically insignificant.[11]

Comparison with other classes of asset managers helps to put in context a number of issues, foremost the relative size of SWFs within the asset management industry. Compared with pension funds, mutual funds, or insurance funds, SWFs account for roughly 6% of all assets managed by institutional asset managers. Only 11 SWFs have assets that exceed US$100 billion. By contrast a global player such as BlackRock, according to its website, had at the end of 2011 AUM totalling US$3.5 trillion comprising equities, fixed income, cash management, alternative investment, real estate and advisory strategies; CalPERS manages about US$234 billion; Carlyle, one of the largest private equity firms, holds nearly US$150 billion in three asset classes – private equity, real estate and credit alternatives. The AUM of the largest American Mutual Funds are in the same league as the largest SWFs: Growth Fund of America has US$137 billion, Vanguard Total Stock Market has US$186 billion, American Funds EuroPacific Growth A has US$113 billion and Vanguard 500 Index Fund has US$203 billion. There are at least 15 American funds with AUM over US$50 billion.[12]

Another useful comparison can be made with the private equity industry. David Rubenstein, co-founder of Carlyle, one of the largest funds, declared in the autumn of 2010: 'By the time the bubble burst in 2007, the industry had over US$1000 billion under management and had become the face of capitalism to some extent.'

Between the third quarter of 2006 and the second quarter of 2007, private equity firms announced deals totalling about US$910 billion, although the crisis had a severe impact: in the 12 months ending in March 2011, the total dropped to a mere US$213 billion, according to Dealogic. In short, these figures indicate that the apprehension over a drastic change in international finance or the ownership structure of large corporates as a result of SWFs activities is grossly exaggerated.

As a final observation we would like to stress another difference between SWFs and privately owned institutions: SWFs are less prone to the accusation often levelled at private equity funds or hedge funds that they are machines for self-enrichment of the partners and more inclined to foster long-term efficiency and accountability in companies they invest in. This characteristic

---

[11] This result, however, could be attributed to the relative small stake held by the Norwegian Fund in those companies, i.e. in the order of 0.5% of total capital equivalent to roughly the daily average trading volume.

[12] Based on website information (February 2012).

would display its maximum benefits in countries where the markets are not fully developed and governance is in its infancy. Here SWFs can take advantage of institutional relationships at the highest level to improve the business environment, spearhead foreign investments and turn into a driver of change.

THE PLAN OF THE BOOK

This book will take a rather eclectic perspective on SWFs. The common theme underlining our views maintains that the emergence of SWFs is an epiphenomenon of the secular rebalancing in the world economy towards emerging markets. The activity by SWFs can be seen from different standpoints.

At a very abstract level most of the issues pertaining to SWFs cannot always be treated within the framework of modern macroeconomic theory which is becoming somewhat detached from reality. The prevailing international economic models do not contemplate that a country can maintain a persistent current account deficit or surplus, so they fail to explain the nature of current global imbalances and the implications for asset pricing and policy recipes. We will strive to separate the hokum of politically motivated arguments from the serious analysis of the role SWFs are playing and will increasingly play in the financial world.

Chapter 1 will explain that the emergence of the SWF resulted from exacerbating macroeconomic imbalance which had many causes and led ultimately to the global crisis of 2008–2009. In this context however we will distinguish two types of economies: the first is that of small countries (and limited population) with sizeable natural resources; the second that of countries that have conspicuous current account surpluses, but a large population, patchy infrastructure and large swathes of underdeveloped regions. The rationales behind the creation of SWFs for the two groups of countries are almost antithetical. The behaviour and the strategies by SWFs that manage revenues from natural resources can be analysed through the models in the economic literature on natural resources management from the classic Hotelling's Rule to the Permanent Income Hypothesis and its variants. The prescriptions of course differ for a developed country with an adequate capital stock and access to financial markets, and for a developing country facing savings shortages, low capital endowment and widespread poverty.

The optimal natural resources management criteria will be put in the context of fiscal systems, comparing a country where revenues are predominantly earned from natural resources (Saudi Arabia) and a country with a widely diversified fiscal base (Norway).

In Chapter 2 we will provide a classification of SWFs and of the economic forces behind their growth, i.e. the sources of persistent current account surpluses. We will start from the optimal management of central bank foreign reserves holdings in order to meet balance of payments needs, offset capital flights or cope with a sudden halt in foreign capital inflows. Once the central bank fulfils its institutional mandate, additional reserves can be managed more actively. In a nutshell, this is the rationale which led to the creation of SWFs. We will provide a forecast of current account surpluses for various economies and therefore the size of SWFs' AUM in 2016.

In Chapter 3 we will classify the SWFs according to their objectives and investment strategies and explain that some of them have (sometimes implicit) liabilities to honour. We will link the long-term objectives of SWFs and FWFs with the options available to them not only in terms of financial investments but also in terms of human capital, green energies, infrastructures, etc. Against this background we analyse the strategies more apt for the pursuit of the various objectives underlining that SWFs display little appetite for politically motivated investments.

In Chapter 4 we will make a digression into the nature of long-term investing and especially risk management, investors' activism and performance benchmarks. SWFs have been slow to adopt a well-rounded risk management culture, preferring, by and large, opportunistic investment strategies combined with a focus on traditional industries. Concerns over risk exposure were shrugged off by the false security of a 'diversified' portfolio. A series of misconceptions about risk management, which we will underscore, have general validity, relevant not only for SWFs. The financial crisis has sent risk managers across the world back to the drawing board and dented the confidence in quantitative techniques such as Value at Risk (VaR), one of the most common and trusted risk metrics. The losses suffered by the SWFs in the aftermath of the Great Recession have opened the eyes to the need for a comprehensive approach to investment, the need to develop a 360 degree view on macroeconomic developments and the fallacy of relying on just one or two indicators to set off the alarm bell. Readers who are more interested in the impact of SWFs on the geopolitical scene might wish to skip this chapter.

Chapter 5 will offer an overview on the mega trends that are redesigning the economic and financial geography as a result of globalization and of which SWFs are but one of the many aspects. The winds of globalization combined with the international financial turmoil and widespread volatility of commodity and financial markets are bound to dislocate and re-assemble economic relations. For example, the Middle East, which was a major economic partner of the US, is shifting its focus towards Europe and lately towards Asia. The old Silk Routes – the sea fare through the Strait of Malacca and the Red Sea and the land route through Central Asia – will in all likelihood become the dominant trade channel – superseding the Atlantic routes – in the course of the twenty-first century. In this chapter we will also discuss the role of SWFs in the post-financial crisis financial architecture where the US dollar is set to play a less important role than in the past 50 years.

Chapter 6 will provide an overview of the main initiatives that international institutions such as the OECD and the IMF are setting up to engage the SWFs in a dialogue on the regulatory framework that would be mutually satisfactory for the recipient countries and the surplus countries. These initiatives, at national and international level, seemed initially to be a hasty response to political pressures and fears instilled in public opinion, rather than a consistently well-designed approach. However, the IMF's Santiago Principles are slowly emerging as the framework of engagement between SWFs and the authorities in recipient countries, prone to meddle into deals they happen to dislike or disapprove of. Within this topic we will make a digression into the shifting border between the role of private and public institutions. The heyday of globalization was characterized by a faith in the virtues of markets. However the pendulum is shifting towards a more pervasive influence of governments in domestic economies and in the redefinition of rules.

Chapter 7 will summarize the most important points, offer some views on future developments and sketch some of the challenges that SWFs and FWFs will face, especially in the discussion over the new financial architecture for the twenty-first century.

The bibliography provides an extensive sample of the enormous literature that has been devoted to the SWFs in the past few years.

1

The Macroeconomic Dynamics
Behind SWFs

The decades around the turn of the century will be remembered in economic history for the process of ever closer economic and financial integration across the world which is synthetically referred to as 'globalization'. This process was propelled by the trade liberalization spurred by the inception of the World Trade Organization (WTO), the economies of scale that ensued in key industries, the technology transfers to emerging countries from relocation of factories, the advances in telecommunications and connectivity, and the revolution in logistics which, by pushing transport costs sharply down, paved the way to a revamp of global manufacturing. (A fascinating account on the effects of the globalization is *The World is Flat* by Friedman, 2006.)

Ironically, the early exegesis of globalization disseminated the illusion that stronger economic ties among remote geographical areas would set the stage for the extension of a US-centric dominance to those countries emerging from decades of stagnation or underdevelopment and eager to embrace free markets after shedding the self-sufficiency myth. Policies promoting economic liberalization, capital flows and Western-style democracy were considered the wings on which this process was destined to take off.

Few envisaged that the globalization would set in motion a momentous dislocation of economic activities, promote a myriad of cross-country relationships at microeconomic level, accelerate the transfer of know-how and attract capital to hitherto forbidding locations. The break-up and reassembly of supply chains favoured the newcomers and not the incumbents. Ultimately this reformatting of the world economic hardware led to a reshuffle of economic power between mature economies and emerging countries.

Even fewer foresaw that Anglo-Saxon finance, instead of gaining strength from globalization, would actually fall victim to this process, in part for its hubris and incompetence, in part because the decision makers in the financial institutions ignored the signals of impending change, as stressed by Mohamed El Erian in his book *When Markets Collide*. Paradoxically the countries (primarily the US and the UK) portraying themselves as the standard bearers and main beneficiaries of globalization have ended up in the relegation zone. By contrast (at least so far) the largest relative gains economically, financially and politically have been enjoyed by Brazil, India and, above all, China, which together with smaller emerging markets were expected to be the 'targets' of the globalization process. In synthesis, contrary to the script of the movie, the extras have become protagonists.

The emergence of SWFs on the world stage must be analysed against the background of this secular process. The SWF phenomenon is fuelled by persistent large current account surpluses pushed by three intertwined phenomena:

1   a boom in commodity prices;
2   a strong, export-led growth model (some may say mercantilist, and we will examine this claim later);
3   a prudent (possibly overcautious) macro-policy framework pursued by the large Asian exporters and many other emerging economies.

The first phenomenon is rather easy to grasp: an unprecedented world growth over the 20 years before the Great Recession propelled the demand for all kinds of natural resources and food commodities stretching supply to the limit, especially after 2005. Among the main beneficiaries were the producers of energy commodities, but also some of the poorest African countries.

The second and third have their roots in the aftermath of the Mexican and Asian crises of the mid 1990s – which represented the first major hiccup of globalization – and the stabilization policies that were embraced (some would say imposed by the IMF), combined, especially in the case of Greater China, with a peg to the US dollar. In the painful aftermath of those crises, the authorities in most emerging countries – with their fingers still burning from the hot money whose flight suddenly sunk their currencies – adopted a cautious fiscal and monetary policy mix. The firmness of this policy stance was measured by the accumulation of foreign exchange reserves, seen as the bulwark against contagion, hot money flows and bouts of risk aversion. With the memory of the crisis fading and stability restored, it became clear that amassing reserves beyond a certain point was bearing substantial opportunity costs, as we will explain in detail in Chapter 2. So the authorities in emerging countries started to look for a better way of managing those funds and found inspiration from the experience of the Arab Gulf commodity exporters.

1.1   PERSISTENT CURRENT ACCOUNT SURPLUSES TRANSLATE INTO ACCUMULATION OF FOREIGN ASSETS

There is no alternative for a country with a current account surplus to invest abroad. The fundamental reason for this is well known to economists, but less so to politicians, editorialists and talk show guests. Countries with a current account deficit, i.e. net importers, need external credit to buy goods and services from abroad. Inevitably, part of the revenues earned by exporters finds its way to foreign bank deposits, foreign stock markets, foreign sovereign or corporate bonds, foreign real estate, etc. For each dollar (or euro or yen or yuan) of current account surplus there is a dollar of foreign assets that the exporting country piles up, corresponding to a dollar of foreign liabilities for the importers.

This flow of funds also implies that there is a direct relationship between current account surplus and aggregate national savings: one is the flip side of the other (economists say there is an identity between current account balance and domestic savings). The reason should be clear. In order to provide credit to the importers, the exporters must save (otherwise they would not have money to lend). Therefore they must forgo some domestic investment in order to finance the purchase of their goods by their trade partners. This can be expressed through a simple relation

$$CAB = S - I \tag{1}$$

where CAB is the current account balance, S is the national savings (of the private and public sector combined) and I is the total investment (again private and public).

In short, a country with a structural current account surplus (such as an oil exporter) builds up a stock of foreign assets. The interest or profits paid on the external liabilities accrues to the current account surplus of the creditor country and to the deficit of the borrowing country.

In advanced, well-diversified economies, these assets are owned primarily by the private sector and, to a much lesser extent, by the public sector, in the form of central bank reserves. Central bank reserves are maintained in low-risk, very liquid assets to ensure that domestic firms and individuals have access to foreign currency needed for their business payments, portfolio transactions and travel requirements. Central banks do not engage much in active asset management.

In economies without significant natural resources, the financial sector is considered by the public, by governments and by most economists as a place where private investors trade securities or foreign currencies, make deals, negotiate terms of contracts such as loans, swaps and derivatives. In fact exporters, banks and asset managers are predominantly private, with some notable exceptions – e.g. civil servant pension funds, such as California Public Employees Retirement System (CalPERS) – and publicly owned banks, which in Europe until 20 years ago were rather common (and still are in Germany). But overall the public hand lost much of its grip on the financial sector in the West by the mid-1990s.

Accordingly, governments' participation in financial markets is now limited to the issuance and management of public debt and occasionally the sale of publicly owned companies. Simply put, in mature economies, governments and their agencies are as a rule on the sell side, not on the buy side. Central banks routinely inject or withdraw liquidity through open market operations and, more rarely, intervene in the foreign exchange market. However these operations are carried out for policy purposes and are not intended to yield a profit.

In small countries with considerable natural resources (which belong to the nation), a large share of export revenues is controlled by the public sector, directly or through state owned entities, which therefore end up managing large funds.

It is awkward for Western public opinion to realize that public entities are engaged in financial transactions as if they were private companies. Is this an aberration or should it be considered a legitimate course of action, and under what conditions?

Before we answer such a question in next section, we need to point to a fallacy that policy makers and media commentators maintain in the back of their minds: **current account imbalances are temporary**. This notion dates back to the venerable Mundell–Fleming model.

In essence, the model posits that real exchange rate corrections and/or productivity adjustments absorb quickly any competitive advantage of net exporters, and therefore an external equilibrium is restored. Also, the magnitude of these surpluses or deficits is supposed to be small relative to the stock of outstanding financial assets, which is largely true in developed countries. In reality, apart from a short period between the end of the Second World War and the demise of the Bretton Woods system, free trade and especially free movement of capital typically generated large and persistent surpluses or deficits. Periodically these imbalances become the focus of international policy diatribes and calls for 'adjustment', but the widespread perception that a large stock of foreign assets or foreign liabilities is an anomaly is hard to dispel.

The size of persistent current account surpluses (and mirroring deficits) has grown steadily in the past decade in some large economies: apart from Japan which has a long track record, Germany, China and OPEC countries have been notable net exporters and are destined to remain in such a position for a long time, contrary to the tenets of the Mundell–Fleming model.

A new generation of models pioneered by Obstfed and Rogoff (1996) embodying an intertemporal framework explains current account imbalances in terms of consumption smoothing and international portfolio allocation.[1] Nevertheless even this more sophisticated theoretical approach neglects the influence on global asset prices from international capital inflows generated by persistent current account deficits. Hence, the links between current account deficits and the financial sector remain poorly understood.[2]

In Chapter 7 we will focus on a particular aspect of this broader issue, namely how energy commodity prices affect what Ben Bernanke, Chairman of the US Federal Reserve, dubbed the savings glut, i.e. an apparent excess of financial flows seeking to be employed across the capital markets.

---

[1] Knight and Scacciavillani (1998) contains a critical review of the mainstream approach to current account balance with an application to the experience of developed and emerging countries.

[2] Hopefully the financial crisis will prompt a flurry of research and data analysis.

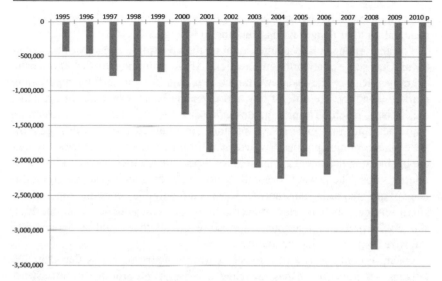

Figure 1.1   US net international position (in US$ millions). p = predicted.

Source: US Department of Commerce.

From the mid-1990s, as the US continued to run a widening current account deficit (Figure 1.1) and countries such as China and Japan (together with other Asian countries and, to a lesser extent, Germany) maintained large permanent current account surpluses, mainstream economists looked increasingly baffled by the lack of any theoretical underpinning.

According to estimates by the Institute of International Finance in the period between 2002 and 2006, the Gulf Cooperation Council (GCC) countries accumulated US$1.5 trillion, twice as much as in the previous five years. As a matter of comparison, this figure is equivalent to about 10% of the domestic market capitalization of the New York Stock Exchange (NYSE) at the end of 2007, more than one-third of the Tokyo Stock Exchange, the Euronext exchanges and the NASDAQ, and it would have almost been sufficient to buy all the companies listed in the Deutsche Börse at the end of 2006. To this flow of money from oil exporters one must add the build-up of foreign assets by China, Korea, Japan and commodity exporters such as Canada and Australia. The financial crisis has only marginally dented these flows, so foreign assets continue to accumulate.

1.2 ABSORPTION CONSTRAINTS: THE RATIONALE FOR ESTABLISHING SWFs AND FWFs

Why would a government reinvest export revenues abroad while neglecting domestic projects or social programmes? After all it would be politically more palatable to raise the living standards of the local population by investing domestically rather than providing funding to foreigners.

The answer depends to a large extent on the absorption capacity of the country and has some noteworthy implications. If we examine two almost opposite examples, Russia and Qatar, we notice that Russia is not a fully functioning market economy. The rule of law and even the basic protection of investors are, at best, patchy. Despite the desperate need for capital for infrastructure, manufacturing, raw materials extraction, etc., bureaucratic hurdles, governance shortcomings, political rivalries and internecine power struggles render the business environment a minefield for those outside the cobweb of powerful relationships. The private corporate sector – i.e. companies outside the influence of national or local authorities – plays a negligible economic role outside small services, such as retail or accounting. As a consequence, even the Russian SWFs prefer to invest abroad those resources that could be deployed to improve domestic living standards.

Qatar, in contrast, is a tiny, mostly barren country with less than 250,000 citizens. Its government has launched a massive programme of infrastructure building and structural transformation of the economy in areas such as finance, tourism, transport services and petrochemicals. As a result, the size of the economy increased almost tenfold in nominal US dollar terms between 2001 and 2011 and the per capita income doubled according to data from the IMF World Economic Outlook.[3] Obviously part of this performance is simply the result of oil price increases, but the non-oil sector has flourished as well. Investments in some years amounted to more than one-third of Qatari GDP, and new investments planned over the next few years are estimated at about three times current GDP. Expatriates already make up over three-quarters of the resident population. A further acceleration of this expansion would run into bottlenecks, which are already evident in terms of housing scarcity, labour and raw materials shortages, and infrastructure insufficiencies. Similar observations can be made of the United Arab Emirates (UAE) and, to a lesser extent, other GCC countries.

In essence, economic development cannot be instantaneous. Absorption capacity needs to be built gradually; hence small oil-exporting countries are compelled to invest a consistent fraction of their export revenues abroad. Stated differently, countries such as Qatar, the UAE, Kuwait, but also the likes of Norway and Singapore – which have already attained a high per capita income – have made a choice to transfer wealth accumulated through exports to future generations. An additional motivation for investing abroad is hedging: if a shock hits the domestic economy or the commodity prices, income levels can be preserved.

---

[3] Per capita income in Qatar increased from US$52,300 to US$103,900 between 2001 and 2011, while nominal GDP rose from US$17.5 billion to US$173.2 billion over the same period; see WEO database in http://www.imf.org.

At the opposite end of the spectrum, large dysfunctional countries such as Russia or Nigeria would be better off if they channelled more of their export proceeds into their domestic economies after liberalizing their business environment and promoting infrastructure development.

A variant of the dysfunctional governance case takes place when the creation of SWFs is motivated by the need to preserve the windfall revenues from the appetite of various pressure groups (and political constituencies) competing for budgetary resources. Ring-fencing the revenues in an entity separated from the central government is a line of defence against pilfering by politicians, waste of resources on pet projects or patronage.

This is a course of action advocated in certain cases by the IMF, although the record is mixed. For example, the 2010 IMF Staff Report on Papua New Guinea argued that 'As country experiences suggest, special fiscal institutions (such as SWFs) themselves are not a panacea, but need to be integrated into a sound fiscal policy framework. [...] In fact, in some countries with special fiscal institutions [i.e. SWFs], government spending followed commodity revenues without averting pro-cyclicality of fiscal policy, and no meaningful difference has been found in the behaviour of spending relative to similar countries without special fiscal institutions (Davis and others, 2001).' In other countries with special fiscal institutions, government spending did not follow commodity revenues, but this was the case before and after the establishment of special fiscal institutions (Ossowski et al., 2008).

Needless to say, the institutional set up, the governance, the check and balances, the accountability, the mandate, the internal audit, etc. need to be well designed for a SWF to manage the funds it has been assigned in conformity with the mandate received.

Nigeria offers a paradigmatic example in this sense. Nigeria had various types of extra budgetary funds financed by oil revenues and used for off-budget expenditure before 1995. Spending was allocated to various investments in the oil sector and development projects for which project evaluation, selection criteria and governance were lax. Moreover, capacity to manage the scale and complexity of the ventures was inadequate. As a result, a number of these projects ended up requiring huge additional financing and displayed low ex post rates of return. Not surprisingly in several cases the expenditures were out of line with the budget and their destinations unaccounted for. However, mindful of that experience, the Nigerian Parliament, under pressure from the new President Goodluck Jonathan – who has gained some reputation in fighting corruption at a high level in a country where past administrations were not widely deemed a model of integrity – passed a law instituting a SWF to manage the oil export revenues after a long and acrimonious debate.

To summarize this section, small economies with huge natural resources face the problem of absorptive capacity of export revenues determined by size, whereas large countries face the problem of absorptive capacity determined by their institutional and legal framework.

In between these extremes there is a whole spectrum of situations. The main one is in China, which has engaged in a breakneck expansion programme over the past three decades, but has not provided modern social services and a universal public pension system that would grant beneficiaries a decent living standard. In practice, the Chinese SWFs constitute a sort of a shadow pension fund, where funds that in other countries would be devoted to social services, as we will see later, consist of a large portfolio of US sovereign debt, and increasingly real assets such as mines, agricultural land, commodities and infrastructure of all kinds in various countries. In other words this sort of gigantic pension fund (we are oversimplifying, because the Chinese government is not formally committed to use SWFs assets to fund any retirement benefits) is being used to foster some broader economic objectives encompassing food security, raw materials and – last but not least for an export-led economy – an extension of credit to the importers of Chinese goods. One can debate whether this crypto-mercantilist policy is still serving the interests of a country such as China and whether it would be more appropriate to redirect its efforts towards improving domestic living standards. In fact this change of objectives is one of the main points of contention in the framework of international policy coordination which takes centre stage during G20 meetings. In other words it involves the global imbalances that in many quarters are considered the main cause of the Great Recession and as such it has much broader implications than the legitimacy of government-sponsored investment vehicles, as we will argue in the next section.

1.3 THE MANAGEMENT OF NATURAL RESOURCES WINDFALL

Why would a country rich in natural resources want to accumulate foreign assets? After all would it not be better to extract only what is needed to sustain its economy and its government budget each year, maybe a little more, just to be on the safe side?

In abstract this seems a more reasonable long-term resource management strategy. In reality it might not be feasible, for example because the extraction technology has increasing returns to scale, hence installed capacity needs to be fully used to recover the investment. In other instances a contract assigns the extraction rights to a private foreign company, so the government collects royalties but has little say over the pace of exploitation.

Generally speaking, a SWF or a Future Wealth Fund (FWF) aims to transform underground wealth into overground wealth. It could very well be the case that the highest long-term return on the natural resource endowment would come from keeping the oil or the minerals untouched for decades and borrow from the financial market in the meantime. For Norway, an already prosperous country, arguably it might be preferable to stop pumping North Sea oil for

20 years rather than accumulate wealth in a wobbly financial market. But no strategy is riskless, especially when it involves decisions over a long time span for which the degree of uncertainty cannot be internalized. For example, if over the next 20 years a new form of energy supplants hydrocarbons, oil and gas reserves might become worthless, and Norwegians would be dismayed.

The optimal management of a natural resource windfall is hardly a novel topic for economists. The literature is extensive and its roots are often traced to the venerable Hotelling's Rule (Hotelling, 1931), which states that under certain conditions the price charged for an exhaustible resource must grow at a rate equal to the rate of interest. From this principle it follows that an optimal extraction policy maximizes intertemporal benefits (see Box 1.1).

Four main assumptions underpin Hotelling's Rule:

1   production can effortlessly be increased in the present or shifted to the future at will;
2   the total reserves of the exhaustible resource are accurately calculated and no technological advances permit an expansion;
3   future demand (in each year) is estimated with accuracy;
4   future interest rates are known.

None of them are realistic, especially in the case of energy commodities. For condition 1, non-renewable commodities require considerable capital expenditures, extraction facilities take a long time to be built and the equipment remains in operation for a long time. Firms take a risk on the price volatility of the natural resource; hence they use cautious price forecasts before undertaking the investment. Once the investment is made, facilities will remain in operation until the price covers operating costs, which are very much lower than the average cost inclusive of fixed capital amortization. Condition 2 is also improbable. Firms engage in exploration of new deposits in response to price signals, largely dependent on demand changes and often deposits grow over or along horizon more or less in conjunction with production. Condition 3 holds only temporarily: as price increases, substitutes for the resource start to emerge or conservation technologies are developed. In essence no one has much of an idea about the backstop price, or the future demand for the use of the resource. Moreover the interest rate itself varies continuously.

Oil prices, to cite a well-known example, have not been increasing at a pace remotely equal to the interest rate, but have fluctuated in response to demand and supply since 1931, when the oil price was low due to the Great Depression and to huge oil discoveries in the Middle East and the USA (mostly Texas and California). Supply overcapacity disappeared during the Second World War, but new discoveries in the Middle East of oil fields that were cheaply exploitable pushed prices down again in the 1950s to 1960s. The success of the OPEC cartel and its embargo in 1973 (triggered by the

Box 1.1 Hotelling's Rule

The optimal extraction rate of an exhaustible resource as posited by Hotelling can be seen as the solution to a profit maximization problem:

$$\frac{\partial X}{\partial t} = Y(t) \tag{2}$$

where X is the stock of the resource and $Y(t)$ is the extraction in each unit of time. The profit is given by

$$\Pi(t) = pY(t) \tag{3}$$

where p is the price of the resource. Future profits must then be discounted. The discount rate in equilibrium is equivalent to the interest rate. Hence the maximization problem, first posed and solved by Hotelling, can be written as:

$$\max \int_0^\infty pY\, e^{-rt} dt \tag{4}$$

where r is the interest rate assumed to be constant over time. The solution that maximizes the present value of total profit is:

$$p_t = p_0\, e^{rt}, \tag{5}$$

i.e. the price of the resource grows over time at the exponential rate r. Extraction continues until a price is reached where an alternative technology or a substitute for the resource becomes economically viable. This is known as a backstop price. It is interesting to note that the natural resource endowment is equivalent to holding a bond which yields r until the backstop price is reached.

The rationale of Hotelling's Rule is simple. If we consider a natural resource as a capital endowment, its present value is determined by the discount rate (which in equilibrium, in a riskless world, is equal to the prevailing market interest rate). Hotelling's Rule is therefore a particular case of the general notion that in competitive (and perfectly functioning) markets, returns on all assets, be they financial or real, will be equal.

The rationale can be explained as follows. If the price of the natural resource rises so that the return goes above the rate of interest, producers will increase their supply or new producers will enter the market, and prices will fall back to their long-term equilibrium. If the price rises more slowly than the rate of interest would warrant, then the supply will decrease and the price will rise back to equilibrium. The profit created by resource scarcity in competitive markets is called Hotelling rent (also known as resource rent or, in a Ricardian flavour, scarcity rent).

Israel–Arab war) inflicted a double blow because the monopoly power was compounded by the higher cost to develop and exploit new oil fields outside the Middle East. After the waning of the second oil shock, triggered by the Iranian Revolution in 1979, until 2003 (with the invasion of Iraq), oil prices remained depressed (except for a brief rebound during the first Gulf War), with continued oil discoveries and the slow growth of oil demand. Over the last decade, the growing demand by emerging economies and geopolitical instability led to a surge of oil prices from a range of US$25–30 to well over US$100 per barrel.

Although Hotelling's Rule is not a coherent theory to guide forecasts relevant for the real world, it does provide an abstract benchmark against which to gauge reality. In particular it contains an important reminder for policy makers: consumption of a resource unit today has an opportunity cost equal to the present value of the marginal profit from selling the resource in the future. A decision maker will always face the choice between the increasing value of the resource, if left unexploited, and its current value if extracted and sold.

Even though the marginal profit cannot be precisely calculated – and in practice it varies continuously – this intertemporal trade-off has been the cornerstone of the Permanent Income Hypothesis (PIH), which represents in a sense the evolution of Hotelling's Rule (Box 1.2). The PIH states that individuals base their consumption (and savings) decisions not on their current income, but on the total expected stream of future incomes from employment, investments, inheritance, etc. during their lifespan.[4] Wealth in this context is defined as the sum of the discounted stream of expected future incomes.

Of course there are other options based on different discounting criteria or that take into account real life constraints or that abide by other definitions of fairness. A country that has discovered deposits of natural resources within its territory but lacks funds to invest in extraction facilities can only resort to external borrowing, providing as collateral the future stream of export proceeds, saving part of the revenues until the natural resource is exhausted, and building up a SWF large enough for interest on the accumulated financial wealth to maintain consumption increments in perpetuity. A widely adopted variant of this strategy consists of auctioning the exploration and extraction rights to foreign companies in exchange for a stream of royalties over a predefined period of time.

In reality even countries that would not face any problem in raising funds for the exploitation of their natural resources or that have enough financial means prefer to auction off the rights, because a key problem is the lack of technology and project management skills. A recent case would be Iraq, where

---

[4] An implication of the PIH is that the choices made by individuals on their consumption patterns are determined not by current income but by their expectations on future incomes. Therefore in a bad year consumption falls less than one would expect because individuals tend to smooth out consumption levels.

Box 1.2 Permanent Income Hypothesis (PIH)

The key intertemporal relation underpinning the PIH states that for an individual (or a community) **optimal consumption in each period is equal to the real rate of return on their wealth.** Translating this principle to a country with an endowment of natural resources, optimal consumption Ct in each period t can be expressed by the formula:

$$Ct = r\,[Ft + \Sigma\,(Tt + 1 + i\,/(1+r)i))]\,,\ i \text{ ranging from 0 to } \infty \qquad (6)$$

where Ft is the value of accumulated (i.e. not spent) net revenues from oil, including interest income, at the beginning of each period t; Tt is the oil revenue the government expects (net of production costs) in each period t; r is the real rate of return on oil wealth (assumed to be constant across time).

When applied to a country, the PIH states that the population in each period should consume an amount equal to the rate of return on accumulated oil wealth multiplied by the net present value of expected future wealth. This intertemporal equilibrium rule insures that the current generation shares the proceeds of the natural resources endowment in a way that preserves the endowment for the next generation. We can interpret the PIH as a sort of fairness benchmark in intergenerational transfer.

---

a large SWF manages the accumulated oil revenues (including those under the Food for Oil Programme managed by the United Nations).[5]

A very prudent approach is the 'bird-in-hand' hypothesis (Bjerkholt, 2002; Barnett and Ossowski, 2003), which posits that all revenues be saved through a SWF and incremental consumption be restricted to the interest earned on the fund. This rule can be interpreted as being equivalent to the PIH, but with the windfall left untouched until it has been fully earned. In other words, the expected imputed interest on the value of the resource still in the ground will be not be spent, but reinvested through the SWF.

A complete account of all the possible optimal rules could probably fill a treatise and it is beyond the scope of this book.[6] Here it suffices to say that the decision on the consumption-saving trade-off over the proceeds from exports of natural resources depends on a wide set of circumstances and collective

---

[5] During the years of the embargo, Iraq was allowed to sell a minimal part of its oil output and the revenues were channelled into a UN account from which only the funds for basic needs were transferred to the Iraqi government.

[6] An overview covering several interesting cases illustrated through two-period models is contained in Venables (2009).

preferences. SWFs are one, often the main one, of the institutions that implement the strategy adopted.

In the real world there is a continuum of practical solutions and theory rarely guides practice precisely, so it is unlikely that any investment policy will follow strictly one of the abstract models. They ought to be considered as purely illustrative, a sort of benchmark shedding light on the broad implications of various alternatives.

One approach cannot be deemed better than another and it might well be that a country decides initially to adopt a certain rule and shift to a different one at a later stage. For example it might make sense for a poor country once commodity deposits have been discovered to borrow against future revenues in order to jump-start the exploitation. Later, when the investment has been amortized (fully or partially), the country could shift more or less gradually to a PIH policy or something akin to the 'bird-in-hand' approach. We will devote the last section of this chapter to a hypothetical shift of Norway to a Saudi Arabian approach. Furthermore, in the real world one faces sudden changes such as the interest rate profile, the fluctuations in commodity prices, security risks, technological advances that impact the demand for the commodity and so on, and therefore the response needs to adapt to circumstances rather than stick once and for all to a predetermined course.

1.4 COMMODITIES DEMAND AND THE SUPER-CYCLE THEORY

Hotelling's Rule and the PIH are relevant for the supply side. The demand side is even cloudier. We have already pointed out how since 2006 there has been an intensification of the upward trend in all commodity prices. This phenomenon was taken as evidence of a secular relentless increase in the use of natural resources which could not be stopped. Peak oil became a favourite theme on the media and internet. Then in the summer of 2008 oil prices dropped sharply, casting doubt on this sort of argument (Table 1.1). The rebound in 2009 and then another drop (not remotely as sharp as in 2008) in late 2011 is evidence that simplistic views are mostly material for talk shows.

To determine whether the SWFs funded by commodity revenues will remain a powerful force in international finance it is paramount to have an idea of the underlying factors affecting commodity demand. In the Appendix to Chapter 2 we will work out a scenario on the growth of AUM managed by SWFs based on the energy prices projected by the IMF. Here we will focus on a more general outlook for commodity demand.

The more popular explanations for the recent oscillations and upward trend in commodity prices follow two lines of argument: the super-cycle and

Table 1.1 OPEC basket oil price (in US$/barrel)

November 2007	88.84
December 2007	87.05
January 2008	88.35
February 2008	90.64
March 2008	99.03
April 2008	105.16
May 2008	119.39
June 2008	128.33
July 2008	131.22
August 2008	112.41
September 2008	96.85
October 2008	69.16
November 2008	49.76
December 2008	39.53
Average 2008	94.15

Source: OPEC.

speculation. The first emphasizes a long-term phenomenon, the second focuses on short run spells out of line with fundamentals.[7]

Typically during the upward phase of an economic cycle, commodity prices increase and once they start to affect everyday life, e.g. when food prices skyrocket, 'speculation' becomes the preferred culprit. Speculation has no face, no country, no names, so it is the perfect target for a rite reminiscent of the Orwellian two minutes of hatred.

Lately fingers were pointed at commodity index funds which could supposedly earn 'substantial risk premiums', and take advantage of considerable leverage. Combined with the availability of deep and liquid exchange-traded futures contracts, investors shifted from equities and fuelled a dramatic surge in index fund investment. Some described this phenomenon as 'the financialization of commodity futures markets' (Tang and Xiong, 2010). Given the size and scope of commodity index funds, for many it followed that they were the prime suspects in the supposed speculative moves that pushed up energy and other commodities' prices. Time and again though, since the onion futures market suppression in the 1950s, following the trails of speculators have always proven difficult. Never mind that for anyone who speculates (i.e. bets) on a price increase there must be someone who speculates on a price decrease, otherwise there would be no trade. Despite the large average position size, the total size of index funds within a given market is not overwhelming. Academic studies and official commissions, routinely appointed to find the smoking gun, have rarely produced conclusive evidence. One of the most extensive recent papers (Irwin and Sanders, 2010), using new data and empirical analysis, found that index funds are not responsible for a bubble in commodity futures

---

[7] Another name often evoked on media and in academic literature is 'bubble'.

prices: 'There is no statistically significant relationship indicating that changes in index and swap fund positions have increased market volatility. The evidence presented here is strongest for the agricultural futures markets because the data on index trader positions are measured with reasonable accuracy'.

If speculation is not a major factor in commodity prices, it follows that fundamental forces are at work. There has been a large body of literature both in academia and among market analysts that points to a 'super-cycle' in commodities driven by emerging markets, which is likely to continue in the foreseeable future (Standard Chartered, 2010). Apart from the obvious effect on commodities demand from the growth of emerging markets, a more specific impulse is attributed to urbanization, which is one of the main ramifications of the secular shift in economic centre of gravity. Urbanization constitutes a commodity-intensive process and, historically, commodity consumption has significantly increased as annual per capita income approaches a level deemed 'middle class'. City dwellers have higher per capita incomes, consume more goods, use more energy and have a diverse protein-rich diet, leading to a higher demand for soft commodities such as grains as well as metals.

According to data from the United Nations,[8] the percentage of the world's population living in urban locations in 2008 exceeded that in rural areas for the first time in human history. This shift is projected to accelerate. By 2030 the world will have almost five billion city dwellers, with urban growth concentrated in Africa and Asia. China alone has about 170 urban areas exceeding one million people – and this number will grow through massive migration from the countryside over the next few years. To give a comparative figure in Europe, only 35 cities reach one million inhabitants. The same process is underway in India – albeit at a slower rate. India, according to UN projections, might be 15 years behind China, in terms of demographics dynamics.

The notion of a long-term cycle was highlighted at the dawn of modern economics by Kondratiev (1925) who extensively studied the price series across the nineteenth century of variables such as wages, interest rates, raw material prices, foreign trade and bank deposits. The Kondratiev waves (also called great surges, long waves, K-waves, long cycles and the now fashionable super-cycle) were described as regular sinusoidal-like cycles with a period of roughly 30 years. Kondratiev's and similar theories on regular secular cycles have not enjoyed widespread acceptance as an elucidation of how economic forces work. The wave of commodity prices surge in the second half of last decade has brought back the interest.

At the heart of the super-cycle lies the idea that all commodities and most other price movements are synchronized. Nevertheless commodities prices behave rather differently even during a long wave for a number of reasons: for some it is easier to increase production, others require specialized transportation facilities, others might be affected by security problems or conflicts,

---

[8] United Nations Population Division. http://www.un.org/esa/population.

etc. Today's technology and logistics are quite different from the nineteenth century which Kondratiev examined.

Oil offers an interesting historical perspective. When it became a major energy commodity around the 1860s, oil production was marred by over-exploitation which led to depletions of reservoirs, and therefore its price was subject to notable volatility. Price controls and two world wars reduced these effects and until 1973 the price remained fairly stable. Wheat prices also varied during periods when other commodities surged. For example the drop in transport costs caused by the spread of the steamships, combined with the gush of American production in the late nineteenth century, tended to depress prices. In the period after the Second World War, the 'green revolution', i.e. the use of improved seeds and fertilizers across the world, boosted production and dampened prices.

A venerable tool describing the effect of demand on prices for commodities with a fixed short-term supply is called the cobweb model (or cobweb theorem) by Kaldor (1938). As usual, reality might be much more complicated, but essentially the cobweb theorem underscores that the super-cycle hypothesis relies on a slow adjustment of supply to demand (see Box 1.3). This might be true more for some metals, oil or rare earths, but agricultural production should correct any major imbalance after a few years. In fact food commodities prices in 2011 retrenched markedly.

For oil and gas, whose exports provide the bulk of fund into several SWFs, making a prediction is not much simpler. Hydrocarbons will maintain their dominant role in the energy supply mix despite the doomsters' refrain that oil will be exhausted in 30 years. This prediction actually remains unaltered since 1970 when the Club of Rome first brought the alarm over the depletion of natural resources to the attention of the wider public. In mid-2008, the media were full of articles on the peak oil theory, and predictions of oil prices at US$200 per barrel made headlines. The frenzy later abated, but the expectation that hydrocarbon reserves are dwindling is still widespread. In reality new discoveries continue to be made, but the extraction costs are increasing because new deposits lie deeper or in a testing environment, often underwater.

Box 1.3 The cobweb theorem

In the basic model of supply and demand, the price adjusts so that the quantity supplied and the quantity demanded are equalized. The precise mechanism that achieves this equilibrium is not always explicit, because essentially it is postulated that supply and demand adjust instantly. In reality if a shock disrupts an equilibrium and as a consequence the total quantity demanded and sold in the market is Q_1 at price P_1 (see Figure 1.2), how will equilibrium be restored? In the short term, supply is fixed so no adjustment can take place. The following year producers will base their production on

P_1 and therefore produce Q_2. But at Q_2 the price buyers are willing to pay is P_2, i.e. much lower than P_1. As a result in the third year producers will adjust production at Q_3 which leads to a price P_3 and so on, until after a few years the equilibrium is restored. The right panel of Figure1.2(a) depicts the time series of the commodity price as it converges to equilibrium. A crucial condition for this convergence is that the slopes of the demand and supply curve are different (if they were the same the process would never reach P_{EQ} but would oscillate endlessly). Specifically, if the supply line is steeper than demand line the process converges. Otherwise the commodity price would spiral out as shown in Figure 1.2(b).

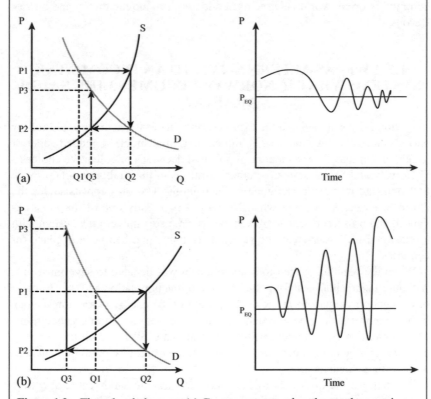

Figure 1.2   The cobweb theorem. (a) Convergent case when the supply curve is steeper than the demand curve. The fluctuations decrease in magnitude with each cycle, so a plot of the prices and quantities over time would look like an inward spiral. (b) Divergent case when the demand curve is steeper than the supply curve. The fluctuations increase in magnitude with each cycle, so that prices and quantities spiral outwards.

Source: http://en.wikipedia.org/wiki/Cobweb_model

Natural gas offers a dramatic and fresh example of how faulty predictions might turn out to be. Until 2008 gas prices were tracking oil prices. Then in 2009 vast discoveries of shale gas in the US and other parts of the world led to a dramatic price drop. In the US, infrastructure for the import of gas had to be transformed into infrastructure for the export of gas. As a result the price dropped and it still remains depressed in the US compared to the 2008 peak.

In conclusion, the evidence that we are experiencing a 'super-cycle' in all commodities is not overwhelming. It is more likely that over the past decade demand pressures combined with a slow supply response has pushed the price of key commodities to a new plateau. Depending on the speed of supply adjustment or the difficulty of extracting in more extreme locations, commodity prices will follow different long-term dynamics. A scenario of ever-increasing commodity prices worldwide seems at odds with economic theory and history lessons.

1.5 SWFs AS ALTERNATIVE TO AN INCOME TAX SYSTEM: WHAT IF NORWAY BECOMES LIKE SAUDI ARABIA?

In section 1.3 we argued that the exploitation of natural resources could follow various patterns. One course of action cannot, in abstract, be judged superior to others. Ultimately it is a matter of political decisions or collective choices.

Norway and Saudi Arabia (or other countries in the Arabian Gulf) provide two opposite real-life paradigmatic illustrations. The oil deposits under the North Sea were discovered when Norway was already one of the most advanced and prosperous economies in the world, had a modern tax system with a renowned welfare system and stable institutions that had been in place for centuries.

When the windfall started to accumulate, it was decided to save most of it without fundamentally altering the lifestyle of the population and the structure of the economy (apart from the development of the energy extraction sector). In practice it was decided to transfer most of the wealth to future generations. The Norwegian government instituted the ultimate FWF, which has recently been transformed into a pension fund that does not require periodic contributions from the beneficiaries.

By contrast, the discovery of oil under the Arabian sands came at a time when the country, under the influence of the British Empire, had a small (predominantly nomadic) population barely above subsistence. Herding camels or goats, fishing, date cultivation and pearl trading were the most common activities.

The oil windfall in Saudi Arabia and the rest of the Arabian Gulf was used to lift the population's standards of living and, especially after the bonanza following the first oil shock in 1973, it was increasingly destined to improve infrastructure, housing and expand the ranks of public employees.

Saudi Arabia and the other Gulf States do not currently have an income tax system and therefore the oil revenues finance all government functions and several welfare programmes for the citizens. In recent years, benefitting from a considerable increase in the prices of hydrocarbons, all Gulf countries to different degrees have embarked on a sustained programme of economic diversification to prepare for when the oil reserves will be exhausted. The Emirate of Dubai was the first and most aggressive in the pursuit of this strategy.

Would it make sense for Norway to become like Saudi Arabia or Qatar? Certainly one could argue that investing considerable oil revenues in financial assets is not exactly a wise choice, considering the parlous state of the world economy and the risks of catastrophic events such as a break-up of the euro. Furthermore, sovereign debts are skyrocketing to a point at which it would be too tempting for government to inflate away the problem. How smart could it be accumulating fixed income securities for long-term wealth preservation? Likewise the financial crisis of 2008–09 shows that the faith in ever-increasing equity valuations is misplaced and long periods of falling or stagnating stock prices in real terms or widespread bankruptcies are not uncommon.

Actually, if we take the data on the eight decades since 1929, we observe that, in three out of eight, stock returns have been nil or negative in the US. This is not really encouraging if one considers that this record was achieved by the country whose economy dominated the twentieth century.

So one could argue that to provide a pension for future generations, a more attractive alternative to financial assets is investing in human capital and research. It would make more sense for the Norwegian government to fund research, make life more pleasant in the vast, sparsely populated North, expand the high- value-added sector through venture capital initiatives, attract talent and labour from abroad on a scale comparable to that occurring in the Gulf, doubling the population over, say, a decade. Boosting demographics and human capital could prove a more successful long-term strategy than counting on expectations of hefty financial returns.

Sceptics might look back at Japan in the 1980s and the huge surplus it accumulated in financial and real estate assets: it is not so far-fetched to assert that it would have been wiser to expand the economy by allowing more immigration rather than buying large swathes of California and the Rockfeller Center at inflated prices.

In Switzerland, a debate along these lines was triggered by the proposal to launch a SWF, given that the country is experiencing a flood of foreign capital in no little part due to fears of a Eurozone dissolution. Those opposing such a proposal have rightly (in our view) argued that for a country like Switzerland it would be preferable to lower taxes or boost research expenditures rather than invest money abroad. It would be paradoxical that while foreign investors take their savings to Switzerland exactly because they feel it is a safe haven, the Swiss authorities would take this money and invest it abroad.

In conclusion, developed countries that are blessed with a sizeable endowment of raw materials could be better off boosting their own economic potential, giving incentives to invest domestically or attracting human capital from outside rather than exacerbate the current account imbalances.

2

Size and Growth of SWFs Assets

Since SWFs have become an issue in the international political debate, estimates of their size and growth have become a matter of intense speculation. New terms such as 'the new power brokers' have been struck to describe the dramatic increase in the assets managed directly or indirectly by governments and their potential implications for the global economy (McKinsey Global Institute, 2007). Some of these estimates have proven to be exaggerated as they were based on unrealistic extrapolations of past trends.

In general, one faces several problems when trying to estimate the size and growth of SWFs. First, despite the recent increase in transparency and disclosure of information about their operations, some SWFs do not report the amount of assets they manage and the composition of their investments. Therefore, for certain SWFs only estimates are available and of course these are subject to substantial uncertainty. The lack of detailed information about the performance and the composition of the underlying portfolio of some SWFs creates difficulties in forecasting the growth of their assets in the future. Second, there is not a single agreed definition of SWFs and depending on which funds are included in the estimates, the results can vary considerably. For instance, the Peterson Institute, which has published extensive research on the topic of SWFs, also includes some pension funds, for instance CalPERS, in the definition of SWFs (Truman, 2010). Last but not least, any estimate about the future growth of the assets managed by SWFs remains very much dependent on how a set of key economic and financial variables in the countries concerned will evolve: current account and balance of payments surpluses, commodity prices, foreign exchange (FX) reserves and exchange rates. In the years preceding the 2008 recession, as the political debate on the growing influence of SWFs intensified, various estimates about the future growth of SWFs were produced. For instance, in May 2007 Morgan Stanley estimated that assets controlled by SWFs would surpass US$10 trillion by 2014.[1] These estimates were based on the assumption that current account surpluses in emerging markets – the key driver for the growth of FX reserves and SWFs' assets as we will discuss shortly – would remain at very high levels for a prolonged period.

As a result of the global recession, according to data from the IMF, the current account surpluses of emerging markets with established SWFs plunged from US$1071 billion in 2008 to US$546 in 2009, reflecting falling international trade volumes and lower commodity prices. The 2008 sharp correction in asset prices that occurred because the financial crisis impacted the market

---

[1] Stephen Jen, Morgan Stanley, Global Economic Forum, How big Could Sovereign Wealth Funds be by 2015?

value of the assets managed by SWFs heavily, thus resulting in a sharp drop in the total size of their AUM. Projections on current account surplus are also revised frequently. For instance, based on the IMF forecasts included in the World Economic Outlook (WEO) of April 2011, the cumulative current account surplus of countries with established SWFs over 2011–2015 amounted to more than US$5 trillion. In the IMF WEO forecasts of September 2011, the same estimate was US$1.6 trillion, a two-thirds drop from April's forecast.

In this chapter we provide our estimates about the future growth potential of the assets of SWFs based on a range of assumptions for some key growth drivers. The Appendix at the end of this chapter contains detailed information on the sources of the data and the methodology used.

2.1 SIZE AND CLUSTERS OF SWFs

In this book we use the definition of SWFs adopted by the International Working Group of SWFs (IWG), established on 30 April 2008 to identify and draft a set of principles that properly reflect their investment practice and objectives (IMF, 2008a). We believe that this definition, finalized with the active contribution of SWFs, better reflects their true nature. The IWG defines SWFs as 'special purpose investment funds or arrangements that are owned by the general government (including both central and subnational governments). Created by the general governments for macroeconomic purposes, SWFs hold, manage, or administer assets to achieve financial objectives, and employ a set of investment strategies that include investment in foreign financial assets. SWFs are commonly established out of balance of payments surpluses, official foreign currency operations, the proceeds of privatisations, fiscal surpluses, and/or receipts resulting from commodity exports'. According to this definition 'SWFs are a heterogeneous group, comprising fiscal stabilisation funds, saving funds, reserve investment corporations, development funds or Investment Holding Companies, and contingent pension reserve funds without explicit pension liabilities' (Table 2.1).

This definition emphasizes three key features of SWFs:

1 the ownership of SWFs must be directly or indirectly under the control of the state;
2 the investment of all or part of the assets in foreign securities;
3 the lack of predefined liabilities.

On the other hand, the IWG's definition is quite broad for sources of funds and the policy objectives they pursue, reflecting the heterogeneity of SWFs across countries and sometimes within the same country. For instance, in the United Arab Emirates (UAE), there are several SWFs, each one with different mandates and investment objectives. The Abu Dhabi Investment Authority (ADIA) is mostly concerned with the investment of excess reserve into foreign markets.

Table 2.1   Classification of Sovereign Wealth Funds

Stabilization Funds	Insulate budget/economy	Chile, Kazakhstan, Azerbaijan, Algeria, Venezuela
Savings Funds	Intergenerational transfer	Kuwait, Qatar, US, Alaska, UAE
Reserve Investment Corporations	Part of reserves; increasing returns	Korea, China
Development Funds/ Investment Holding Companies	Socio-economic objectives	Malaysia, UAE, Singapore
Contingent Pension Reserve Funds	Finance unspecified; contingent pension liabilities of governments	Australia, New Zealand

Source: International Working Group on Sovereign Wealth Funds.

Likewise, Mubadala Development Company, also from Abu Dhabi, is funded with foreign reserves, but it is mostly engaged in diversifying the economy away from oil extraction. The Investment Corporation of Dubai is a special investment vehicle controlled by the Dubai government and in charge of managing the various activities relating to the economy of the Emirate. China Investment Corporation (CIC) invests both in domestic and international assets. The variety of policy goals, structure and investment style of SWFs is an aspect often neglected in the political and economic debate. According to the Sovereign Wealth Fund Institute (SWFI), our main source of data on the current size of SWFs, assets managed by SWFs by the end of 2011 amounted to about US$4.7 trillion, of which US$2.6 trillion was accounted for by commodity-based SWFs and US$2.1 trillion by non-commodity-based SWFs (see Appendix for a detailed list of SWFs). Despite the relatively high number of SWFs – 55 according to the SWFI – their assets are very concentrated: the largest 11 SWFs, those with assets in excess of US$100 billion, account for more than 80% of the total (Table 2.2).

Of the US$2.6 trillion managed by commodity-based SWFs, assets are concentrated in the UAE, Norway, Saudi Arabia, Kuwait and Russia. In the UAE there are seven SWFs. In Norway, there is the third largest SWF in the world, the Government Pension Fund Global (GPFG), with assets worth US$540 billion. Among the large commodity-exporting countries, Saudi Arabia is unique because it has no separate sovereign fund and the Saudi Arabia Monetary Authority (SAMA), the central bank, is actually in charge of managing both the foreign reserves and the accumulated wealth.[2] Russia is

---

[2] In addition to the funds managed by SAMA, the SWFI includes also the Saudi Public Investment Fund (PIF), originally established in 1971 to facilitate the development of the Saudi economy and since 2008 allowed to make investments in foreign corporations. In 2009 Saudi Arabia announced the establishment of a new SWF named Sanabil al-Saudia. However, due to the lack of sufficient information about this new fund, the SWFI does not include this fund in its list of SWFs.

Table 2.2   Top 20 largest SWFs

Fund name	Country	AuM – US$ bn
1. Abu Dhabi Investment Authority	UAE	627.0
2. SAFE Investment Company	China	567.9
3. Government Pension Fund – Global	Norway	560.0
4. SAMA Foreign Holdings	Saudi Arabia	472.5
5. China Investment Corporation	China	409.6
6. Kuwait Investment Authority	Kuwait	296.0
7. Hong Kong Monetary Authority Investment Portfolio	China – HK	293.3
8. Government of Singapore Investment Corporation	Singapore	247.5
9. Temasek Holding	Singapore	157.2
10. National Social Security Fund	China	134.5
11. National Wealfare Fund[1]	Russia	113.9
12. Qatar Investment Authority	Qatar	85.0
13. Australia Future Fund	Australia	73.0
14. Investment Corporation Dubai	UAE	70.0
15. Libyan Investment Authority	Libya	65.0
16. International Petroleum Investment Company	UAE	58.0
17. Revenue Regulation Fund	Algeria	56.7
18. Alaska Permanent Fund	US	40.3
19. Kazakhsatan National Fund	Kazakhstan	38.6
20. Korea Investment Corporation	South Korea	37.0
SWF commodity-based		2651.0
SWF non-commodity-based		2104.0
SWF total		4755.0

[1] Including the Oil Stabilization Fund.
Source: See Appendix.

one of the last oil-exporting countries to have established a SWF. The Russian Stabilization Fund – initially established in 2003 – was restructured in 2008 by splitting it into two different funds: the Reserve Fund, a stabilization fund with a primary purpose to cushion the fiscal budget in case of a substantial drop in oil prices and the National Wealth Fund, primarily intended to cover future deficits of the National Pension System.[3] All the other oil-commodity-based SWFs have less than US$100 billion of assets under management, as displayed in Table 2.2.

Among non-commodity-based SWFs, China, Hong Kong and Singapore account for nearly 90% of the total assets. Singapore has two SWFs: Temasek, established in 1974, a holding company with equity stakes in several domestic and foreign companies, and the Government of Singapore Investment Corporation (GIC), whose assets are entirely invested abroad. Together, these two SWFs manage assets worth more than US$400 billion and, given their long

---

[3] In Table 2.2, the two Russian funds are considered as one individual SWF.

history and track record, these two SWFs are often taken as a model by other countries when considering establishing new SWFs.

The Hong Kong Monetary Authority (HKMA), the central bank established in 1993 via the consolidation of two pre-existing entities, manages the so-called Exchange Fund, a fund that serves two main purposes: holding US dollar denominated assets to back up Hong Kong's currency board and investing the remaining liquidity in global markets. This latter tranche, named Investment Portfolio, is generally considered to be Hong Kong's SWF. For China, the SWFI lists four SWFs and altogether they manage assets estimated at over US$1100 billion. The largest SWF is a subsidiary of the State Administration of Foreign Exchange (SAFE), the institution responsible for managing China's FX reserves, the largest in the world. SAFE has a subsidiary in Hong Kong named the SAFE Investment Company which is considered a SWF. The second largest Chinese SWF is the CIC, established in 2007. Despite its relatively short life, with more than US$400 billion under management, the CIC has emerged as one of the most active SWFs in the world, as we shall see later. Its multibillion investments in foreign companies often hit the news but it is sometimes forgotten that the largest share of its funds are actually invested domestically, mostly in banks through a wholly owned subsidiary named Central Huijin Investments. The Chinese authorities have recently announced that they will further separate the domestic and international assets managed by CIC. The National Social Security Fund (NSSF) is the third-largest Chinese SWF, established in 2000 but which only recently has started investing part of its assets internationally.

While some SWFs are very old and have been operating in global markets for several decades, the majority of the funds listed by the SWFI were established during 2000 to 2010, reflecting soaring commodity prices and large current account surpluses, as we will discuss later. Their number continues to rise as several countries are in the process of setting up a SWF or are considering this option. In Asia, Papua New Guinea has already finalized the legislative framework for a new stabilization and development fund. Its primary goal will be to insulate its economy from volatility in gas prices (this recently established SWF is already listed by the SWFI; Table 2.A.2 in the Appendix). Mongolia, benefitting from rising mining revenues, is also in the process of setting up a stabilization fund. Macao, the special administration zone of China with a booming gambling industry, has already surpassed Las Vegas in terms of annual visitors to its casinos and has recently established a new Reserve Fund with a mandate to invest globally. In other Asian countries with large FX reserves – including Thailand, Philippines, India and Japan – the political debate over the pros and cons of establishing a SWF is ongoing and we might well see some action in the future. In Australia, where the Australian Future Fund is funded by budget revenues, there is a very lively debate among politicians and academics on whether an additional fund financed by booming commodity revenues should be established. In China, according to media reports,[4] the central bank plans to create a new SWF to manage FX reserves worth US$300 billion. This new SWF would be affiliated with SAFE and would include two funds: the Hua Ou (or China–Europe in Chinese), targeting investments in Europe, and the Hua Mei (China–US), targeting investment in the United States. The two funds would be similar to the already existing SAFE Investment Company and they would focus on the acquisition of equity stakes.

The other regions with an increasing number of SWFs are Africa and the Middle East. Israel is considering the establishment of a SWF following the discovery of two massive offshore natural gas fields about 130 km west of Haifa. According to some estimates, by 2020 gas exports will raise Israel's already high trade surplus by a third (Milken Institute, 2011). Israel already has more than US$70 billion of FX reserves managed by the central bank and the new fund would aim to invest part of this for macroeconomic stabilization and long-term saving. In sub-Saharan Africa, Nigeria was the first African country to establish a SWF (the Excess Crude Account in 2004); most of these funds were withdrawn following the global crisis and the Nigerian government has recently launched a new sovereign fund, named the Nigerian Sovereign Investment Authority. Ghana has already passed the legislation required to set up a SWF and is now starting operations. Angola and other commodity-exporting countries including Namibia, Mozambique, Uganda and Tanzania, are in the process or are considering the establishment of separate state-controlled investment vehicles.

Overall, following a decade that witnessed the establishment of nearly 30 new institutions, the trend is expected to continue.

How big are SWFs compared to other institutional asset managers? By using estimates of the size of other institutional asset managers provided by McKinsey, SWFs' assets are larger than hedge funds (US$2.8 trillion) and private equity funds (US$0.9 trillion) but they are much smaller than the three largest institutional asset management sectors: insurance funds (US$19.2 trillion of assets under management), mutual funds (US$25.9 trillion) and pension funds (US$23.3 trillion). The picture changes somewhat when SWF assets are considered together with the FX reserves held by the central banks in these countries (nearly US$6 trillion): the total 'sovereign wealth' controlled by governments would rise to over US$10 trillion, five times the size of the assets managed by hedge funds but still smaller than the assets of insurance, pensions and investment funds.[5]

---

[4] China Central Bank to Create US$300 billion FX Investment Vehicle, Thomson Reuters, 9 December 2011.

[5] However, one might argue that FX reserves and SWFs' assets are much more concentrated. While it is true that there are very large pension funds (e.g. The California Public Employees' Retirement System, CalPERS, manages assets in excess of US$200 billion) and some insurance companies control very large amount of assets (e.g. Zurich Financial Service, an insurance

2.2 DRIVERS OF SWFs ASSET GROWTH

The common denominator of most countries with SWFs is that they have a positive trade balance with the rest of the world, reflecting either large oil export receipts, in commodity-exporting countries, or manufactured good export receipts, in Asian export-led economies (Vietnam is a hybrid case).[6] Of the 35 countries with SWFs considered in the Appendix, during 2000–2010 only eight countries had a current account deficit: three advanced economies (Australia, New Zealand and Ireland) and five emerging markets (Brazil, Mexico, Kazakhstan, Mauritania and Vietnam). Excluding these eight countries, the combined current account surplus of all the countries with SWFs increased from a yearly average of US$51 billion in 1990–2000 to more than US$500 billion in 2000–2010 (Table 2.3). In the peak year of 2008, it surpassed US$1.1 trillion, equally split between commodity- and non-commodity-exporting countries.

As we have repeatedly stressed, soaring current account surpluses translate into rising FX reserves (Table 2.4). For commodity-exporting countries, the rise in foreign reserves has been largely associated with the energy price boom that started in early 2000. Since then, their current account surpluses have soared as expenditure has grown less than exports, leading to a rapid accumulation of financial wealth. In the 1990s, their FX reserve-to-GDP ratio averaged 12% of GDP; in 2000, this ratio started rising and this rise continued uninterrupted throughout the decade stabilizing at more than 40%. As a result, in one decade, total FX reserves held by commodity-exporting countries climbed from around US$66 billion to US$1440 billion, corresponding to a

Table 2.3 Current account surplus in commodity- and non-commodity-exporting countries with SWFs (US$ and as a percentage of GDP)

	1990	2000	2010	1990–2000 average	2000–2010 average
Current account surplus (US$ billion)					
Commodity	28	166	367	23	293
Non-commodity	17	61	425	28	250
Commodity and non-commodity	45	227	792	51	543
Current account surplus (% GDP)					
Commodity	5.2	14.1	8.8	1.8	11.3
Non-commodity	1.9	2.8	5.5	1.7	5.2
Commodity and non-commodity	2.8	6.7	6.6	1.7	7.5

Source: See Appendix.

company, manages US$120 billion), the majority of the assets managed by investment and pension funds are controlled by thousands of different independent entities across several countries.

[6] Foreign exchange reserves can also grow as a result of positive net capital inflows. This factor is not particularly relevant for commodity-exporting countries but it is quite important for Asian exporters, which in the past few years, in addition to soaring current account surpluses, have also enjoyed rising financial inflows.

Table 2.4   FX reserves in commodity- and non-commodity-exporting (in US$ and as a percentage of GDP)

	1990	2000	2010	1990–2000 average	2000–2010 average
FX reserves (US$ billion)					
Commodity	66	170	1441	23	293
Non-commodity	112	485	3759	28	250
Commodity and non-commodity	178	656	5199	51	543
FX reserves (% GDP)					
Commodity	12.1	14.4	34.5	11.2	25.3
Non-commodity	12.9	22.2	48.3	17.0	35.3
Commodity and non-commodity	11.2	19.5	43.5	14.4	31.6

Source: See Appendix.

yearly compound growth rate of more than 20%. Two countries – Saudi Arabia and Russia – account for the lion's share: 60% of the total by the end of 2010.

The growth in the official FX reserve of non-commodity countries has been equally spectacular: from around US$500 billion in 2000 to nearly US$4000 billion in 2010, also corresponding to a yearly compound rate of more than 20% (Table 2.4). The yearly growth rate of Chinese reserves, exceeding US$3 trillion in 2011, was more than 30% over the decade.

The FX reserves allocated to government securities are often invested in bonds with short maturity to minimize capital losses. Overall, in the trade-off between liquidity and return faced by any private or institutional investor, central banks have a preference for the former and therefore foreign reserves traditionally produce a low return. The World Bank which runs a Treasury service for central banks (http://treasury.worldbank.org/sip/htm/index.html), suggests that the opportunity cost of this policy can easily reach 1% of GDP.

The diversification of foreign reserves into more lucrative investments does not necessarily require the establishment of a separate investment vehicle such as a SWF. A central bank or the Treasury, after having assessed that reserves exceed the level considered adequate for monetary or precautionary motives, can adopt a more dynamic style. This trend was already observable before the financial crisis when several central banks relaxed their prudential criteria and invested in less liquid, higher return assets. This trend paused as a result of the financial crisis but restarted more recently as the impact of the financial crisis gradually faded away and asset prices recovered (see Park, 2011). Alternatively, a central bank can split its portfolio in different tranches, each one with a different policy goal: for instance a policy tranche, aimed at providing the central bank with the working capital required for its daily FX operations; a liquid tranche, capable of enhancing yield with low volatility and high liquidity; and an investment tranche for long-term return maximization. Or finally, it could opt for the establishment of a SWF with the explicit mandate to invest part of the national wealth in less liquid and more risky assets with a long-term investment horizon (Saidi and Scacciavillani, 2011).[7]

According to this rationale, the growth of SWFs is largely associated with the rise in FX reserves which in certain countries have reached a level beyond that required for monetary policy or contingency motives.

2.3 THE OPTIMAL LEVEL OF FOREIGN EXCHANGE RESERVES

Any estimate of their potential growth should be based on an accurate estimate of the future growth of foreign reserves as they represent – together with the return obtained on the accumulated assets – the main source of additional funds. This is indeed the methodology adopted in the Appendix for estimating the growth of SWFs' assets over the period 2011–2016.

The key question, therefore, concerns what level of foreign reserves is adequate for policy and liquidity purposes. The academic debate dates back to the 1960s and 1970s (for a review see Flood and Marion, 2002). Two approaches emerge: the descriptive approach and the optimal level approach. The descriptive approach focuses on the demand of international reserves by central banks, in analogy to the determination for money demand by individuals. Central banks maintain foreign assets for three motives:

1 a transaction motive, i.e a means of payment for FX transactions;
2 a precautionary motive, i.e. a buffer against unforeseen events like wars or a sudden drop in cross-border capital flows;
3 the speculative motive, i.e. the return on foreign assets compared to domestic ones.

In the descriptive approach, therefore, the adequacy of the reserves is often expressed in terms of their ratio to another economic variable, for instance:

- months of imports of goods and services;
- short-term debt immediately coming due;
- GDP or to any other measure of money supply;
- a combination of the above.

---

[7] Each alternative has its pros and cons. Reserves management under one roof and within a single portfolio has the advantage of permitting an integrated investment policy, low operational costs and high liquidity. But it also increases the reputational risk for the central bank in cases of losses and can lead to conflicts of interest in the management of the different portions of the total portfolio. Splitting the portfolio into different tranches increases operational costs and decreases the average liquidity of the reserves, but increases the gains from diversification. Finally, the establishment of a SWF increases operational costs and decreases liquidity even more but reduces the reputational risks for the central bank and allows the capture of more diversification gains.

These indicators on the adequacy of FX reserves put emphasis on either the use of reserves for transaction purposes (ratio to monetary base or GDP) or for precautionary purposes (ratio to months of imports or ratio to short or total external debt), but they neglect the speculative motive as they do not take into account the opportunity cost of holding the reserves.

The problem with these descriptive measures is that there is not a level of these ratios that can be considered optimal in absolute terms and outside the economic, financial and institutional context of the countries under consideration.[8] The best-known descriptive 'rule of thumb' for the adequacy of FX reserves is the Guidotti–Greenspan,[9] assuming that a 100% coverage of short-term external debt makes a country less vulnerable to external crises.

According to the alternative optimization approach, the optimal level of reserve is estimated by maximizing a government's objective function subject to certain constraints. For instance, Jeanne and Ranciere (2006) conclude that the optimal level of reserves for an average middle-income economy with an average probability of a sudden stop in capital flows is around 8% of GDP. This is well below the level observed in most emerging markets and very close to the level determined with the Guidotti–Greenspan rule. The rise in official reserves in most emerging markets – particularly in Asia – in 2000–2010 should therefore be considered excessive.

Overall, the academic and empirical debate over what is the 'optimal' level of reserves has not reached a final consensus because in practical terms the accumulation of reserves is not a simple optimization process based on an accurate estimation of costs and benefits.[10] Rather, it is a by-product of the decisions taken by each individual country in the area of fiscal, monetary and exchange rate policies. In addition to the precautionary or self-insurance motive, some countries such as China accumulate FX reserves in the process of keeping their currency undervalued, according to a policy sometimes defined as mercantilist. If this country were to let its currency appreciate and its current account surplus fall, the build-up of reserves would stop or reverse. It is very difficult to draw a clear distinction between the relative importance

---

[8] According to the descriptive approach, the key variable for the adequacy of the reserves is the likelihood of a financial crisis in the country under consideration. This probability tends to be negatively correlated with the level of development of the country in question and that is why most advanced economies have relatively low reserve-to-GDP ratios while emerging markets tend to have higher ratios. Higher integration into global capital markets also requires higher reserves as the potential impact of a sudden outflow of foreign capital becomes larger.

[9] The rule is named after Pablo Guidotti – Argentinian former minister of finance – and Alan Greenspan – former chairman of the US Federal Reserve – and was first stated in 1999 at an international summit.

[10] Some countries have carried out an accurate analysis of the adequate level of foreign exchange reserves, for instance Chile (Jadresic, 2007). In Chile a reserve optimization exercise was carried out by the central bank between 2001 and 2003, calculating both marginal costs and benefits of holding reserves. Following this exercise, the level of foreign reserves has actually been reduced. Another country that has carried out a similar exercise is Mexico (Ortiz, 2007).

of self-insurance and mercantilist policies in explaining the rapid build-up of FX reserves following the Asian crisis in the middle of the 1990s. One could observe that in the period following the Asian crisis and the Russian crisis in the second half of 1990, the use of reserves to counter the depreciation of the currency has become a rarity. Much more common has been intervention to stem the appreciation of the domestic currency. Apart from the demise of the currency board in Argentina (which is a one-of-a-kind situation), only a handful of episodes involving sizeable countries come to mind, and mostly during or as a consequence of the disruption caused by the Great Recession in 2008 or, more recently, some selected cases of depreciation as a result of the negative impact of the euro debt crisis on global markets. Otherwise intervention has always taken the form of concerted actions, for example the euro being propped up in 2002 by the European Central Bank (ECB), the Federal Reserve and the Bank of Japan. A similar move was initiated after the tsunami in Japan to offset the appreciation of the yen. Often these interventions are carried out through swap agreements between central banks, rather than outright purchases of FX on the markets.

So it would not be too far-fetched to assert that, with the evolution of markets and the coming of age of many large emerging countries, the optimal level of FX reserves is lower. Ultimately, the desire of central banks to hoard reserves, beyond the parameters such as the Guidotti–Greenspan rule could find its rationale in the 'Mrs Machlup rule', the concept developed by the Austrian-born economist Fritz Machlup in 1966. According to this rule, the demand of central bankers for international reserves would be comparable to that 'of a woman for clothes' and regarded as 'a simple desire for a little more than last year'. According to this witty comparison, central bankers would always tend to target an increase in their reserves and consider as negative any drop in their level.

2.4 FUTURE GROWTH IN FX RESERVES: COMMODITY- VERSUS NON-COMMODITY-EXPORTING COUNTRIES

Whether the recent build-up of reserves is temporary and largely a reflection of the global macroeconomic imbalances and high energy prices or a trend that will continue unabated in the future is up for discussion. The 2008–2009 global crisis slowed down the accumulation of foreign reserves in emerging markets, mostly as a result of the fall in commodity prices in the summer of 2008 and the collapse in international trade the following year. However, this slowdown seems to have been just a pause and FX reserves in most emerging markets started growing again in 2010 and 2011, some surpassing the pre-crisis peak (for instance in China, Brazil and South Korea). Will FX reserves continue to rise?

According to the latest forecasts by the IMF in its WEO (September 2011, see the Appendix for details), the majority of countries with established SWFs will continue enjoying high and persistent current account surplus over 2011–2016. Their cumulative current account surplus over this period will be nearly US$7 trillion, US$2 trillion more than that of the previous six years (2005–2010). This US$2 trillion of additional surplus is almost entirely accounted for by China, where the current account surplus in 2012 is already expected to pass the peak reached before the crisis. In commodity-exporting countries, the external trade surplus is expected to remain positive but will gradually fall over the next few years leaving its cumulative value over 2011–2016 at levels pretty similar to that of the previous five years (Table 2.5). Overall, therefore, the current account surpluses of most economies with SWFs will remain high over the next few years unless a new recession hits the global economy, energy prices fall substantially from current levels or the macroeconomic imbalances are addressed through a political agreement between the Western world and emerging markets.

Will persistent current account surplus translate into rising FX reserves at the pace experienced in 2000–2010? We believe that a further substantial increase in the level of reserves when measured relative to GDP in emerging markets is unlikely. First, as discussed in the previous section, the level of FX reserves reached in most of the countries considered here seems more than adequate for precautionary or self-insurance motives. This is indirectly proven by the fact that during the last crisis – one of the worse recessions in the post-war era – the median reserve loss experienced in emerging markets was 27% of peak reserves (Prasad, 2011). Second, the costs and the risk associated with holding an ever-growing stock of reserves invested into government bonds of advanced economies have substantially increased in the post-financial crisis era. Before the crisis of 2008, there was already considerable pressure on central banks to diversify given the historically low level of interest in most advanced economies. Following the crisis, not only have returns on these assets fallen even further but the risk associated with the sustainability of public finances in the US, Europe and Japan has grown. Finally, the most likely trend for most Asian countries is for a revaluation of their currencies as they reorient their growth model towards domestic consumption; this will make the cost of

Table 2.5 Cumulative current account surplus in 2011–16 in commodity- and non-commodity-exporting countries (in US$ billion)

	2011	2012	2013	2014	2015	2016	2011–2016 cumulative
Commodity	578	489	439	391	383	350	2629
Non-commodity	476	550	654	758	869	978	4283
Total	1053	1038	1092	1149	1251	1328	6913

Source: See Appendix.

holding large reserves invested in the currencies of advanced countries even higher. Hence our key assumption is that FX reserves will continue to rise in absolute terms, but relative to GDP they will be on par with the level reached at the end of 2010. In Table 2.A.6 we illustrate our estimates for FX reserves in countries with SWFs (and with current account surplus) by 2016 by making a clear distinction between commodity- and non-commodity-exporting countries.[11]

In absolute terms, FX reserves will grow from about US$5200 billion in 2010 to over US$8700 billion in 2016, corresponding to an increase of about US$3500 billion over the period (Table 2.6). Relative to GDP, they will remain unchanged at the average level of 2005–2010, corresponding to a compound yearly growth rate of around 9%, in line with their forecasted nominal growth over 2010–2016. This rate of growth is less than half the rate experienced in 2000–2010. Non-commodity-exporting countries, with China accounting for the lion's share, will add US$2600 billion of reserves, about two-thirds of the total. Commodity-exporting countries will add nearly US$900 billion.

2.5 SIZE OF SWFs BY 2016

After having forecasted the growth in the official FX reserves, the growth of the assets managed by SWFs is determined by three factors: the return on the wealth accumulated, the fiscal policy framework adopted by the countries concerned and the new funds transferred from the current account surpluses. With regards to first factor, we have taken into account three different return scenarios:

1   a conservative scenario, with a yearly average return of 3% over 2011–2016;
2   a baseline scenario with a return of 6% per year;
3   an aggressive scenario with a yearly average return of 9%.

The baseline return scenario reflects the average return obtained on a balanced portfolio (60% fixed income and 40% equity) in the past few decades and is a good approximation of the average long-term return experienced by SWFs (discussed in more detail in Chapter 3).

---

[11] To simplify our analysis and also considering that our forecast of the future level of FX reserves is just instrumental to our final goal, i.e. forecasting the future growth of SWFs assets, we have not taken into account the return obtained on the accumulated reserves. This assumption seems reasonable considering the current level of interest on the shortest end of the fixed income curve and the fact that central banks are not generally concerned with the return obtained on their reserves. However, for some of the largest FX holders, even a small return on accumulated reserves can be a substantial amount. For instance, for China, 1% of return on the current level of reserves would translate into a gain of US$30 billion.

Table 2.6 FX reserves in 2010–2016 and cumulative (in US$ billion)

	2010	2011	2012	2013	2014	2015	2016	Change 2010–2016	CAGR 2010–2016 (%)
Commodity-exporting countries of which:	1441	1649	1763	1897	2030	2174	2331	891	8.4%
Russia	444	558	627	694	761	832	914	471	12.8%
Saudi Arabia	445	460	477	509	540	571	605	160	5.3%
Non-commodity exporting countries of which:	3759	3931	4333	4773	5254	5780	6366	2607	9.2%
China PRC	2866	3027	3354	3729	4141	4594	5102	2236	9.9%
Commodity and non-commodity exporting countries	5199	5580	6097	6670	7284	7954	8697	3498	8.9%

Source: see Appendix.

Fiscal policy is assumed to be largely unchanged from the current stance. In other words, both countries relying on commodity export revenues and those in structural surplus will maintain the share allocated to public expenditure constant as a share of GDP.

For the third factor driving the growth of SWFs assets, the inflow of additional funds, we simply assumed that the residual of countries' current account surplus not being allocated to foreign reserves is entirely shifted to SWFs.[12]

The overall results of our forecasts for the commodity and non-commodity SWFs' assets are illustrated in Table 2.7. For commodity funds, SWFs assets increase from US$2651 billion in 2011 to US$5451 billion in 2016 in the likely scenario (US$4742 billion and US$5977 billion in the conservative and aggressive scenarios respectively). This growth corresponds to a compounded annual growth rate of between 12.3 and 17.7% depending on which return scenario is considered.

For non-commodity funds, SWFs' assets swell from US$2104 billion in 2011 to US$4378 billion in 2016 in the baseline scenario (US$3935 billion and US$4855 billion in the conservative and aggressive scenarios respectively). This corresponds to an annual compounded growth rate ranging between 13.3

Table 2.7   Growth of SWFs 2011–2016 (in US$ billion)

	2011	2012	2013	2014	2015	2016	CAGR 2011–2016
Conservative scenario – return on assets 3%							
Total commodity	2651	3128	3558	3958	4357	4742	12.3%
Total non-commodity	2104	2286	2586	2961	3415	3935	13.3%
SWF total	4755	5414	6144	6919	7772	8677	12.8%
Likely scenario – return on assets 6%							
Total commodity	2651	3223	3770	4311	4875	5451	15.5%
Total non-commodity	2104	2347	2719	3179	3736	4378	15.8%
SWF total	4755	5570	6489	7490	8611	9829	15.6%
Aggressive scenario – return on assets 9%							
Total commodity	2651	3287	3918	4562	5251	5977	17.7%
Total non-commodity	2104	2408	2854	3404	4074	4855	18.2%
SWF total	4755	5696	6771	7966	9325	10832	17.9%

Source: See Appendix.

---

[12] The majority of countries with SWFs have and will continue to have current account surpluses over 2011–2016. For those countries with a projected current account deficit (nine countries: Canada, Australia, Brazil, Mexico, Indonesia, New Zealand, Vietnam, East Timor and Mauritania), the assets managed by their respective SWFs are assumed to grow at the average rate of those included in our forecasts. It is important to keep in mind that the assets managed by SWFs from countries with current account deficits represent only 5% of the total assets managed by SWFs globally. See the Appendix for more details on the methodology adopted.

and 18.2%. **Overall, by 2016 SWFs assets are forecasted to reach US$8,657 billion in the baseline scenario, almost double the amount estimated by the SWFI at end 2011**.

On these forecasts, a number of observations can be made. First, while the return on accumulated assets has an impact, as shown by the results of the sensitivity analysis, the most important driver for the future growth of SWFs assets is the inflow of additional funds. This is of course a reflection of the widening current account surpluses. For China and the other Asian exporting countries, a robust revaluation of their currencies as often advocated by the US and other Western countries would change our forecasts dramatically as their current account surpluses would shrink significantly in such a scenario (in addition to determining a loss on their FX reserves largely invested in US dollar denominated assets). For the oil-exporting countries, a fall in commodity prices or a substantial increase in domestic expenditure – for instance as a result of the political turmoil in the Middle East and North Africa region – would also reduce the future inflows of funds into SWFs. The second observation concerns the fact that – according to our forecasts – the relative size of assets held by commodity- and non-commodity-based SWFs remains almost unchanged during the period, with the former accounting for around 55% of the total. However, this is also because commodity-based SWFs are estimated to be larger in the baseline year (2011), thus benefitting from higher returns on the accumulated wealth in the following years.

In our forecasts non-commodity-based inflows into SWFs are expected to become larger than those in commodity-based SWFs during 2011–2016. This is largely a reflection of the IMF projections on the future development of current account surpluses in commodity- and non-commodity-exporting countries. The current account of the two largest commodity exporters, Saudi Arabia and Russia, are expected to gradually fall over 2011–2016, reflecting rising domestic expenditure in both countries as they try to raise their growth potential by investing in infrastructure and intangible assets. In contrast, the IMF forecasts that the current account surplus for China – following the pause of 2009–2010 due to the global recession – will continue to rise in the next few years.

The third observation concerns the increasing concentration of the assets managed by SWFs in a relatively small number of countries. Of some US$10 trillion of assets that SWFs will manage by 2016, about 85% is concentrated in only eight countries: Norway, Saudi Arabia, UAE and China, whose SWFs will manage more than US$1 trillion each; and Kuwait, Qatar, Hong Kong and Singapore (detailed forecasts by individual countries are available in the Appendix).

A word of caution is warranted about the prospect that non-commodity-based funds will eventually outgrow the commodity-based ones. On the one hand, new discoveries or the exploitation of oil and gas reserves in places such as Brazil, Iraq or Israel, and the launch of new SWFs in places such as Nigeria,

Angola and other African countries, might very well change the picture. On the other hand, the sustainability of current account surpluses in China hinges on the expectation of a gradual readjustment of global imbalances as embedded in the IMF scenarios. However, there lurks a risk that at some point a traumatic event, such as a sizeable sovereign default, will set in motion a chain of events that leads to a sudden adjustment.

APPENDIX: HOW BIG COULD SWFs BE BY 2016?

As we discussed in Chapter 2, the most common feature of countries with established SWFs or countries considering the establishment of a SWF is persistent current account surpluses, leading to the accumulation of FX reserves. Persistent surpluses in the trade balance, determined either by soaring commodity exports or by increasing shares in the export market of manufactured goods, translate into the accumulation of assets held abroad. In the terminology of national accounting, the net international investment position of a country – essentially, its balance sheet in relation to the rest of the world – improves as its external assets grow faster than its external liabilities. In 1990–2010, one of the most remarkable developments was the increasing dominance of FX reserves in the asset position of most emerging markets. By the end of 2010, FX reserves accounted for more than half of the total external assets in emerging markets; in countries such as China and India they accounted for about two-thirds of total external assets (Prasad, 2011). Given their self-insurance purpose, FX reserves are generally invested in safe and liquid assets, typically government bonds of advanced economies. With the dramatic increase in FX reserves experienced in 1990–2010, the opportunity cost of holding FX reserves invested into low-yield (albeit more recently less safe) government bonds of advanced economies increased dramatically, thus leading to the proliferation of SWFs.

According to this rationale, the starting point of any estimate of the growth potential of SWFs should be the projection of the current account balance.

We assume that a portion of each country's surplus is allocated either to FX reserves or existing (or eventually newly established) SWFs. With regard to the data on current accounts, we rely on the IMF's September 2011 World Economic Outlook (WEO) Database, one of the most complete data sets of country coverage providing a complete set of key macroeconomic forecasts covering the period 2010–2016.[13] As to the forecast of FX reserves, projecting the trend prevailing in emerging markets over 1990–2010, we assume that the level of FX reserves relative to GDP remains broadly unchanged over 2011–2016 at the average level of the second half of 2010. Then, by using the GDP forecasts provided by the IMF WEO, we estimate the future level of FX reserves across countries. The rationale is that FX reserves have reached a level that is considered more than adequate for liquidity and precautionary motives, and any additional flow of funds generated from current account surpluses should be allocated to stabilization and/or savings funds. To make our forecast more robust, we will also show the results obtained by using the country-by-country ratio of the yearly change in FX reserves to the current account balance over the second half of 2010 to determine the future level of FX reserves. According to this alternative approach, we assume that rather

---

[13] The entire World Economic Outlook Database can be downloaded at: http://www.imf.org/external/pubs/ft/weo/2011/02/weodata/index.aspx

than aiming at a target level of FX reserves relative to GDP, countries allocate a pre-set share of their yearly current account surplus to FX reserves. The two approaches lead to remarkably similar results in commodity-exporting countries, while some differences emerge for non-commodity-exporting countries. We believe that the diverging results between the two groups of countries actually make sense and reflect the different nature of the accumulation in their reserves, as discussed later.

Once the future level of FX reserves has been determined, the future flow of funds to SWFs is simply the residual from the annual current account surplus. In short, we assume that any current account surplus not allocated to FX reserves is transferred to separate state-controlled investment vehicles. This approach naturally works only for those countries with a current account surplus (the majority of the countries with SWFs considered here and representing about 95% of the total assets managed by SWFs globally). For those countries with current account deficits, we will assume that the assets controlled by SWFs will grow in line with the expected inflow of funds provided by their respective governments. We stress that given the relatively small size of the SWFs' assets controlled by countries with a current account deficit, the influence of this simplification on the future size of SWFs estimated here is negligible.

The second driver of the growth in SWFs' assets is the return on the accumulated assets[14] which depends on several factors, some external (market returns across asset classes) and some internal (the investment profile of the specific fund). As the purpose of this exercise is not to provide an estimate of the future size of each single SWF but rather to forecast the global size of SWFs based on current macroeconomic trends, we estimate the average yearly return on total SWFs assets on the basis of three different scenarios: a baseline scenario, a conservative scenario and an aggressive scenario.

The baseline scenario assumes an average annual nominal return of 6% over 2011–2016 and reflects the average return obtained by an investor on a standard balanced portfolio (60% fixed income and 40% equity) over the past few decades. The conservative scenario assumes an average annual nominal rate of 3%, reflecting the current low level of interest rates prevailing across advanced economies and the low return on global equities experienced in 2010. The aggressive scenario is based on an average annual nominal return of 9%, on the assumption of a return of interest rates to their long-term historical means and positive returns on equity over the next few years.[15]

---

[14] The return on accumulated assets is also a driver for FX reserves. However, as FX reserves are largely invested into government bonds and because of the current very low level of interest rates, we ignored this factor in the forecast of the future level of FX reserves.

[15] For an overview of the historical returns across asset classes and different investment strategies see Antti (2011, table 2.1, p. 25).

Before presenting the results of our estimates, we draw attention to two key factors that play a key role in the determination of the final results: energy prices and the current account surplus of China.

With regard to the former, the IMF assumes that energy prices (in Table 2.A.1, the case for oil and gas is also illustrated) will remain at relatively high level over the next few years. In its forecasts, therefore, the IMF seems to be also leaning towards the existence of a super-cycle in the commodity sector expected to endure throughout 2010–2016. Thus, commodity-exporting countries will continue experiencing large and sometimes growing current account surpluses: over 2011–2016, the average yearly current account surplus of commodity-exporting countries with SWFs (excluding Canada, Brazil, Mexico and Australia that will experience current account deficits) is projected at US$440 billion, above that experienced on average in 2000–2010 (around US$300 billion). Commodity-exporting countries will therefore remain a major source of capital invested in global capital markets by central banks or SWFs.

For the Chinese current account surplus, the IMF forecasts that, following the 2009 sharp slowdown in Chinese exports due to the global recession (when the current account surplus dropped to around US$260 billion), its current account surplus will continue rising over the next years. It is forecasted to surpass the pre-crisis peak touched in 2008 during 2012 and reach the staggering amount of US$852 billion in 2016. If the IMF forecasts prove to be correct, over 2011–2016 the cumulated Chinese current account surplus would exceed US$3000 billion, more than any other country in the world and equivalent to the current stock of FX reserves accumulated by China so far. This huge amount will eventually translate into either growing FX reserves or will be transferred to existing or newly created SWFs. Based on the IMF forecasts, as we will show below, over 2011–2016 China is set to account for more than 60% of the increase in FX reserves and nearly 40% of the additional flow of funds into SWFs.

Table 2.A.1 Simple average of crude oil prices (US$ per barrel) and gas (Index, 2005 = 100)

	1990–2000	2000–2008	2009–2010	2011–2012
Oil[1]	20	47.8	70.4	101.6
Gas[2]	43.5	89.6	11.5	138.4

[1] Crude oil (petroleum), simple average of three spot prices (APSP); Dated Brent, West Texas Intermediate, and the Dubai Fateh.
[2] Commodity natural gas price index includes European, Japanese, and American natural gas price indices.
Source: World Economic Outlook, September 2011.

Current size of SWFs

Table 2.A.2 illustrates the amount of assets controlled by SWFs globally at December 2011 according to the SWFI.[16] We will use this data set as our baseline to forecast the size of assets controlled by SWFs throughout the period 2011–2016. The SWFI lists a total of 55 SWFs; in our forecasts we excluded 17 funds for the following reasons.

1 Lack of reliable macroeconomic forecasts (2): Iran (Oil Stabilisation Fund, US$23 billion) and Kiribati (Revenue Equalization Fund, US$0.4 billion).
2 Sub-national SWFs, all in the US (4): Alaska Permanent Fund, US$40.3 billion; Texas Permanent School Fund, US$24.4 billion; New Mexico State Investment Council, US$14.3 billion; and the Permanent Wyoming Mineral Trust Fund, US$4.7 billion.
3 Countries with projected current account deficits over 2011–2016 (9): Canada (Alberta's Heritage Fund, US$15.1 billion); Australia (Australian Future Fund, US$73 billion); Brazil (Sovereign Wealth Fund, US$11.3 billion); Mexico (Oil Revenue Stabilisation Fund, US$6 billion); Indonesia (Government Investment Unit, US$0.3 billion); New Zealand (Superannuation Fund, US$13.5 billion); Vietnam (State Capital Investment Corporation, US$0.5 billion); East Timor (Timor-Leste Petroleum Fund); and Mauritania (National Fund for Hydrocarbon Reserves).
4 Different source of funding (2): France (Strategic Investment Fund, US$28 billion); Italy (Italian Strategic Fund, US$1.4 billion)

The 17 SWFs not included in our estimates control assets worth US$263 billion, representing around 5% of the total assets managed by the SWFs in December 2011. In our estimates on the growth of SWFs' assets over 2011–2016, to allow a comparison with the data provided by the SWFI, we will include these 17 SWFs by assuming that their assets will grow at the same rate as those included in our forecasts. As already mentioned, this simplification does not alter in any way the soundness of our methodology given the relatively small size of these funds when compared to the total size of assets currently managed by SWFs.

FX reserve forecasts to 2016

To estimate the future level of FX reserves, we use the average FX reserve-to-GDP ratio over 2005–2010 to project their value to 2016. In other words,

---

[16] The Sovereign Wealth Fund Rankings are updated quarterly by the Sovereign Wealth Fund Institute. All figures quoted are from official sources, or, where the institutions concerned do not issue statistics of their assets, from other publicly available sources. Some of the figures are best estimates because market values change daily. The databank used can be downloaded from http://www.swfinstitute.org/fund-rankings/. Source: The Sovereign Wealth Fund Institute.

Table 2.A.2 Sovereign wealth fund rankings

Country	Fund name	Assets (US$ billion)	Inception	Origin
UAE – Abu Dhabi	Abu Dhabi Investment Authority	627	1976	Oil
China	SAFE Investment Company	567.9[2]	1997	Non-commodity
Norway	Government Pension Fund – Global	560	1990	Oil
Saudi Arabia	SAMA Foreign Holdings	472.5	n/a	Oil
China	China Investment Corporation	409.6	2007	Non-commodity
Kuwait	Kuwait Investment Authority	296	1953	Oil
China – Hong Kong	Hong Kong Monetary Authority Investment Portfolio	293.3	1993	Non-commodity
Singapore	Government of Singapore Investment Corporation	247.5	1981	Non-commodity
Singapore	Temasek Holdings	157.2	1974	Non-commodity
China	National Social Security Fund	134.5	2000	Non-commodity
Russia	National Welfare Fund	113.9[1]	2008	Oil
Qatar	Qatar Investment Authority	85	2005	Oil
Australia	Australian Future Fund	73	2004	Non-commodity
UAE – Dubai	Investment Corporation of Dubai	70	2006	Oil
Libya	Libyan Investment Authority	65	2006	Oil
UAE – Abu Dhabi	International Petroleum Investment Company	58	1984	Oil
Algeria	Revenue Regulation Fund	56.7	2000	Oil
US – Alaska	Alaska Permanent Fund	40.3	1976	Oil
Kazakhstan	Kazakhstan National Fund	38.6	2000	Oil
South Korea	Korea Investment Corporation	37	2005	Non-commodity
Malaysia	Khazanah Nasional	36.8	1993	Non-commodity
Azerbaijan	State Oil Fund	30.2	1999	Oil

Ireland	National Pensions Reserve Fund	30	2001	Non-commodity
Brunei	Brunei Investment Agency	30	1983	Oil
France	Strategic Investment Fund	28	2008	Non-commodity
UAE – Abu Dhabi	Mubadala Development Company	27.1	2002	Oil
US – Texas	Texas Permanent School Fund	24.4	1854	Oil and other
Iran	Oil Stabilisation Fund	23	1999	Oil
Chile	Social and Economic Stabilization Fund	21.8	1985	Copper
Canada	Alberta's Heritage Fund	15.1	1976	Oil
US – New Mexico	New Mexico State Investment Council	14.3	1958	Non-commodity
New Zealand	New Zealand Superannuation Fund	13.5	2003	Non-commodity
Brazil	Sovereign Fund of Brazil	11.3	2008	Non-commodity
Bahrain	Mumtalakat Holding Company	9.1	2006	Oil and gas
Oman	State General Reserve Fund	8.2	1980	Oil and gas
Botswana	Pula Fund	6.9	1994	Diamonds and minerals
East Timor	Timor-Leste Petroleum Fund	6.3	2005	Oil and gas
Mexico	Oil Revenues Stabilization Fund of Mexico	6.0	2000	Oil
Saudi Arabia	Public Investment Fund	5.3	2008	Oil
China	China-Africa Development Fund	5.0	2007	Non-commodity
US – Wyoming	Permanent Wyoming Mineral Trust Fund	4.7	1974	Minerals
Trinidad and Tobago	Heritage and Stabilization Fund	2.9	2000	Oil
US – Alabama	Alabama Trust Fund	2.5	1985	Oil and gas
Italy	Italian Strategic Fund	1.4	2011	Non-commodity
UAE – Ras Al Khaimah	RAK Investment Authority	1.2	2005	Oil
Nigeria	Nigerian Sovereign Investment Authority	1	2011	Oil

(Continued.)

Table 2.A.2 (*Continued.*)

Country	Fund name	Assets (US$ billion)	Inception	Origin
Venezuela	FEM	0.8	1998	Oil
Vietnam	State Capital Investment Corporation	0.5	2006	Non-commodity
Kiribati	Revenue Equalization Reserve Fund	0.4	1956	Phosphates
Gabon	Gabon Sovereign Wealth Fund	0.4	1998	Oil
Indonesia	Government Investment Unit	0.3	2006	Non-commodity
Mauritania	National Fund for Hydrocarbon Reserves	0.3	2006	Oil and gas
US – North Dakota	North Dakota Legacy Fund	0.1	2011	Oil and gas
Equatorial Guinea	Fund for Future Generations	0.08	2002	Oil
UAE – Federal	Emirates Investment Authority	NA	2007	Oil
Oman	Oman Investment Fund	NA	2006	Oil
UAE – Abu Dhabi	Abu Dhabi Investment Council	NA	2007	Oil
Papua New Guinea	Papua New Guinea Sovereign Wealth Fund	NA	2011	Gas
Mongolia	Fiscal Stability Fund	NA	2011	Mining
	Total Oil & Gas Related	2667.9		
	Total Other	2104.0		
	TOTAL	4771.9		

[1]This includes the oil stabilization fund of Russia.

[2]This number is a best guess estimation.

All figures quoted are from official sources, or, where the institutions concerned do not issue statistics of their assets, from other publicly available sources. Some of these figures are best estimates as market values change daily.

Updated December 2011.

Source: Sovereign Wealth Fund Institute.

we are assuming that this ratio will remain broadly unchanged at the current level over 2010–2016. In the last column of Table 2.A.3, we also illustrate the average value of the ratio between the yearly change in FX reserves and the current account surplus in that year over the same period. This ratio measures the yearly portion of the current account surplus that countries have allocated to FX reserve accumulation in the second half of the last decade. The difference between commodity-exporting and non-commodity-exporting countries is noteworthy. The first, on average, allocate about 40% of their annual current account surplus to FX reserves. In non-commodity-exporting countries, whose results are heavily influenced by China, FX reserves grow more than the yearly current surplus. How is this possible and how can the different behaviour between the two groups of countries be justified?

In commodity-exporting countries, the accumulation of reserves is the result of soaring export receipts as energy prices increase. In these countries intervention in the FX market is not a main concern of macroeconomic management, and capital inflows (portfolio flows and foreign direct investments) play a minor role. In China and other Asian countries, in addition to increasing current account surpluses, the accumulation of reserves is also determined by constant intervention by the central bank in the FX markets to maintain the competitiveness of the export sector. This active exchange rate management results in rising FX reserves as large quantities of foreign currency is bought in the FX market. Furthermore, in the past few years China and other Asian countries have become large receivers of foreign investments that improve their net international investment position. In other words, while in commodity-exporting countries the largest source of foreign currencies to be allocated to either FX reserves or SWFs is exports, in Asian economies the active management of the exchange rate and the inflow of capital provide additional sources of foreign currencies, thus leading to an accumulation of FX reserves that in some cases, for instance China, can exceed the surplus in their trade balance.

The ratio between the yearly change in FX reserves and the current account surplus also shows how each country allocates its accumulated wealth between FX reserves and SWFs. As mentioned earlier, commodity-exporting countries on average allocate about 40% of their surplus to FX reserves; the other portion is likely to flow into the coffers of their SWFs. In countries with established SWFs – for instance Norway and Kuwait – only a very small share of the yearly current account surplus is allocated to FX reserves, while the bulk of foreign currencies flowing into the country is allocated to the Government Pension Fund Global and the Kuwait Investment Authority. The same observation can be made for Singapore which has two well-established SWFs – GIC and Temasek. In Singapore, in contrast to China, less than half of the current account surplus actually translates into rising FX reserves.

Based on the average ratio of FX reserves to GDP in 2005–2010, Table 2.A.4 illustrates our forecasts for FX reserves over 2010–2016. Overall, the FX reserves increase from US$5200 billion in 2010 to US$8700 billion in

Table 2.A.3 FX reserves 1990–2010, US$ and percentage GDP

| | US$ billion | | | % GDP | | | | Change in FX reserve/CA surplus, % |
	1990	2000	2010	1990	2000	2010	Average 2005–2010	Average 2005–2010
Commodity-exporting countries	66.1	170.3	1440.7	12.1%	14.4%	34.5%	32.5%	40.0%
Algeria	0.7	12.0	162.6	1.2%	22.0%	103.1%	82.8%	309.5%
Azerbaijan	0.0	0.7	6.4	NA	12.9%	11.8%	12.0%	21.0%
Bahrain	1.2	1.6	NA	27.3%	19.6%	NA	NA	NA
Botswana	3.3	6.3	7.9	81.7%	111.9%	53.1%	67.7%	54.2%
Brunei	0.0	0.4	1.6	0.0%	6.8%	12.9%	7.6%	3.7%
Chile	6.1	15.0	27.8	19.2%	20.0%	13.7%	13.4%	207.5%
Kazakhstan	0.0	1.6	25.2	NA	8.7%	17.0%	16.0%	−43.5%
Kuwait	2.0	7.1	21.2	10.7%	18.8%	16.0%	14.0%	5.9%
Libya	5.8	12.5	99.6	19.1%	32.6%	139.7%	119.0%	54.9%
Nigeria	3.9	9.9	34.9	12.3%	21.4%	17.2%	25.8%	24.1%
Norway	15.3	27.6	52.8	13.0%	16.4%	12.8%	14.3%	3.4%
Oman	1.7	2.4	13.0	14.3%	12.2%	22.5%	19.7%	27.1%
Papua New Guinea	0.4	0.3	3.0	12.5%	8.1%	31.9%	26.8%	58.5%
Qatar	0.6	1.2	30.6	8.6%	6.5%	24.0%	13.7%	26.7%
Russia	0.0	24.3	443.6	NA	9.3%	30.0%	29.6%	68.2%
Saudi Arabia	11.7	19.6	444.7	10.0%	10.4%	99.2%	82.1%	49.8%
Trinidad and Tobago	0.5	1.4	9.6	9.7%	17.0%	47.1%	37.7%	16.9%
UAE	4.6	13.5	42.8	9.3%	13.0%	14.2%	15.3%	40.5%
Venezuela	8.3	13.1	13.1	17.2%	11.2%	4.5%	10.9%	−25.5%

Non-commodity-exporting countries	111.7	485.8	3758.6	12.9%	22.2%	48.3%	42.1%	115.6%
China	29.6	168.3	2866.1	7.6%	14.0%	48.8%	43.3%	136.5%
Hong Kong	24.6	107.5	268.6	32.0%	63.6%	119.7%	90.1%	120.0%
Ireland	5.2	5.4	1.8	10.9%	5.5%	0.9%	0.5%	0.4%
Malaysia	9.8	28.3	104.9	22.2%	30.2%	44.1%	48.6%	25.5%
Singapore	27.8	80.2	225.7	71.6%	85.0%	101.3%	95.7%	46.8%
South Korea	14.8	96.1	291.5	5.5%	18.0%	28.7%	26.3%	−208.5%
Commodity- and non-commodity-exporting countries	178	656	5199	11.2%	19.5%	43.5%	38.5%	80.2%

Source: World Bank Development Indicators, 2011.

Table 2.A.4 FX reserves in 2010–2016 (in US$ billion)

	2010	2011	2012	2013	2014	2015	2016	Change 2010–2016	CAGR 2010–2016 (%)	Change 2010–2016[1]
Commodity-exporting countries	1441	1649	1763	1897	2030	2174	2331	891	8.4%	1132
Algeria	163	152	156	163	168	175	181	18	1.8%	358
Azerbaijan	6	8	10	11	12	13	14	7	13.7%	16
Bahrain	0	NA	NA	NA	NA	NA	NA	NA	NA	–5
Botswana	8	11	12	13	14	15	15	8	11.8%	0
Brunei	2	1	1	1	1	1	1	0	–3.7%	2
Chile	28	33	33	35	36	39	42	14	7.2%	15
Kazakhstan	25	29	32	36	40	45	52	27	12.8%	–20
Kuwait	21	24	25	26	28	29	31	10	6.7%	20
Libya	100	105	110	115	121	127	134	34	5.0%	33
Nigeria	35	64	68	73	79	85	93	58	17.6%	38
Norway	53	68	71	73	74	76	78	25	6.7%	13
Oman	13	13	14	14	15	16	17	4	4.6%	13
Papua New Guinea	3	3	3	3	4	5	6	2	10.4%	–1
Qatar	31	24	25	26	27	28	29	–2	–1.0%	79
Russia	444	558	627	694	761	832	914	471	12.8%	182
Saudi Arabia	445	460	477	509	540	571	605	160	5.3%	225
Trinidad and Tobago	10	8	9	10	11	12	12	3	4.5%	5
UAE	43	55	57	60	64	67	71	28	8.8%	81
Venezuela	13	34	34	35	35	36	37	24	18.7%	–23
Non-commodity-exporting countries	3759	3931	4333	4773	5254	5780	6366	2607	9.2%	4536
China	2866	3027	3354	3729	4141	4594	5102	2236	9.9%	4863
Hong Kong	269	222	241	261	279	298	320	51	2.1%	136
Ireland	2	1	1	1	1	1	0	0	–6.7%	0
Malaysia	105	120	130	140	151	163	176	71	9.2%	45
Singapore	226	255	271	283	296	310	324	98	6.5%	142
South Korea	291	306	335	359	385	413	443	152	7.2%	–218
Commodity- and non-commodity-exporting countries	5199	5580	6097	6670	7284	7954	8697	3498	8.9%	5667

(1) Using the 2005-10 average ratio of the change in FX Reserves to the current account surplus as the driver for the forecasts.

Source: Authors' calculation on data from World Economic Outlook September 2011 and World Bank Development Indicators, 2011.

2016. Over this period, commodity-exporting will add around US$900 billion of additional funds to their FX reserves, with Russia and Saudi Arabia representing the lion's share of the total. Non-commodity-exporting countries will add US$2600 billion, with China accounting for 85% of the total.

In the last column of Table 2.A.4, we also report the results of our estimations when the 2005–2010 average FX reserve-to-GDP ratio is replaced by the 2005–2010 average ratio of the change in FX reserves to the current account surplus as the key driver of our forecasts. For commodity-exporting countries, the results of the two approaches are broadly similar. For non-commodity-exporting countries, the alternative approach leads to an additional increase in FX reserves of around US$2000 billion. This additional increase in FX reserves is entirely due to China's and reflects the underlying assumption of an unrelenting increase in China current account surplus over 2011–2016 and the additional flow of FX reserves originated through intervention in the FX market (and inflows of capital). This last factor remains largely undetermined and dependent on how China will manage its exchange rate over the next few years, eventually allowing for a faster appreciation of the Renminbi against other currencies. That is also why in forecasting the future size of SWFs we rely more on the current account surplus, which in both commodity- and non-commodity-exporting countries is a more reliable driver of the future growth in FX reserves.

Flows into SWFs in 2011–2016

In Table 2.A.5 we illustrate the estimated flow of funds to SWFs obtained by subtracting the projected yearly increase in FX reserves from the yearly current account surplus of each country. Over 2011–2016, we forecast that US$3415 billion of new funds will be transferred to existing or newly established SWFs; of which, US$1739 billion will be transferred to commodity-based SWFs and US$1676 billion to non-commodity-based SWFs.

Among commodity-exporting countries, Norway, Kuwait, Qatar, UAE and Saudi Arabia account for over 75% of the total.[17] Noteworthy is Russia where – according to our estimates – the residual flow of funds into SWFs will eventually become negative over the next few years. In other words, given the IMF's forecasts on the evolution of its current account balance over 2011–2016, the net international investment position of Russia is set to worsen. In fact, the IMF forecasts that the current account surplus will gradually fall over 2011–2016; if Russia intends to grow the assets managed by its SWFs for stabilization purposes or in favour of future generations, it will have to either reduce the size of FX reserves, as a percentage of GDP, or improve its trade balance. Russia is not unique among commodity-exporting countries;

---

[17] For Saudi Arabia, where SAMA manages both FX reserves and sovereign wealth, the flow to SWFs is reported for illustrative and comparative purposes.

Table 2.A.5 Flows to SWFs in 2011–2016 (US$ billion)

	2011	2012	2013	2014	2015	2016	Cumulative 2011–2016
Commodity-exporting countries	369	374	305	258	239	193	1739
Algeria	36	16	12	11	10	12	97
Azerbaijan	14	14	13	11	10	9	70
Bahrain	3	4	4	4	4	4	24
Botswana	–4	–1	–1	–1	0	0	–7
Brunei	8	7	7	7	8	8	46
Chile	–3	1	–1	0	–1	–2	–7
Kazakhstan	7	6	4	2	1	0	19
Kuwait	55	53	53	55	58	62	336
Libya	5	5	5	4	4	4	26
Nigeria	5	25	21	19	16	14	99
Norway	52	61	61	59	58	56	346
Oman	10	8	8	6	7	6	44
Papua New Guinea	–2	–2	–1	–1	0	2	–5
Qatar	63	53	49	47	44	41	297
Russia	–11	5	–15	–46	–56	–80	–204
Saudi Arabia	15	18	32	31	31	33	160
Trinidad and Tobago	6	4	4	4	4	4	27
UAE	25	32	27	27	30	29	171
Venezuela	2	18	14	13	11	9	67
Non-commodity-exporting countries	303	148	214	277	343	392	1676
China PRC	200	104	160	225	293	344	1327
Hong Kong	60	–4	–2	1	3	6	62
Ireland	5	4	3	4	3	3	21
Malaysia	13	19	19	19	19	18	107
Singapore	24	36	40	37	36	34	206
South Korea	3	–11	–6	–9	–11	–13	–47
Commodity- and non-commodity-exporting countries	672	522	519	535	582	584	3415

Source: Authors' calculation on data from World Economic Outlook, September 2011 and World Bank Development Indicators, 2011.

Saudi Arabia is also forecast to experience a gradual decrease in its current account surplus over the next few years, reflecting the recent sharp increase in domestic expenditure after the Arab Spring. However, contrary to Russia, by 2016 Saudi Arabia is forecasted to still have a current account surplus of around US$50 billion (while in Russia it will be almost nil).

Among the non-commodity-exporting countries, the weight of China is overwhelming. According to our forecasts, over 2011–2016 Chinese SWFs are set to receive US$1327 billion of additional funds, about 80% of the total additional flows to be received by non-commodity-based SWFs. The second largest flow of funds will be in Singapore, US$206 billion, followed by Malaysia and Hong Kong. South Korea will have to decrease the FX reserves to GDP ratio if it wants to transfer additional funds to the Korea Investment Corporation.

Growth in SWFs' assets over 2011–2016

Table 2.A.6 reports the development of SWFs' AUM over 2011–2016 across three different return scenarios (conservative, baseline and aggressive). According to our estimates, by 2016 SWFs' AUM will be worth between US$8.7 trillion in the conservative return scenario (yearly return of 3%) and US$10.8 trillion in the aggressive return scenario (yearly return of 9%).

In the baseline scenario (yearly return of 6%), AUM will grow by more than 15% per year and over 2011–2016 their value will double. According to these forecasts, assets managed by SWFs are set to be the fastest growing segment in the institutional investment market as the pension, insurance and investment fund markets will only grow at a single digit rate over the same period.

By 2016, in the likely return scenario, in four countries – Norway, Saudi Arabia, UAE and China – assets controlled by SWFs will be larger than US$1 trillion. In China, AUM controlled by SWFs will amount to over US$2.7 trillion, corresponding to nearly 30% of the total SWFs' AUM. Following these four largest holders of SWFs, there is another group of countries – Kuwait, Qatar, Hong Kong and Singapore – where assets controlled by SWFs will amount to several hundred billions but will remain below US$1 trillion. Overall, these eight countries will control about 85% of the assets managed by SWFs globally.

Table 2.A.6 Growth in SWFs' AUM by country, 2011–2016

Growth in SWF assets, by country[1,2]	2011	Conservative return scenario (3%)		Likely return scenario (6%)		Aggressive return scenario (9%)	
		2016	CAGR 2011–2016	2016	CAGR 2011–2016	2016	CAGR 2011–2016
Commodity-exporting countries	2651	4742	12.3%	5451	15.5%	5977	17.7%
Algeria	56.7	131.4	18.3%	146.0	20.8%	162.1	23.4%
Azerbaijan	30.2	95.5	25.9%	105.1	28.3%	115.6	30.8%
Bahrain	9.1	32.4	28.9%	35.3	31.2%	38.6	33.5%
Botswana	6.9	4.3	–8.8%	5.3	–5.2%	6.4	–1.6%
Brunei	30	75.1	20.2%	82.9	22.5%	91.5	25.0%
Canada	15.1	26.6	12.0%	30.5	15.1%	33.5	17.3%
Chile	21.8	21.4	–0.4%	25.3	3.0%	29.6	6.3%
East Timor	6.3	11.1	12.0%	12.7	15.1%	14.0	17.3%
Kazakhstan	38.6	58.4	8.6%	66.6	11.5%	75.8	14.4%
Kiribati	0.4	0.7	12.0%	0.8	15.1%	0.9	17.3%
Kuwait	296	641.2	16.7%	711.8	19.2%	789.8	21.7%
Iran	23	40.5	12.0%	46.5	15.1%	40.0	11.7%
Libya	65	73.4	2.5%	84.9	5.5%	97.8	8.5%
Mauritania	0.3	0.5	12.0%	0.6	15.1%	0.7	17.3%
Mexico	6.0	10.6	12.0%	12.1	15.1%	13.3	17.3%
Nigeria	1	102.1	152.2%	109.4	155.8%	117.2	159.3%
Norway	560	962.3	11.4%	1082.3	14.1%	1215.5	16.8%
Oman	8.2	46.4	41.4%	50.4	43.8%	54.7	46.1%
Papua New Guinea	0	1.0	NA	1.0	NA	1.0	NA
Qatar	85	348.1	32.6%	379.7	34.9%	414.2	37.3%
Russia	113.9	–66.6	–189.8%	–51.6	–185.4%	–34.4	–178.7%

Saudi Arabia [3]	477.8	859.6	12.5%	1075.5	27.7	1075.5	17.6%
Trinidad and Tobago	2.9	25.8	54.9%	27.7	57.1%	29.8	59.3%
UAE	769.5	1047.2	6.4%	1194.6	9.2%	1359.0	12.0%
US	69.4	122.3	12.0%	140.2	15.1%	154.1	17.3%
Venezuela	0.8	70.4	144.9%	75.6	148.4%	81.1	151.9%
	2104	3935	13.3%	4378	15.8%	4855	18.2%
Non-commodity-exporting countries							
Australia	73	139.3	13.8%	155.3	16.3%	172.0	18.7%
Brazil	11.3	21.6	13.8%	24.0	16.3%	26.6	18.7%
China	1117.1	2472.9	17.2%	2725.8	19.5%	3005.2	21.9%
France	28	53.4	13.8%	59.6	16.3%	66.0	18.7%
Hong Kong	293.3	342.2	3.1%	394.0	6.1%	452.0	9.0%
Indonesia	0.3	0.6	13.8%	0.6	16.3%	0.7	18.7%
Ireland	30	52.3	11.8%	58.9	14.4%	66.2	17.1%
Italy	1.4	2.7	13.8%	3.0	16.3%	3.3	18.7%
Malaysia	36.8	142.6	31.1%	155.5	33.4%	156.9	33.6%
New Zealand	13.5	25.8	13.8%	28.7	16.3%	31.8	18.7%
Singapore	404.7	663.0	10.4%	747.6	13.1%	841.7	15.8%
South Korea	37	−9.7	−176.5%	−6.1	−169.7%	−1.9	−155.3%
US	14.3	27.3	13.8%	30.4	16.3%	33.7	18.7%
Vietnam	0.5	1.0	13.8%	1.1	16.3%	1.2	18.7%
Total SWF	4755	8677	12.8%	9829	15.6%	10832	17.9%

[1] In countries with more than one SWF this refers to the sum of all assets managed by SWFs.

[2] In these countries AuM grow at average growth rate of the relative group.

[3] In the case of Saudi Arabia, the total of the FX reserves managed by SAMA is included.

Source: Authors' calculation on data from World Economic Outlook, September 2011, World Bank Development Indicators, 2011 and Sovereign Wealth Fund Institute, 2011.

3

SWFs as Investors in Global Markets

SWFs are often considered as a homogenous group of investors. In reality, SWFs include a variety of institutions with different objectives, investment behaviour and risk appetite. Generally speaking, SWFs and FWFs invest excess FX reserves (i.e. above the amount needed by the central bank) into global financial and real assets.[1]

In the UAE, for example, the central bank is in charge of investing less than 10% of sovereign reserves, while the bulk of oil receipts are invested by the Abu Dhabi Investment Authority (ADIA), one of the largest SWFs in the world, and other vehicles such as ADIC or Mubadala. Among large commodity-exporting countries, only Saudi Arabia has not set up a SWF. Saudi Arabia assigns to its central bank, SAMA, both the management of the liquidity needed for monetary policy purposes and the investment of excess reserves.[2] Russia had some investment vehicles, in particular a stabilization fund, but the central bank is directly or indirectly responsible for managing most of the sovereign wealth, because due to entrenched macroeconomic instability and periodic episodes of capital outflows the central bank must hold substantial liquid 'fire power'. We must make a distinction, however, between the source of reserves managed by the SWFs and FWFs.

In commodity-exporting countries, the reserves managed by SWFs and the investment income they yield are primarily used to offset any unexpected shortfall in fiscal revenues during periods of lower commodity prices – the so-called stabilization function of SWFs. The reserves above the level considered adequate for fiscal stabilization, are invested for the benefit of future generations. Sometimes the two functions are assigned to different entities: in Oman for example there exists a State General Reserve Fund which receives funds during good years and releases them to the Treasury in bad years, while the Oman Investment Fund can be best described as a FWF focusing on long-term investments.

---

[1] As pointed out in the Introduction the first large SWFs were established by energy commodity-exporting countries in the period after the Second World War, Kuwait being the first. Nowadays a number of other commodity-exporting countries have followed suit.

[2] In 2009, Saudi Arabia announced the establishment of a new investment vehicle controlled by the government called Sanabil, but so far its role in the management of FX reserves seems to be marginal.

For non-commodity exporting countries, the rationale for establishing a SWF and its function has historically been different and has been evolving through time. Singapore was the first Asian non-commodity exporter to set up a SWF, Temasek, in the early 1970s, with an explicit domestic mandate: support the economic development of Singapore. Accordingly, its investment profile is distinct from that of stabilization fund or a FWF: Temasek is fundamentally a state holding corporation investing in strategic industries on behalf of the government, largely resembling the public companies established in some European countries in the 1930s and 1940s to sustain economic development and support strategic sectors. In many cases they survived well into the 1990s. Khazanah Nasional, the Malaysian SWF established in the early 1990s, has a similar mandate and invests mostly domestically in sectors such as financial services, media and communication, and utilities that are obviously considered strategic for growth.

With the surge in FX reserves experienced by most Asian exporters in 1990–2010, the scope of separate state-controlled investment vehicles has been expanded beyond domestic development to include the need of diversifying FX reserves internationally. In China, for instance, the first investment vehicle devoted to diversify FX reserves, the State Administration of Foreign Exchange (SAFE), was established in 1997; and China Investment Corporation (CIC) was established in 2007. The Korea Investment Corporation (KIC) was established only in 2005. Despite the rising trend in establishing SWFs, and unlike commodity-exporting countries, the largest Asian exporters generally allocate the bulk of their sovereign assets to central banks (Figure 3.1). In China, for example, even after the shift of a substantial amount of reserves to CIC in 2007, the central bank is still in charge of 85% of the total FX reserves and the same is true for countries such as Malaysia or South Korea.[3] Also in Singapore, despite two well-established SWFs, the central bank still holds about 40% of total reserves. The large role played by Asian central banks – where FX reserves have exceeded the level considered optimal for purely monetary purposes – mostly reflects the use of FX reserves for macroeconomic management, notably the intervention in FX markets to maintain export competitiveness. In these countries, the growth of FX reserves is mostly the result of sterilization operations carried out by the central bank to mop up the excess liquidity injected into the domestic economy as a result of FX intervention.[4] In commodity-exporting countries, the increase in FX reserves is simply an income windfall. There is no corresponding increase in the domestic money supply as the dollars received in

---

[3] At end 2011, the Chinese government announced the creation of another SWF in addition to CIC with a US$300 capital to be used in the acquisition of equities and raw materials worldwide.

[4] The purpose of sterilization is to avoid FX intervention translating into a swelling domestic money supply with repercussions for interest rates and inflation. China (which also maintains tight capital controls) and other Asian countries buy US dollars in the FX market to prevent an appreciation of their currencies. Sterilization involves the sale of a corresponding amount of bonds to domestic investors, thus reducing the domestic money supply.

exchange for the commodities sold on international markets are received by the treasury or the central bank and invested abroad – after skimming the portion needed for government expenditures. In these countries, the competitiveness of the exchange rate is not a key concern for economic performance, which is mostly linked to the commodity price cycle.

An alternative way to look at the different roles played by SWFs in commodity-exporting and non-commodity-exporting countries – and the ensuing diverse investment behaviour – focuses on the different nature of their sovereign wealth. For commodity-exporters SWFs and FWFs hold the net wealth of the country, so their primary purpose is to fund domestic expenditure either when commodity prices fall below a certain threshold or when such endowment is eventually depleted. Given their nature, these assets could be considered the equivalent of the capital of the country or – in financial connotation – as 'equity'. Accordingly, investment will target real return, risk appetite will be high and there will be no particular investment constraint as there are no (explicit) items on the liability side.

In non-commodity-exporting countries, the central bank reserves are 'borrowed' funds as they are funded through domestic short- to medium-term debt issued for sterilization purposes. The debt nature of these reserves has implications for their investment: first, the existence of an implicit 'hurdle rate', the interest rate paid to domestic lenders that can be higher than the return obtainable in international short- to medium-term lending. Second, these funds face a FX risk given that they are accumulated through continuing currency appreciation (Berkelaar *et al.*, 2010). Third, their investments will be targeting nominal rather than real returns as the interest rate paid on the liability side is expressed in nominal terms.

The different nature of the liabilities in the balance sheet of SWFs from commodity-exporting and non-commodity-exporting countries is often

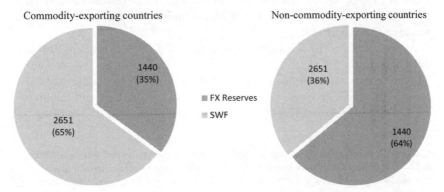

Figure 3.1   Sovereign wealth management in commodity- and non-commodity-exporting countries, 2010.

Source: See Appendix, Chapter 2.

neglected. We will devote section 3.5 to these critical implications, after having analysed the investment behaviour of SWFs in more detail.

3.1 CLUSTERING SWFs BY OBJECTIVES AND INVESTMENT PROFILES

Table 3.1 reports the policy mandate, investment objective, asset allocation, risk appetite and liabilities for a selected group of SWFs.[5] The classification into five clusters illustrated in the previous chapter will be maintained across the book to explain their investment behaviour. However, SWFs can have multiple and overlapping objectives and their policy mandate can change through time, so in reality one SWF can belong to more than one cluster. For instance, the CIC – classified as a saving fund – invests more than half of its assets into domestic banks to support the domestic financial sector. This objective is typical of investment holding companies such as Khazanah or Mubadala rather than saving funds. The monetary authorities of Hong Kong and Saudi Arabia (institutions akin to central banks) are also in charge of investing excess reserves with a long-term investment horizon. A SWF established as a pure stabilization fund can evolve into a saving fund once accumulated reserves grow beyond the amount needed for macroeconomic stabilization. This is the case of Russia where the stabilization fund, established in 2003 with the primary objective of managing fiscal reserves during periods of high oil prices, was reorganized in 2008 with the establishment of two separate funds, the Reserve Fund and the National Wealth Fund.

Each different policy mandate translates into different operational objectives that define the return target, the nature of the investments, the constraints, the investment horizon and the risk tolerance. Taken together these elements define what in asset management is often referred to as Strategic Asset Allocation (SAA), i.e. the framework through which any institutional investor manages and invests its assets. The SAA determines the risk-return profile of any investment portfolio.

At the bottom of the risk tolerance spectrum, Reserve Investment Corporations manage the FX reserves of central banks.[6] Their primary task is optimal liquidity management through improved diversification but within tight risk constraints; therefore assets are generally invested cautiously and the investment horizon is relatively short (1–3 years). However, compared with central

---

[5] Most of the information included in Table 3.1 is derived from the annual reports of SWFs and from some additional public sources such as Monitor, a strategy consultancy, and other published articles on SWFs. We included only those SWFs for which a minimum amount of information about their asset allocation is available.

[6] In some cases, the central bank is directly in charge of the management of these funds, as for the Hong Kong Exchange Fund and the Saudi sovereign assets. In other cases, a separate entity is established as for SAFE, which is an agency of the People's Bank of China.

banks, they can adopt a more diversified investment strategy as their secondary objective is preserving the long-term value of the reserves. Thus, in addition to investing in safe and liquid government bonds such as US Treasuries, Reserve Investment Corporations generally also invest in corporate bonds and equities, asset classes in which many central banks do not generally invest as they are too volatile for monetary management purposes. For instance, the HKMA Exchange Fund is split into two tranches: (1) the Backing Portfolio, which holds highly liquid US dollar-denominated assets and whose primary purpose is to provide full backing to the monetary base as required under the Currency Board arrangements; (2) the Investment Portfolio, invested in a broader set of fixed income and equity securities primarily across OECD countries.

Another large player, the China SAFE, does not disclose much information over its asset allocation, but there is indirect evidence of significant allocations to global equity markets: according to the *Economist* (Chinese Investment in Europe, *The Economist*, 2 July 2011), in June 2011 SAFE held around US$20 billion of stocks in the UK, representing about 1% of the UK's stock market capitalization. It is very likely that SAFE holds similar or larger equity stakes in other stock markets across Europe, America and Asia. Overall, Reserve Investment Corporations maintain very liquid assets. Nevertheless the recent acquisition of a 3% stake in Munich Re by SAFE underscores a bolder attitude.

Stabilization Funds are generally set up by countries rich in natural resources: their primary goal is to insulate the budget from terms of trade-of-trade shocks and to meet contingent financing requirements. Examples of stabilization funds include the Russian Stabilization Fund, Khazakhstan National Oil Fund, the State Oil Fund of Azerbaijan and the Social and Economic Stabilization Fund in Chile. In terms of investment behaviour, these funds have a SAA that is very similar to that of Reserve Investment Corporations, as they put great emphasis on liquidity and capital preservation. As a result, their investment universe is broadly similar and includes money market funds, bank deposits and high grade sovereign and corporate bonds. Some SWFs, for instance the Timor-Leste Petroleum Fund, invest in equities as well. Given the broadly similar investment profile and relatively short-term investment horizon, Reserve Investment Corporations and stabilization funds are often grouped together.

Saving funds, which can be considered a subset of the FWFs, on the other hand aim at long-term value creation and can be found in both commodity- and non-commodity-exporting countries. This is the largest group both in terms of number and assets; they hold more than half of the total assets managed by SWFs. The saving funds' prime operational objective is the maximization of real annual pay-out; by not having any specific short-term liabilities, these funds have a longer investment horizon and invest in less liquid and more risky assets such as emerging markets equities, speculative grade corporate bonds, real estate, hedge funds, private equity and – as we will discuss shortly – direct equity investments in listed and unlisted corporations. Among the

Table 3.1   Investment profile of selected SWFs*

	Country	Policy mandate[1]	Investment horizon	Investment objective[2]
Reserve investment corporations and stabilization funds				
Hong Kong Monetary Authority Exchange Fund	Hong Kong	To affect, either directly or indirectly, the exchange value of the currency of Hong Kong; to maintain the stability and integrity of Hong Kong's monetary and financial system	Medium–long	Subject to preserving capital, achieve an investment return that will help preserve the long-term purchasing power of the fund
National Reserve Fund (1) & National Wealth Fund (2)	Russia	Macroeconomic stability (1), support pension system (2)		Capital preservation & stable long-term investment return
Social and Economic Stabilisation Fund	Chile	Finance fiscal deficit during periods of weak growth and low commodity prices	Medium	Current investment policy based on that adopted by the CB. A more aggressive investment policy postponed due to the global crisis
State Oil Fund	Azerbaijan	Maintain reasonable liquidity to ensure that planned money and other transfers to the fiscal budget can be made in an accurate and timely manner	Medium	Target duration (not exceeding 48 months) of its investment portfolio in line with condition in financial markets
Heritage and Stabilisation Fund	Trinidad & Tobago	Cushion the impact on or sustain public expenditure during periods of revenue downturn; provide a heritage for future generation	Medium–long	Long-term investment objective within defined risk levels
Timor-Leste Petroleum Fund	East Timor	Liquidity, capital preservation	Medium–long	FI and equity benchmarks
Saving funds				
Abu Dhabi Investment Authority	UAE	Invest funds on behalf of the government of the Emirate of Abu Dhabi to make available the necessary financial resources to secure and maintain the future welfare of the Emirate	Long-term	Deliver sustained long-term financial return

Risk appetite	Explicit liability	Long-term average nominal return on assets, %[3]	Asset allocation[4]	Direct investments
Medium	Monetary base	5.90%	Fixed income: 75% Equity: 25%	No
Low	Meet shortfall In government revenues		Fixed income: 95% Supranational: 5%	No
Low	Meet shortfall in government revenues	6.10%	Sovereign bonds: 66.5% Money markets: 30% Inflation-linked bonds: 3.5%	No
Medium	Meet shortfall in government revenues	3.40%	Only fixed income (currently under revision with more asset classes eligible)	Yes
Medium	Meet shortfall in government revenues	NA	US FI short duration: 25% US FI: 40% US equity: 17.5% Non-US equity: 17.5%	No
Medium	Meet shortfall in government revenues	4.15%	Fixed income (94%) Equity (4%)	No
High	Abu Dhabi budget shortfalls	8.10%	Developed equities: 35–45% ME equities:10–20% Small cap equities: 1–5% Government bonds:10–20% Credit: 5–10% Alternative: 5–10% Private equity:2–8% Infrastructure: 1–5% Cash: 0–10%	Yes

(Continued)

Table 3.1   *(Continued)*

	Country	Policy mandate[1]	Investment horizon	Investment objective[2]
Saving funds (continued)				
Government Pension Fund Global	Norway	Intergenerational wealth sharing, maximizing returns	Long-term	Return maximization within certain risk levels
China Investment Corporation	China	Hold, invest and manage a portion of FX reserves	Long-term	Maximization of risk-adjusted returns
Government of Singapore Investment Corporation	Singapore	Preserve and enhance the purchasing power of Singapore reserves	20 years	Achieve long-term returns above inflation over the investment time horizon
Alaska Permanent Fund	USA	The Permanent Fund is made of two parts: no spendable (principal) and assigned (realized income). The no spendable portion of the fund is invested permanently and cannot be spent without a change in constitution. Decision about uses of the assigned portion are made each year	Long-term	Generate the maximum return while protecting the principal
Korea Investment Corporation	South Korea	Enhance sovereign wealth and contribute to the development of the financial industry by managing the assets entrusted by the government and the Bank of Korea	Long-term	Preserve long-term purchasing power of the assets add exceed investment target return with a justifiable level of risk
Alberta's Heritage Fund	Canada	Produce income supporting government programs (e.g. health/education)	Long-term	4.5% above the Canadian inflation rate
New Mexico State Investment Council	USA	Ensure that future generations receive the same benefits as current beneficiaries	Long-term	Preserve and enhance capital over the long term. It includes several funds

Risk appetite	Explicit liability	Long-term average nominal return on assets, %[3]	Asset allocation[4]	Direct investments
Medium– high	No specific llablllty (pension outflows will start after 2020)	5.00%	Equities: 60% Fixed income:35–40% Real estate: 5%	No
High	No explicit liability	6.40%	Equities: 48% Fixed income:27% Alternative: 21% Cash: 4%	Yes
Medium– high	50% of the long-term real investment return can be transferred to the fiscal budget	7.20%	Developed equities: 34% EM equities:15% Nominal bonds:20% Inflation-linked bonds:2% Real estate: 10% PE infrastructure: 10% Absolute return: 3% Natural resources:3% Cash: 3%	Yes
High	Payout dividends to the Alaska government	9.10%	Stocks: 36% Bonds: 23% Real estate: 12% Private equity: 6% Absolute return: 6% Infrastructure: 3% Cash: 2% Other: 12%	No
High	No explicit liability	NA	Equity: 43.4% Fixed income:49.1% Alternatives: 5.8%	Yes
High	Part of the return is transferred to general revenues	5.30%	Equities: 51% Fixed income:25% Alternative: 24%	No
High	Well-defined spending policy	4.72%	Domestic equity: 51% International equity:10% Real estate: 3% Private equity: 6% Hedge funds: 10% FI IG: 15% FI HY: 3%	No

(Continued)

Table 3.1   *(Continued)*

	Country	Policy mandate[1]	Investment horizon	Investment objective[2]
Contingent pension reserve funds				
Australia Future Fund	Australia	Meet unfunded superannuation liability that will become payable in the future	Long-term	4.5–5.5% above the inflation rate
National Pension Reserve Fund	Ireland	Meet as much as possible of the costs of social welfare and public service pension	Long-term	Maximize the terminal value of the Fund and as a supplementary objective to outperform the cost of government debt over rolling five-year periods. Benchmark consistent with SSA
New Zealand Superannuation Fund	New Zealand	Reduce the tax burden on future NZ taxpayers of the cost of NZ superannuation	Long-term	Maximizing return over the long term

* We only include a selected number of SWFs: those that publish sufficient information in their annual reports.
[1] The policy mandate is often included in the annual reports.
[2] Investment objective as described in the annual reports.
[3] In some cases this is the return rate since inception; when this is not available, we report the return for the longest period available as from annual report.
[4] When available we report the strategic (or policy) asset allocation; when not available we report the most recent asset allocation as from annual reports.
Source: SWFs' annual reports, various years.

largest Saving Funds are ADIA, the Norwegian Government Pension Fund Global (GPFG), CIC, GIC, the Kuwait Investment Authority (KIA) and the Oman Investment Fund.

Sovereign pension reserve funds provide for contingent unspecified pension liabilities on the government's balance sheet. Their primary purpose is to accumulate capital to be used as an additional source of wealth to counteract the impact of demographic changes on the pension system. Funds included into this group of SWFs are the Australia Future Fund, the Irish National Pension Reserve Fund, the New Zealand's Superannuation Fund and the recently established Russian Wealth Fund. The Norwegian GPFG could also be included into this category as one of its goals is to 'to support government savings to finance the pension expenditure of the National Insurance Scheme'. However, given that its mandate also includes macroeconomic stabilization and long-term saving, the GPFG is classified mostly as a saving fund. In terms of assets,

Risk appetite	Explicit liability	Long-term average nominal return on assets, %[3]	Asset allocation[4]	Direct investments
High	Future pension liability from 2020	5.20%	Equities: 40% Fixed income:15% Tangible assets: 25% Alternative: 15% Cash: 5%	No
High	Future pension liability from 2025	3.50%	Global equity: 55.4% Fixed income:23.3% Alternative assets: 21.3%	Yes
Medium– high	Future pension liability from 2031	7.83%	Global equity: 70% Domestic equity:5% Global real estate: 5%	No

pension reserve funds are the smallest group of SWFs. These funds have a traditional asset liability management approach to investment and as such they are more similar to traditional pension funds; however, by being a supplementary source of income for retirees, they have a longer investment time horizon and can tolerate more short-term volatility. Their asset allocation is obviously very similar to that of a normal pension fund.

The first four clusters of SWFs – Reserve Investment Corporations, Stabilization Funds, Saving Funds and Sovereign Pension Reserve Funds – represent the bulk of the assets globally managed by SWFs and can be broadly defined as 'asset managers', in the sense that they have an investment approach very similar to that of conventional institutional investors. From a policy point of view, their asset management activities in global capital markets are almost 'invisible', as their operations blend into those of thousands of pension and investment funds operating across global capital markets. While they often manage part of their investments internally (for instance, passive equities index tracking), they also partly outsource the asset management to external fund managers in the same way as most institutional investors in Western countries do. The asset management activities of these funds have never raised any political concern in Western countries and their activity has actually been by and large considered positively as they provide liquidity and stability in the global bond and equity markets.

The fifth group of SWFs includes investment institutions of a different nature, i.e. Investment Holding Companies (or development funds). They have specific socio-economic objectives such as economic diversification, the development of strategic industries or poverty alleviation. Their primary policy mandate is 'strategic' in the sense that they have an objective beyond pure return on investments; they are mostly investment holding corporations with large controlling stakes in national companies and strategic investments in foreign corporations. The largest funds falling in this category are Temasek, Qatar Investment Authority, Khazanah Nasional in Malaysia and Mubadala in the UAE. Overall, these funds manage assets worth around US$400 billion.

These SWFs are more aggressive in their asset allocation, make individual acquisitions and dispose of strategic assets, and therefore are more similar to private equity funds rather than pension or investment funds. Within this group, we can distinguish between funds having a predominantly local or regional scope and those with an international reach. For instance, Malaysian Khazanah invests the bulk of its assets within the country including financials, communications and utilities according to its stated policy mandate: 'develop selected industries in Malaysia on behalf of the government'. On the other hand, about a third Temasek's investments are domestic while the majority of the assets are invested across Asian and OECD countries. The Qatar Investment Authority is particularly active in the international arena despite having some large stakes into some domestic ventures that are key for the diversification of Qatar into non-oil sectors. In some cases, the SWF has a sector specialization, for instance the International Petroleum Investment Company invests globally in the energy sector. The key distinctive feature of these SWFs is that they acquire large or small strategic equity stakes in listed/unlisted corporations.

This strategic attitude is not, however, a prerogative of Investment Holding Companies only. Most saving funds and a few stabilization funds also make direct investments, in domestic or foreign markets. In the last few years, ADIA, CIC, KIA and GIC have made multibillion direct investments into listed and unlisted foreign corporations, including international banks during the financial crisis. By having the majority of their assets under management invested into liquid securities either directly in global markets or via fund management companies, these funds can count on a large pool of liquidity ready available for the purchase of large unleveraged stakes into listed or non-listed corporations. These are the investments that most often hit the news and occasionally make a splash into the Western political world.

Direct investments clearly fall within the mandate of Investment Holding Companies. How do they fit into the risk/return profile of Savings and Stabilization Funds? The rationale for such strategy lies in the search for alpha hinging on the distant horizon. SWFs such as ADIA, GIC and KIA have been investing in global capital markets for a very long time and have developed in-house investment team capable of handling such complex transactions. It is not unusual that within these institutions, besides the asset management arm investing the bulk of the assets according to a well-defined SAA, there is a 'specialized' investment department with the technical and financial expertise required to screen and select strategic equity investments in listed and non-listed corporations. For instance, within GIC there are three investment groups: the public market group, dealing with the investment in publicly listed securities; the real estate group; and the special investments group, dealing with strategic investments (GIC, 2011). At CIC, investments and mandates are managed by four investment departments: public market investment, tactical investment, private market investment and special investment. The special investment department is in charge of making and managing direct long-term large-scale investments (Sekine, 2011). The main goal of these departments is to identify any temporary mispricing opportunity in global markets that can become an opportunity for above-average returns (later, we will indeed argue that this is the main driver behind the multibillion investments made by SWFs into Western banks during the financial crisis).

SWF large direct investments into listed or unlisted, domestic and foreign corporations should therefore be considered either as the only and exclusive activity of Investment Holding Companies such as Temasek or Mubadala, in full accordance to their policy mandate, or as one leg of the broader investment approach adopted by Saving Funds. As large direct investments attract media attention and raise suspicion in the Western world, it is now time to look at them in detail.

3.2 SWFs AS STRATEGIC INVESTORS IN DOMESTIC AND GLOBAL MARKETS

The share of SWFs' assets invested into listed and unlisted corporations – while still representing a small share of the total assets managed by SWFs – has grown dramatically in 2000–2010 (Figure 3.2). According to the Monitor-FEEM database[7], publicly reported equity investments by SWFs increased from around US$4 billion in 2000 to US$109 billion in 2008; their

---

[7] Data on direct equity investments carried out by SWFs is scarce, reflecting various factors. First, as we will discuss in Chapter 7, while the level of transparency on SWFs is generally increasing due to international political pressure, some of the largest SWFs still do not disclose detailed information about their investments. Second, similarly to most private equity funds, SWFs are more reluctant to disclose information about direct investments in listed or unlisted companies as confidentiality is regarded as even more important given the price sensitivity of this type of deal. Among the various studies on SWFs direct investments, in this chapter we will largely rely on the work carried out by Monitor, a strategy consulting firm that since 2008 has provided data and analysis on publicly reported direct SWF investments. The Monitor databank is built by combining different sources of information, including financial transaction databases such as Bloomberg, SDC Platinum, Datamonitor and Datastream, information provided by SWFs in their websites and annual reports, target company and partner organization press releases and news reports by newswires such as Dow Jones and Reuters. For a detailed description of the methodology see Monitor Group (2011).

value dropped in the following two years as a result of the global financial crisis, but in 2010 – at more than US$50 billion – it was about 12 times larger than in 2000. Why did direct investments by SWFs rise so markedly during 2000–2010? Does this rise reflect an increased use of these funds by their sponsoring governments for 'non-commercial' purposes as sometimes feared by Western politicians, or are they motivated by exclusively commercial and financial reasons?

The surge in SWFs' direct investments is in line with the growth in total assets controlled by SWFs as FX reserves ballooned (Figure 3.2). Indeed, the acceleration in SWF direct investments started around 2005 when FX reserves

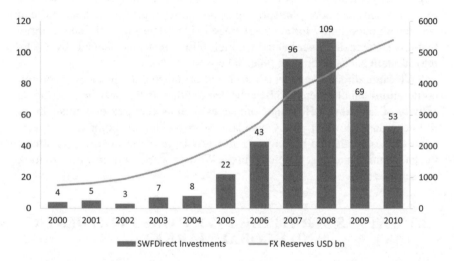

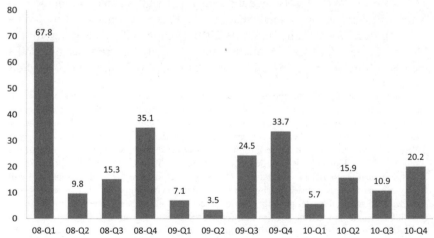

Figure 3.2   SWF investments 2000–2010 (US$ billion).

Source: Monitor-FEEM Transaction Database.

were increasing by more than half a trillion dollars per year. As discussed earlier, direct investments are the primary activities for certain types of SWFs such as Temasek or QIA and a secondary but growing activity for established SWFs such as ADIA, GIC and KIA and many newcomers. The number of SWFs involved in direct investments has also been gradually increasing during this period as either new funds with an aggressive policy mandate were established or existing funds improved their technical and financial capabilities to handle these operations. For instance, the Qatar Investment Authority (QIA) – one of the most active in direct investments – was established in 2005; the Libyan Investment Authority, equally if not more active, was established in 2006; and CIC – whose multibillion investments often hit the news – was established in 2007. Some SWFs whose investment approach has not historically included direct investments have recently changed their attitude: for instance, the State Oil Fund of the Republic of Azerbaijan, created in 1999, made its first direct investments in 2010; and the Norwegian GPFG is investing in real estate as well (see Austvik, 2007).

The financial environment prevailing in 2000–2010, characterized by low inflation and historically very low interest rates, was also conducive to a so-called 'search for yield', a dominant investment theme in the past few years. SWFs are created to boost the return on FX reserves and in an environment of very low nominal yields like that prevailing in the last decade, their sponsoring governments have increased the political pressure for higher returns, resulting in more aggressive investment behaviour.

Finally, SWF direct investment should also be considered in the context of the latest trends in how institutional investors manage their assets. Large institutional investors are increasingly adopting an investment approach often referred to as 'core and satellite'. The portfolio is split into two main components: the core component, representing the bulk of the total portfolio, consists mostly of stable, passive investments in fixed income and equity securities giving broad exposure to markets. These investments are often managed internally, thus avoiding the fees paid to external asset managers. The satellite component consists of eclectic investments, to some extent uncorrelated to global financial markets, aiming at long-term returns in areas where the liquidity premium is substantial. The satellite typically involves more sophisticated strategies, involving derivatives, structured products and private equity investments.[8]

Direct investments are less liquid and more volatile than passive strategies but with higher expected returns due to liquidity premium. Of course, higher

---

[8] For example, a large SWF such as ADIA reportedly allocates up to 60% of its assets to index tracking strategies. But if an interesting opportunity arises it might snap it up, such as investing US$7.5 billion into Citigroup during the financial crisis. This investment in Citigroup can be viewed as part of the satellite portfolio, targeting a rare opportunity of entering the capital of a major bank.

returns do not always materialize, as in the case – which we will discuss shortly – of investments made by SWFs into Western banks during the financial crisis.

Likewise investment in highly risky structured products might backfire, such as the position acquired by the Libyan Investment Authority (LIA) during the financial crisis. Information provided by Wikileaks over a confidential LIA's Management Information Report from June 2010 provides a rare in-depth view of its asset allocation. More than 60% of the portfolio (excluding the LIA's holding into its subsidiaries) was safely invested in cash and deposits; about 6% into high-rated bonds and externally managed funds. About US$6 billion, equivalent to 17% of its portfolio, was invested into listed equities, of which about half were classified as 'strategic investments' and consisting of large equity stakes into companies such as Unicredit, an Italian bank, the Italian oil company ENI with strategic interests in the Libyan oil sector and other blue chips such as Siemens, a German manufacturer. More than 10% of assets were invested into externally managed alternative products including hedge funds, private equity funds, structured products and equity derivatives. Some of these equity derivatives, purchased for a total of about US$1.3 billion, became worthless following the financial crisis.

3.3 GEOGRAPHICAL AND SECTOR DISTRIBUTION OF SWF STRATEGIC INVESTMENTS: THE 2007–2008 SURGE OF INVESTMENTS IN WESTERN FINANCIALS

The activism in SWF direct investment over 2000–2010 tracked the evolution of the global economy. The regional and sector distribution of SWFs' actions (Figure 3.3) shows how SWF direct investment decisions have been influenced by:

- the shifting centre of gravity of the global economy from advanced countries to emerging markets;
- the boom of the 2000s in financials and real estate and the subsequent collapse;
- the rising importance of the commodity and energy sectors.

SWFs are mostly located in emerging markets, therefore it is not surprising that they display a preference for investing in these economies (induced also by the domestic focus in some SWFs' guidelines). For instance, the majority of Temasek's investments are in Asia; Mubadala invests primarily in the UAE and other Gulf countries; the Vietnamese State Capital Investment Corporation's portfolio is entirely domestic; CIC is primarily active in mainland China. In 2000–2005, emerging markets accounted for the lion's share of the direct investments of SWFs but these were still relatively small in absolute terms. In 2005–2010, reflecting the surge in SWFs' investment volumes, the flow of investment to emerging markets soared. The apparent contradiction between

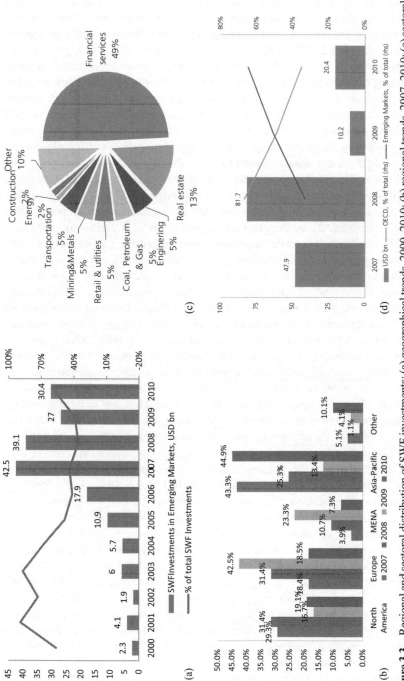

Figure 3.3 Regional and sectoral distribution of SWF investments: (a) geographical trends, 2000–2010; (b) regional trends, 2007–2010; (c) sectoral trends; (d) investment in financial service industry, 2007–2010.

Source: Monitor-FEEM Transaction Database.

the soaring value of investment in emerging markets in absolute terms and their falling share as a percentage of total investments in 2007–2008 is largely explained by the surge in acquisition of stakes into Western banks during the financial crisis of 2007–2008.

The global financial crisis slowed down the investment trend towards emerging markets as uncertainty over the global economic outlook curbed the SWFs' risk appetite. However, this slowdown seems to have been just a pause as the trend resumed in 2009–2010. Emerging markets – particularly in Asia and Latin America – very quickly overcame the Great Recession and showed their capability for 'decoupling' from advanced economies still struggling to resume their pre-crisis pace of growth. What the financial crisis changed, however, is the regional distribution of SWF investments into emerging markets. Before the crisis, the Middle East and North Africa (MENA) region was experiencing a surge of investments from SWFs outside the region, particularly Asian ones attracted by the growing opportunities in oil and real estate sectors. The 'Arab Renaissance' was epitomized by booming Dubai: in the years before the financial crisis, massive capital sums from around the world were flowing to this tiny emirate. Following the crisis, the MENA's share of SWF investments dropped substantially and the deals carried out in the region were mostly the result of the activities of local SWFs put under pressure by their respective governments to sustain their economies. The MENA region is still suffering from the consequences of the financial crisis, with Dubai struggling to rebound towards the pre-crisis years. The ongoing political turmoil after the Arab Spring and the uncertain regional security outlook (especially for Iraq and Iran) are powerful headwinds for a trend reversion in the near future.

The Asia-Pacific region – not only China and India but also Indonesia, Malaysia, Singapore and Vietnam – emerged from the financial crisis as the main destinations of SWF direct investments both in absolute and relative terms (45% of total SWF direct investment in 2010). In response to the financial crisis, SWFs doubled their investments to Latin America, Russia and so-called frontier economies all classified as 'Others' in Figure 3.3(b). Latin America – and Brazil in particular – seems to have become an important receiver of SWF investments. In 2010, the initial public offering (IPO) of Brazilian giant Petrobras worth US\$70 billion, attracted significant (but undisclosed) investments from Asian and Middle Eastern SWFs and paved the way for other major deals such as the roughly US\$1 billion invested by CIC, GIC and ADIC in BTG Pactual, a Brazilian investment bank. Qatar Holding, a subsidiary of QIA, invested US\$2.7 billion in Banco Santander Brazil, in exchange for a 5% stake in the Brazilian subsidiary of the Spanish bank. ADIA is also active in the Latin American private equity market (Santiso, 2011). Frontier markets in sub-Saharan Africa are also gradually attracting SWF resources – particularly in agricultural land, mobile, telecoms and mining. Recent examples include the establishment of a fund by Invest AD, a private equity company owned by the ADIC, in partnership with Japan's SBI Holdings, and the investments by the KIC and the State Oil Fund of the Republic of Azerbaijan (SOFAZ) in the International Finance Corporation's new Africa, Latin America and Caribbean Fund.

Two sectors have historically prevailed in the portfolio allocation of SWFs: financial services and, to a lesser extent, real estate. With regards to real estate, the oldest funds such as ADIA, KIA and GIC set up a dedicated property arm more than two decades ago: less liquid and more risky but with a lower correlation to the equity and debt markets, a good income stream and features that make it a good hedge against inflation, real estate is a natural asset class of choice and a powerful risk diversifier for long-term investors such as SWFs. As real estate prices rose in 2003–2007, the flow of SWF investments into the sector also increased sharply as the youngest SWFs such as LIA and QIA (but less so the most established funds such as ADIA and KIA with more robust risk management frameworks and therefore binding limits to a single sector) jumped on the real estate bandwagon. In 2007, at the height of the global real estate bubble, more than US$11 billion was invested in real estate, corresponding to about 12% of the SWFs' investments in that year. Booming British and Dubai real estate sectors were the largest beneficiaries of this huge flow of capital: Middle Eastern SWFs buying iconic properties in London regularly hit the news. Following the burst of the real estate bubble, SWF investments into real estate fell dramatically: in 2010, to only US$3.5 billion, a quarter of the level touched in the pre-crisis years and less than 7% of the total SWF investments. The SWFs that sharply increased their allocation to real estate in 2007–2008 – particularly in hot spots such as Dubai or London – have probably suffered heavy losses on their investments. However, this has not deterred SWFs from continuing their enthusiasm for bricks and mortar. In the aftermath of the crisis, Chinese and Middle Eastern SWFs were attracted by the bargain prices they could take advantage of for prime properties in international cities. In 2010, CIC bought a 7.4% stake in General Growth Properties, a US-based property developer in the commercial real estate sector; and QIA bought 100% of the iconic Harrods store in Central London for about US$2.2 billion. These operations add to the evidence of opportunistic behaviour by SWFs, in line with the behaviour of other long-term institutional investors such as large pension funds that have recently re-entered the real estate market.

Even before the sub-prime crisis erupted in 2007, the financial service industry accounted on average for about 40% of the value of SWFs direct investments, by far the sector attracting the largest share of SWF direct investments (Monitor Group & Fondazione Enrico Mattei, 2009). The historical 'bias' of SWFs towards financials reflects several factors. First, in the past few decades, the financial service industry delivered stellar performances as one of the main beneficiaries from globalization. As countries opened up their economies to foreign investments and international trade soared, the intermediation by banks and capital markets also rose substantially. Furthermore, the dismantling of trade barriers and the deregulation made financial services one of the sectors most open to foreign investments. Another reason for the traditionally high investment of SWFs into financials – particularly Asian SWFs – is that the financial sector holdings may be a conduit for investment opportunities overseas. For instance, acquisitions by SWFs of large stakes in private equity and alternative asset managers such as Blackstone, JC Flowers and GLG partners can provide access to high-quality investment opportunities before other competitors. SWFs might even try to attract staff away to build up their internal expertise. Providing financial support to US and European banks during the crisis – given the Western pressure on SWFs to become more open and transparent – could also have been seen by some SWFs as a smart public relations move.

However, all these factors seem to be less relevant when compared with the above average profitability of financials until 2007. The subprime crisis provided SWFs a supposedly unique opportunity for a potentially lucrative investment. When the first wave of losses suffered by US and European banks began to be unveiled in the course of 2007, the financial crisis was expected to remain confined to a specific and relatively small asset class, the subprime market. At that time, banks were mostly seen as suffering a temporary liquidity crisis as their capital fell short due to the write-downs on the toxic assets and the legal uncertainty surrounding the true magnitude of their exposures. However, very few analysts expected the sub-prime crisis to escalate into the worst financial crisis since the Second World War and eventually push the global economy into the Great Recession. SWFs from Asia and the Middle East, with growing assets and with commodity prices at still historic highs, spotted the opportunity in an already familiar sector actively seeking fresh capital and willing to provide very attractive conditions to liquid investors.[9]

The Economist had a vivid (and possibly not entirely imaginary) account of the efforts to save banks in the Anglosphere: 'Your phone rings at 3am. It's a senior American banker sounding desperate. An unidentified heavy-breather – the Treasury Secretary? – is also on the line. It's the opportunity of a lifetime, the banker swears: the chance to buy a multibillion-dollar stake in a big Wall Street firm. By the way, he adds breezily, any chance of an answer right away?'[10] And SWFs actually provided their answers right away: in a matter of six months (from the last quarter of 2007 to the first quarter of 2008; Figure 3.4) SWFs invested around US$70 billion to recapitalize the biggest investment banks in mature economies, a figure that paradoxically is larger than the analogous flow going in the opposite direction as a result of an emerging-markets crisis. During this period, GIC invested more than US$30 billion in two banks, UBS and Citigroup; the KIA invested about US$6 billion in Citigroup and Merrill Lynch; Temasek invested US$7.8 billion in Merrill

---

[9] Many of the investments made by SWFs in Western banks included a discount on the stocks acquired and in some cases payment of a fixed interest rate coupon payment on the nominal value of the investment for a certain number of years, partly limiting the downside risk of investment.

[10] Falling Knives: The Smart and the Not-so-Smart, *The Economist*, 10 December 2009.

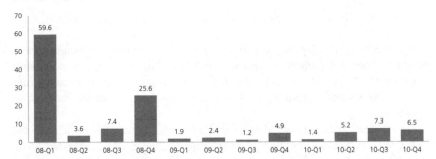

Figure 3.4   Quarterly flows of SWF direct investments in Western Banks, 2008–2010.

Source: Monitor Database.

Lynch; ADIA invested US$7.5 billion in Citigroup; and CIC invested US$5 billion in Morgan Stanley.

The SWFs' enthusiasm for Western banks diminished as soon as the extent of losses was ascertained. In the following quarters the flow of investments into OECD banks slowed down: only two investments were recorded (QIA put US$3.5 billion in Barclays and Temasek an additional US$3.5 billion in Merrill Lynch). In the last quarter of 2008 – following Lehman's default – the only active SWF in the Western bank sector was QIA with two follow-up investments in Credit Suisse and Barclays. Unsurprisingly, in 2010 the total value of direct investments by SWFs into financials collapsed from the level touched in 2008 from US$96.2 billion to about US$20 billion.

Some SWFs came under sharp criticism from their governments for the losses incurred on these investments, which seem to have involved some mis-judgement of the magnitude of the crisis.

Without the benefit of hindsight, however, an assessment of these opera-tions is not straightforward. An often repeated claim is that at the inception of this crisis the recapitalization of financial institutions had a stabilizing effect and reduced the contagion at a critical juncture. Furthermore, as large inves-tors in global capital markets (and financial institutions), the indirect benefit from a stabilization of the Western banking sector was significant for SWFs themselves. However, this argument could also be turned around by observing that so much capital being poured in banks that had piled up undue risk led to further value destruction. It would have been better to let these institutions fail and clean up the system rather than exacerbate the problem with a new injec-tion of funds. Clearly we will never know which of the two arguments is right, but this example illustrates how issues can defy the sometimes simplicistic analysis that fill the media and airwaves.

SWF's love affair with the financial services industry seems to be gradually on the mend since late 2010 but with a focus on emerging markets, which ac-counted for 60% of total investments with a more diversified exposure across sub-sectors such as private equity, insurance and asset management (Monitor Group, 2011).

Again SWFs are adapting their strategies to the changing environment, expanding in countries where the financial sector is still in a phase of expansion (e.g. Brazil, China and Russia) and in those sub-sectors presenting few regulatory challanges and continuing to deliver superior profits over the medium to long term.

Diversification also involved other sectors including manufacturing, natural resources and technology. For instance, during 2009, SWFs invested more than US$17 billion in the motor vehicle industry taking advantage of stock prices at historic lows and ailing US car manufacturers kept alive by government's financial oxygen. In addition to the opportunity of potentially very lucrative investment, leading automotive companies also provide access to first-class technology and partnership for the launch of new business ventures. This is, for instance, the rationale of the US$2.7 billion investment by Abu Dhabi-based Aabar (a subsidiary of the International Petroleum Investment Company) in the German car manufacturer Daimler. In addition to investing in a leading top brand car manufacturing company, the deal also paved the way for the establishment of a partnership between Daimler and Aabar to launch a new industrial plant in Algeria, to establish a joint venture for the development of electric vehicles and to create a training centre in Abu Dhabi. A purely financial rationale was instead behind the QIA's investment of nearly US$5 billion in Volkswagen in exchange for a 10% stake in the German car manufacturer. The 'passive' nature of the QIA's investment in Volkswagen did not prevent the Doha-based SWF from having two senior officials sitting on the supervisory board of the German company.

Energy commodities and mining also received a growing share of SWF investments during the Great Recession. In 2009, SWF investments in energy sources such as coal, oil and natural gas rose to more than US$11 billion from just US$1 billion the year before. In 2010 the additional flow of investments into mining and metal, and energy generation and transmission, highlight the strategic shift of SWFs towards not only the primary commodity sector but along the whole value chain (Monitor Group, 2011). The most active investors in these sectors have been the SWFs from energy-hungry countries in Asia, with China in the lead. In 2010, for instance, CIC invested US$1.7 billion in coal, petroleum and natural gas exploration, particularly in North America, and US$1.6 billion in AES Corporation, a power generation and transmission company. In 2011, CIC further expanded its investments in the energy sector by joining forces with GDF Suez, one of the biggest utility firms in the world operating in the gas, power, water and waste, and energy efficiency services. CIC and GDF Suez signed a Memorandum of Understanding for cooperation across multiple businesses and regions, in particular in Asia-Pacific. As a first milestone of this cooperation, CIC invested more than US$3.15 billion in the exploration and production division of the French company and US$850 million in the Atlantic LNG liquefaction plant located in Trinidad and Tobago.

In addition to CIC, Temasek and GIC have also been particularly active in South Africa (mining), Canada (mining) and Russia (aluminium) in the past few years. The SWF activism was not restricted to Asian funds and to traditional energy sources: for instance, during the same period, the KIA invested in Areva, the French nuclear energy company and Mubadala invested heavily in the alternative energy sector, most famously in Masdar, a 'zero emissions' city under construction on the outskirts of Abu Dhabi.

This analysis of regional and sector distribution of SWF direct investment has been long but also illuminating as it shows some crucial features of the behaviour of SWFs, which can be summarized in three points:

- SWFs invest in sectors and regions with long-term profitability potential, in line with their mandate, especially in financials and real estate before the crisis, and in energy and commodities afterwards and in emerging markets as the global economic barycentre shifts.
- SWFs do not eschew large bets, depending on macroeconomic and financial conditions, in distressed assets as reflected by investments made into Western banks and in the automotive sector during the crisis.
- While investing in advanced economies is almost inevitable given the depth of these markets and the need of diversification, SWFs increasingly look at those regions with the highest long-term growth potential such as South East Asia, Latin America and sub-Saharan Africa.

Does the sector/regional distribution of investments show any non-commercial motive by SWFs or their respective sponsoring governments? What emerged from our analysis is that the dominant motivation behind SWFs' investment was and remains financial long-term returns as determined by macroeconomic and financial developments. Other considerations or 'strategic benefits' that can potentially be extracted from their international investment activity play a less prominent role. Unfortunately the two aspects cannot be precisely disentangled. This is the case, for example, of the investments made by some Middle Eastern SWFs in the car industry and the recent wave of investments by Asian SWFs into the energy and commodity sector. In fact, these acquisitions not only have a strong financial rationale (cheap prices in the case of car companies' stocks and long-term attractiveness in the case of the energy/commodity assets), but also the strategic value of directly or indirectly supporting the countries' economic priorities (economic diversification into manufacturing in the case of oil-dependent Abu Dhabi and access to energy/commodity sources in the case of China and other Asian countries). We will return to this issue in Chapter 5 where the role of SWFs in areas of geopolitical interest for their sponsoring governments is discussed in depth.

3.4 INVESTMENT PERFORMANCE OF SWFs AND THE IMPACT OF THE FINANCIAL CRISIS

The heterogeneity of SWFs in policy mandates and investment styles makes it difficult to provide an accurate assessment of their investment performance through time. Investment performance is a relative concept as the return obtained by an investor on a portfolio can be assessed either in absolute terms or in comparison with a benchmark. Benchmarking is not an exact science and lack of information on SWFs' benchmarks does not allow a systematic assessment. According to a survey carried out by the International Working Group of Sovereign Wealth Funds, the majority of SWFs have specific investment objectives, expressed either in terms of absolute return or relative to a benchmark. Most respondents to the survey also mentioned that performance is reviewed regularly in relation to an index and portfolio rebalancing is done at regular intervals. Many SWFs do have an internal performance evaluation framework but there are also funds – often the recently established or smaller SWFs – that do not have specific return objectives aside from vaguely defined long-term financial returns (IMF, 2008a).

The financial crisis has challenged the risk framework of most institutional investors, including SWFs, as we explain extensively in Chapter 4.

It would be an important exercise for the management and the board to devise a yardstick, for two reasons:

- it would help to clarify the objectives of the investment strategy in terms of time frame and expected returns;
- it would sharpen the concentration on the risks that the decision makers are willing to bear.

The most common piece of investment information provided by SWFs is a description of their Strategic Asset Allocation and long-term yearly return (since inception or over the past 5 or 10 years). These two pieces of information, while not allowing a systematic assessment of their investment performance, provide however a broad understanding of their risk profile and long-term returns. The return on assets since inception or over a long period of time (10 or 20 years) is the right performance indicator for saving funds that invest for the long term.

Among reserve investment corporations and stabilization funds, the HKMA reports a long-term historical return on the Exchange Fund (including both the Backing and the Investment portfolio) of 5.9% per annum since inception (HKMA, 2011). The Chilean Social and Economic Stabilization Fund – investing exclusively in fixed income securities – has an average return on assets of 6.1% p.a. (Ministry of Finance Chile, 2010); the Timor-Leste Petroleum Fund – investing in both fixed income and equities – has an average return of 4.2% (Petroleum Fund of Timor-Leste, 2011). Over the long term, therefore, stabilization funds and Reserve Investment Corporations have a return on assets oscillating between 4 and 6% p.a.

Saving funds and Investment Holding Companies have a more diversified investment allocation and a long investment horizon; their returns are therefore expected to be higher. For instance, the Norwegian SWF has a traditionally balanced asset allocation (60% in equity and 40% into fixed income, though recently under modification) and reports a long-term return on assets of around 5% p.a. (NBIM, 2011). Those funds with a more diversified asset allocation – including alternative asset classes such as private equity, real estate, hedge funds and direct investments – generally report higher returns: for instance, the GIC claims a long-term return on assets of above 7% p.a. (GIC, 2011); ADIA, another SWF with an extremely diversified asset allocation, reports a long-term average return of around 8% p.a. (ADIA, 2010); the Alaska Permanent Fund reports long-term average returns also of almost 9% (but over the five years to 2010 the return was only 3.7% p.a.; Alaska Permanent Fund, 2011). CIC – despite a short track record of only three years – reports an average return of 6.4% p.a. since its inception in 2007 (CIC, 2011). With regards to Investment Holding Companies, Temasek reports that since inception it has delivered an annualized compounded return of 17%, certainly an impressive feat (Temasek, 2011); Khazanah Nasional reports a long-term return of around 10% p.a. (Khazanah, 2010). Considering that Temasek also invests outside Singapore while Khazanah's investments are almost entirely domestic, the difference in performance seems to be justified. Unfortunately, QIA and Mubadala – the two most active Investment Holding Companies in the Middle East – do not provide detailed information over their long-term investment performance so a comparison between Asian and Middle Eastern Investment Holding Companies is impossible.

For reserve investment corporations and stabilization funds, given their preference for liquidity and capital preservation, a return above 5% p.a. seems to be reasonable, when taking into consideration the low inflation and low interest rates prevailing during 2000–2010. But for Savings Funds that have considerable 'freedom' in investments and can invest in less liquid assets, is a long-term return of 7% p.a. satisfactory?

For diversified institutions such as Saving Funds or more generally FWFs, to assess their performance one could resort to a comparison with a stock market index, which would in practice be a measure of the opportunity cost of capital. During 1980–2010, the global equity markets provided an average annual return of around 6% in nominal terms (MSCI World): however, during 2000–2010, the return has fallen to around zero, reflecting the impact of the bursting of the tech bubble early in the decade and the financial crisis in 2007–2008. Saving Funds traditionally maintain a large exposure to global equity markets, particularly those of advanced economies given their depth and liquidity and the need for investment diversification. A long-term performance of 7% – considering the recent return levels in global stock markets and the lack of leverage in SWFs – seems overall more than reasonable. It is also reasonable that those SWFs that are more diversified into alternative asset classes seem to be capable of better compensating the poor equity returns with some additional sources of alpha. From this point of view, it is not surprising that the Norwegian GPFG has recently decided to revise its strategic asset allocation to include real estate.

As Investment Holding Companies are basically private equity houses owned by the government, returns are expected to be similar to those obtained by private equity funds. As the portfolio of these funds covers a wide range of assets in listed and non-listed companies, spanning a number of sectors sometimes with a rather broad geographical diversification, the performance evaluation is beset by subjective valuations. Moreover, during a bear market the performance would be negatively affected by the difficulty of liquidating investments. In other words, returns might be lumpy, meagre in the initial years and questionable for lack of accounting standards, and therefore much tougher to assess in comparison with, say, mutual or pension funds.

This kind of predicament also affects venture capital and private equity funds, so it is not unique to SWFs, but there exist indices that have been developed by specialized firms such as Venture Economics owned by Thomson Financial or Prequin or Standard & Poor's. For instance, the Private Equity Performance Index (PEPI) produced by Standard & Poor's shows a return of 10.9% p.a. over 20 years and 3.7% p.a. over 2000–2010.

SWFs' long-term performance is an important indicator given their long-term investment horizon. Short-term annual performance, however, is inevitably scrutinized very closely by the SWFs' principals, for example Parliament, the Treasury or the central bank. As for any other large investor in global markets, the financial crisis also hit the portfolio of SWFs. While the oldest SWFs have experienced several periods of falling asset prices, for most of the SWFs established in during 2000–2010, the 2007–2008 financial crisis was the first real test in fund management during a period of unprecedented financial and economic distress. According to the OECD, in 2008 pension funds experienced on average a negative return of 21.4% in nominal terms (OECD, 2010); given the generally higher exposure of saving funds to equity, an average loss equal to or greater than that of pension funds seems reasonable. Several SWFs – like several pension funds and endowment funds – also invest in alternative asset classes that have fallen heavily during the financial crisis despite their alleged low correlation with equity prices. A large part of these losses was recovered in 2009 as stock markets around the world experienced one of the largest bull runs of the past few decades. The recovery in asset prices continued in 2010 but at a low pace when compared with the year before, then stalled in the spring of 2011 and reverted sharply until year end. This is true provided that the SWFs did not substantially alter their equity exposure in response to the losses occurred in 2008; all in all this seems to be the case for most SWFs which remained committed to their long-term investment strategy.

A good approximation of the average performance of SWFs during this period of extreme financial distress is provided by the OECD data on Public Pension Reserve Funds (PPRFs), which includes some SWFs such as the Australian Future Fund, the Irish NPRF and the Norwegian GPFG. PPRFs' average yearly nominal rate in 2008–2010 was 4.4% p.a. in nominal terms (2.6% in real terms), which is meagre when compared with long-term performance but definitely remarkable considering the extent of the financial crisis and the recession it triggered.

With regard to SWFs' strategic investments, on a total of US$126 billion invested in listed stocks from inception to March 2009 (the trough in stock prices), these SWFs have suffered substantial paper losses, totalling US$57 billion, corresponding to an adjusted return of around −47% (Monitor Group, 2010). Most of these losses were actually suffered in a cluster of investments, those concerning the injection of capital into Western banks: the largest ten SWF direct investments in Western banks lost about US$41 billion, corresponding to more than 70% of their initial value. The following recovery in stock prices partly reduced these losses but the bulk of investments made by SWFs into Western banks remained in the red for a long time. What is important, however, is that Monitor's analysis also shows that the average long-term returns on SWF direct investments is generally positive. Over a two-year period, the average return on SWF investments is equal to over 40%, reinforcing the argument that with hindsight the investments made by SWFs into Western banks in 2007–2008 have not been as successful as perhaps they hoped.

3.5 EXPLICIT AND IMPLICIT LIABILITIES OF SWFs

It is very common to read in the press that SWFs are long-term investors without any liabilities on their balance sheets. To a large extent, this is broadly correct and indeed this is what makes SWFs unique among institutional investors. As we consistently argue in this book, however, SWFs are a very heterogeneous group of investors and this is also true of their liabilities (Rozanov, 2007). For any investor, whether individual or institutional, the definition of a liability profile is a fundamental step in the design and set-up of the investment process. In the case of traditional funds – pension funds and insurance companies – the liability profile can be identified with a certain degree of confidence (for pension funds, for instance, the age profile of the fund's participants, expected pension payments and life expectancy can be used to determine the future payments of the fund). For SWFs, given the heterogeneity of their policy mandates and the different features of their economies, the question of defining their liabilities is more complicated but still fundamental to understanding their investment behaviour. There are implicit liabilities that might significantly affect investment behaviour, particularly during periods of economic downturns or financial distress.

Stabilization funds (see Table 3.1) have a contingent liability: cover the shortfall in government revenues due to volatility in exchange rates or commodity prices. For instance, in Chile the Economic and Social Stabilization Fund (ESSF) is integrated in the broader fiscal management of the country and according to a well-defined withdrawal policy and a long-term structural fiscal policy, the ESSF can be drawn down to finance fiscal deficits or pay down public debt. Due to this explicit fiscal liability, stabilization funds maintain a liquidity profile very similar to the FX reserves. In Russia, for instance, the assets of the Reserve Fund are deposited with the Central Bank of the Russian Federation and the central bank acts as operational manager under the guidance of the Ministry of Finance. The Reserve Fund, designed to cushion the budget against the impact of a drop in oil prices, is invested in very liquid assets, mostly AAA-rated sovereign securities.

Sovereign pension reserve funds such as the Australia Future Fund or the Irish National Pension Reserve Fund have fixed liabilities, consisting of contractually defined and measurable obligations. They have a higher degree of freedom in terms of how funds can be invested when compared to stabilization funds but this tends to decrease over time as they start meeting their contractual obligations. Savings funds have mixed liabilities as they have some contractually defined payout obligations but a very long investment horizon (typically no less than 10 years) and enjoy a wide choice of investment profiles. Investment holding corporations have open-ended liabilities and no contractually defined interim or final payout obligations. Thus these funds have a high degree of flexibility in investment strategies and can accept low or even negative returns to meet policy objectives or to reap longer term gains.

In addition to the explicit liabilities, explicitly integrated in the policy mandate, the liabilities faced by SWFs are broader and can include implicit guarantees to the private sector or emergency situations. Obviously a stash of funds sitting within the reach of governments is a temptation very difficult to resist, especially during tough times and with elections around the corner.

The most notable example is the Irish National Pension Reserve Fund (NPRF): in the original statutory mandate set in 2001, funds from the NPRF could not be used before 2025, so that the commitments of Ireland's social welfare and public service pensions system could be sustained until 2055. The Irish government, however, amended the rule in 2009 and used €7 billion, i.e. all cash balances and part of sovereign bond holdings, to recapitalize the ailing banking system. An additional €3.7 billion was made available in November 2010 as part of another bailout. In essence the fund objectives were drastically redirected to deal with an emergency, but the original objectives are now clearly out of reach. In other words future pension payments have been used to bail out the banks.

Ireland is not alone in dipping into its sovereign fund to revive the economy, although it may be the first one to have changed its mandate to do so. The Kuwait Investment Authority and Russia's National Wealth Fund have been asked by the Treasuries to bail out troubled banks and companies in their domestic economies. Under a government-ordered rescue plan, the Kuwait Investment Authority in January 2009 took a 16% stake in the struggling Gulf Bank to help the company raise KWD375 million (US$1.3 billion) in emergency funding,[11] and it injected about KWD400 million (US$1.4 billion) into a dedicated fund to support the local stock market in the first four months of that year.[12] Within the Arabian Gulf region the QIA also intervened to support the domestic banking sector. In Russia the government used the National Wealth Fund, a pool designed to be invested abroad for future generations, to support the domestic stock market at the peak of the crisis. Kazakhstan's Samruk-Kazyna has also bailed out the domestic financial sector hit by the credit crisis, spending US$9 billion transferred from the government (Reuters, 2010). What all these episodes show is that during a crisis, any financial entity subordinated to the state – central bank, SWF, pension funds or public corporations – can become fungible (Bodie and Briere, 2011). There is no simple solution to prevent redirection of public funds for short-term objectives. One means could be a constitutional law or a supermajority to change the fund's destination. In times of economic difficulties, however, any law can be revised if there is enough political support for such a move, including a constitutional one.

3.6 LONG-TERM INVESTMENTS: SWFs AS THE ULTIMATE RISK BEARERS

Very few asset managers would resist the temptation, when speaking in public or to their clients, to claim that they are 'long-term investors'. Almost none would admit that their focus is inherently short term. When pressed on what exactly they mean by long-term investment, however, chances are that they would offer some blurb on selecting companies with long-term potential or 'safe assets'. How does a long-term investment strategy differ from the investment strategies of traditional institutional investors? And do SWFs actually embrace long-term investment strategies?

The most distinguished advantage of long-term investment is the ability to take significant market risk, meaning that a fund with a very long investment horizon can tolerate losses in the short term and also stick to its long-term investment strategy during periods of high volatility in the prices of risky assets. This is not always the case: the sovereign nature of the wealth managed by SWFs is perceived as a reserve of state-owned capital and this does not make it easy for politicians, often not familiar with financial market matters, and the population at large, to accept heavy capital losses, whatever the justification might be. According to the International Forum of Sovereign Wealth Funds,

---

[11] Gulf Bank Statement of the Board of Directors, 18 November 2008.
[12] Kuwait Pumps 1.4bn in Kuwait Bourse: Report, Emirates 24/7, 27 April 2009.

'there is some evidence of pressure on withdrawals and a focus on short-term performance in time of volatility, which can create challenges for a long-term investment strategy' (IFSWF, 2011). Indeed, SWFs have often come under heavy political pressure during times of market turbulence. For instance, in the early 2000s, following a heavy stock market sell-off, the Norwegian GPFG was criticized for its decision to increase exposure to equities taken a few years before. Thanks to high transparency and regular interaction with policy makers, however, the management of the GPFG was able to resist the pressure and left its equity exposure unchanged, despite the losses caused by the burst of the internet bubble. An eventual reversal in the fund's exposure to equity following political pressure would have cost it dearly in light of the subsequent market price recovery. Political pressure on short-term performance of SWFs is not limited to advanced economies where transparency is generally higher. China's CIC was criticized in the national media for the losses suffered on the investments made in Western financial institutions in 2007–2008. In the 2010 annual report of the CIC, the Chinese government mentions a 10-year investment horizon and a rolling 10-year annualized return as an important measure of investment performance but 'annual portfolio return will continue to be monitored' (CIC, 2011).

A distinct advantage of long-term investment is the possibility of investing in less liquid assets such as private equity, real estate or infrastructure, or other forms of alternative asset classes. SWFs – Saving Funds and Investment Holding Companies in particular – are indeed among those investment institutions with a relatively high allocation to these asset classes. However, their exposure to these asset classes is lower than that of other long-term institutional investors such as family offices, endowments and foundations where illiquid assets can also reach 35% of their total assets (Monk, 2011), signalling a relatively higher preference for liquidity among SWFs despite their long-term investment horizon.

A long-term strategy should aim to track the long-term growth (and hence long-term returns on investments). Long-term aggregate economic growth depends essentially on three factors: physical capital, human capital and technological progress. Physical capital is the sum of machinery, real estate and infrastructure, while human capital includes demographics, health and education. Furthermore there is an imponderable element, which economists call total factor productivity, related to the efficient combination of these elements, the competence of the public sector and the quality of the legal system.

Forecasting long-term growth prospects is hardly straightforward and often misleading even when based on sensible hypotheses and theories. For instance, in the 1960s several studies comparing the long-term development prospects of the Philippines vis-à-vis Korea, Japan and other Asian countries concluded that the Philippines was much better placed to achieve an outstanding economic performance. The argument relied on factors such as land fertility, natural resources abundance, English language skills and stability (Korea for example was recovering from a devastating and still unfinished war). In 1960, of the population aged over 10 years, 72% were literate, a similar level to Singapore, Korea and Hong Kong, and superior to Malaysia and Indonesia. It already had a domestic savings rate of more than 25% in the mid-1960s, a level comparable to that of the first generation 'miracle economies'. Various agreements with the US gave the Philippines preferential access to US markets and created a level of political comfort that made the Philippines a favourite destination for US foreign investment. It even had a well-developed industrial sector, much larger than Korea's share of GDP (28%), and a thriving services sector (46% of GDP). Nevertheless in the following 30 years the Philippines has been a laggard in economic development compared to almost all its peers in South East Asia. While countries like Taiwan, Korea and Singapore, not to mention Japan and Hong Kong, sooner or later took off, the Philippines underperformed.

In searching for long-term investment opportunities, one can rank countries using a series of indicators on population, infrastructure, education level, business environment, health system and so on. Actually there is a cottage industry devoted to this task and, as a consequence, a number of indicators have been designed as a weighted (or even simple) average of certain variables and/or rankings. The best known are the rankings produced annually by the World Economic Forum, a Switzerland-based think tank and by the World Bank. What emerges from these reports is the view that long-term growth (and hence long-term returns on investments) in the first half of the twenty-first century will be mainly spurred by demographics in emerging economies with a well-established business-friendly environment, i.e. stable macroeconomic conditions, sound legal framework, economic freedom and financial openness. Technology and innovation, on the other hand, will be the key factors driving growth in mature economies. Among emerging markets, in general East Asia comes up strongly and Africa is the place to ride the last demographic wave before the world population starts to stabilize. Among developed countries, Australia, Singapore, Norway, Sweden and South Korea are those with a noteworthy outlook. In Europe only the Baltic states (Latvia and Estonia) and Turkey stand out; North and South America do not appear much on the radar screen, while Western Europe suffers from a poor demographic score, mediocre technological prowess and fiscal mismanagement.

Is there any evidence that SWFs differentiate themselves from other institutional investors by investing according to 'long-term economic value' rather than 'short-term financial value'? As we discussed earlier, at least in terms of direct investments, SWFs seem to lean towards those regions or countries with long-term growth potential. In 2010 about half of direct equity investments were in emerging markets with Asia capturing almost half of these flows, and there is also an increasing strategic focus on African countries. With regard to purely financial investments in listed equities, while the allocation to emerging markets is relatively higher than other institutional investors such as pension funds, the bulk of the assets are still invested in mature economies, reflecting the depth and liquidity of their equity and bond markets. This reflects a major obstacle to matching better long-term economic growth prospects with better long-term returns on capital: the lack of a sufficient number of investment opportunities in those economies with higher long-term growth potential, due to underdeveloped financial markets, a convoluted legal framework, providing little protection for foreign investors, or simply the lack of adequate openness to foreign investments (India is a high-profile case). Furthermore, while emerging markets might have 'decoupled' from developed economies in terms of growth, as shown by their resilience during the last recession, the correlation between listed securities in emerging and advanced economies is very high. And it has actually risen as a result of globalization. This might also explain why SWFs are increasingly turning to direct investment into emerging markets: the scope for diversification through balanced investments in global stock markets has been reduced in the past few years as a result of correlation across markets.

Sectors where SWFs investment behaviour seems to be driven by long-term fundamentals rather than short-term returns are green technology and infrastructure. Both Asian and Middle Eastern SWFs have become increasingly active in the green tech revolution. For instance, the Norwegian GPFG increased the size of its environmental investments to nearly US$5 billion in 2010 (NBIM, 2011); CIC is active in solar and wind energy (Behrendt, 2011); and Mubadala is pumping billions of dollars into Masdar City.[13] Investments by SWFs in the 'green economy' not only provide a hedge against a global scenario of declining oil-based economies but also support the strategic goals of their principal governments. For instance, the adoption of a 'sustainability-enhanced' investment orientation such as that adopted by Mubadala with Masdar satisfies two long-term goals:

- to reduce the domestic dependency on oil as the global economy embraces stricter carbon emissions policies and the oil reserves diminish;
- to provide for a new domestic source of economic development and employment creation.

In fact, the Masdar initiative fits very well into the diversification agenda outlined in 'The Abu Dhabi Economic Vision 2030', a long-term roadmap created by the Emirate's government to guide the sustainable evolution of its economy. For China, investing in solar and wind energy sources is not only a response to the international pressure faced by China to reduce carbon emissions but it also provides the country with a competitive edge in an industry

---

[13] Masdar has the ambition to build the world's first carbon-neutral, zero-waste city powered entirely by renewable energy (Castelli, 2010). The project, however, has been progressively scaled down and the implementation is behind schedule.

that is gradually emerging as an important source of profitability as climate change tops the international agenda. The Chinese focus on green technology should be considered in the context of the broader push by Chinese authorities in research and development from the 2006 'National Medium and Long-Term Plan for the Development of Science and Technology', a blueprint for turning China into a tech powerhouse by 2020. While the green technology sector is still in a nascent phase and investments from SWFs are relatively small, in 2010–2020, the huge wealth accumulated by SWFs could well become a propeller of the 'green revolution'.

With regard to infrastructure, according to the McKinsey Global Institute, relative to GDP emerging markets invest more than twice as much as mature economies in infrastructure: in 2008, China and India alone spent more than US$500 billion on new infrastructure, nearly as much as all of Western Europe (McKinsey Global Institute, 2010).

4

Risk Management for SWFs

To the majority of practitioners, and almost all regulators, the quasi-meltdown of the financial markets in the autumn of 2008 came as a shock, because they were genuinely convinced that they were relying on state-of-the-art models which would capture accurately the exposure to risk and provide early signals of impending mayhem. They were genuinely convinced that fancy formulas and complex numerical solutions to partial differential equations were an accurate description of reality. They were genuinely convinced that they had reliably estimated within a narrow confidence interval stable correlation coefficients between asset prices, including those of derivatives contracts, notwithstanding that not even the lawyers (or the quants) that had designed them knew what the clauses entailed. And, above all, they took for granted that a triple A assigned to a tangle of intricate structured products really meant that their default risk was as remote as the default of the US or German sovereigns.[1]

This false sense of security spread like gangrene to the trading floors, the auditors and the boardrooms, where few bothered to challenge the assumptions or examine the underpinnings of the rosy picture. It was much more comfortable to receive a hefty pay check for nodding silently and congratulating top management on yet another quarter of forecast-beating profits. Sadly even in hindsight it was the right behaviour because, as experience proved, ultimately almost nobody was held liable. The search for responsibilities did not even start. No fuss was raised and the flow of hefty pay cheques did not stop, nor did the bonuses. Apart from those at the helm of Lehman Brothers who lost their job (but suffered no penalties and are enjoying their considerable accumulated wealth), few faced any consequences or even questioning. The meltdown of financial markets has, for all practical purposes, been considered by the authorities a sort of natural cataclysm. On the contrary it resulted from years of abnormally low interest rates, lax regulation, conflicts of interest in rating agencies, abysmal credit standards, reckless behaviour by banks and other intermediaries, and incompetent risk-taking by insurers and asset managers. A host of entrenched deficiencies in the international financial architecture and loopholes in the regulatory framework adopted by developed economies were exposed. Private agents, such as ratings agencies entrusted to enforce transparency and provide timely and accurate information, misled investors to pursue short-term benefits. In a nutshell, investors were misled

---

[1] Among all securities which received a rating, during the crisis of 2008–2009 those rated AAA suffered the most frequent and largest losses due to default.

by the boards, the risk managers and the regulators who got off the hook after being granted impunity.

By the way, while all worries before the crisis had been concentrated on hedge funds and speculative funds, the quake originated from the supposedly dullest intermediaries: commercial banks and credit unions.[2]

SWFs that had participated in the recapitalization of the major American and British banks (see Chapter 3) were among the prime victims of this mixture of careless risk taking, fraudulent actions, and negligent regulatory oversight, because many of them lacked a strong risk management unit which would monitor macroeconomic risks, liquidity shortages and the cracks that were emerging in the Western banking sector.

Sizeable SWFs did not have any unit or staff in charge of macroeconomic analysis and forecasts. Management, asset managers and strategists were relying on the inputs provided by commercial and investment banks with conflicts of interest. Financial analysts, often with little more than desk experience and scant knowledge of real life, would merely analyse the balance sheets of target companies through the alphabet soup of financial indices (ROE, ROI, EBITDA, etc.), unaware of off-balance sheet positions and neglecting stress tests or at least more stringent valuation models. They were not aware of the regulatory framework in which banks operated, the treatment of derivatives in the books, and had only a cursory understanding of the global macroeconomic picture. In short, many SWFs were run with a degree of sophistication more reminiscent of small family offices rather than leading financial institutions.

They were misled by the microeconomic picture depicted in the financial analysis of (often unreliable) balance sheets which conflicted with the macroeconomic clouds on the horizon. Worse, the microeconomic analysis was distorted by accounting smoke and mirrors that concealed the banks' leverage, built through a shadow banking system and the imbalances between short-term liabilities and long-term risky assets that beset Bear Sterns and Lehman brothers and many other large financial institutions.

Shadow banking is the tangle of contracts and positions built outside the regulated perimeter of depositories, investment banks, or bond funds. It grew out of control because, being outside the reach of regulators, it became the carpet under which to sweep the murkiest operations. According to certain estimates, more than 30% of assets in the US are kept off balance sheet. Nevertheless regulators seemed quite happy to ignore this area and confine their role to the tick-box approach cherished by bureaucrats. Hence, to this day,

---

[2] With some prescience Simon Johnson, at the time Chief Economist at the IMF, wrote in the IMF Survey in 2007: 'The emergent approach to "regulating" hedge funds is not to regulate them, but rather to watch carefully over the regulated intermediaries that lend to them (that is, commercial and investment banks). The idea is that this protects the core of the financial system while allowing innovation and risk taking.'

limited data are available on toxic assets. Even after the financial crisis, the efforts to rein in the phenomenon have been feeble.[3]

A dedicated risk management function could have alerted the investment committees of SWFs that – starting from the Mexican Crisis of 1994 – the financial sector was increasingly fragile despite, or probably due to, the higher profitability propelled by a much higher level of aggregate risk. And to those convinced that the crises of the 1990s were mostly confined to emerging economies, the lessons from the Long Term Capital Management (LTCM) default should have served as a reminder of the shaky foundations of globalized financial markets.[4] Paradoxically emerging markets in 2008–2009 were better equipped to withstand the shockwaves thanks to improvements in banking regulation and supervision, higher bank capitalization, and curtailment of non-performing loans. Most credit institutions in emerging markets did not have sizeable off balance sheets items and had limited exposure to structured products, CDOs or ABS. In many cases (exceptions include Argentina, Iceland, Baltics, Ukraine and South Africa) peripheral economies had been transformed from potential sources of systemic instability to 'safe havens'.

But without any lantern to shed light on the actual precarious state of the world economy, the unsustainability of global imbalances and the inadequacy of financial supervision in the main markets, the management of the SWFs relied on external assessment and forecasts swaying a positive spin on the economic outlook. Few SWFs had access or paid attention to high-quality independent research and their due diligence process in terms of macroeconomic scenario analysis was in many instances cursory.

As a rule of thumb the costs for an asset manager are in the order of 1% of its AUM. A SWF with US$50 billion AUM could therefore devote half a billion dollars to cover these costs. Allocating even one-tenth of this amount to research, intelligence and risk management would allow setting up a world class economic research and intelligence function to rival those of leading banks and international institutions. It would be money well spent given the magnitude of the losses incurred trying to navigate blindfold in unchartered territory. Smaller SWFs could pool resources with comparable institutions from the same country or geographical area to fund economic research (which would also provide governments with valuable inputs for economic policy).

In this chapter we will touch upon key issues involving risk management with broader implications for financial markets and for the geopolitics of the

---

[3] As regulators continue to abdicate their responsibilities, markets participants cannot be confident of securing access to liquidity in case of systemic crises without heavy government intervention. In July 2011 the European Council extended the support of the European Financial Stability Fund (EFSF) to the banking system, without putting the banking system under a pan-European supervisory agency. In short the national regulators will have an incentive to downplay the riskiness of bank assets, knowing that in case of trouble the losses will be socialized.

[4] A comparison between the Asian crises of the 1990s and the sub-prime crisis identifies a common backdrop with abundant liquidity and excessive, imprudent credit expansion.

twenty-first century. Before we direct our attention to the specifics of risk management for SWFs, it is worth setting the record on:

1 the roots of the Great Recession, its aftermath and the 'New Normal', i.e. the economic environment that will prevail in this decade after the dust settles;
2 the nature of risk in financial markets and how it differs from the notion that has prevailed among practitioners.

The rest of the chapter treats issues that are rather technical and might be skipped by those interested only in the themes pertaining specifically to SWFs operations and their geopolitical role.

4.1 THE CRISIS IN RETROSPECT

The implosion of financial markets in the autumn of 2008 had a long gestation. Its roots can be traced back to the dotcom bubble at the beginning of the twenty-first century. Technological advances in information technology, combined with the spread of internet, led to an overinvestment in the US technology sector colloquially called the dotcom. Virtually free capital flowed from all over the world to Silicon Valley and Wall Street, producing a steep jump in US economic growth, investment, consumption and wealth. Unfortunately resources available at zero cost are always used inefficiently and financial capital is no exception. When the bubble exploded, the US authorities shunned the idea of engineering an orderly readjustment of the economy, with the inevitable fall in standard of living, to more sustainable levels (i.e. levels compatible with long-term growth patterns, not those artificially boosted by the euphoria) and restoring savings rates.

Instead a stolid political decision led in the opposite direction, substituting the stimulus from private investments with a hike in private consumption supported by lower taxes and higher household debt. In this policy response the US government was sheepishly supported by the Federal Reserve which maintained interest rates unduly low, fuelling an abnormally high level of private debt and leverage across all financial institutions. In essence in the early years of the twenty-first century while the corporate sector was purging its debt overhang, the household sector was pressed to increase its consumption and its already swollen liabilities (thanks to home equity loans and mortgage refinancing). The US government added soaring budget deficits resulting from large tax cuts and ballooning military expenditures for the wars in Afghanistan and Iraq. Before 2001 an intense policy debate focused on how to use the budget surplus (e.g. to fund Social Security); a few months later the US public finances were sinking in a sea of red ink, a prelude to a much larger red ocean 10 years later.

A key role played in this process was the reaction to 9/11 and the priorities of a US presidency with a serious legitimacy problem following a contested electoral victory assigned by a contentious Supreme Court ruling. The flood-gates of liquidity and public expenditure were kept wide open in an attempt to reassert US global prominence despite the blows suffered. The US assumed the role of consumer of last resort for the world economy while, as a result, its current account deficit and external liabilities ballooned. Against this background one cannot fail to point out that the responsibility for the growing global imbalances were shared by the European Central Bank that maintained rates at a higher level sapping European growth, and by the mercantilist at-titude of Japan, Germany and China which relied heavily on export-led growth and compressed domestic demand.

The financial system increased leverage, risk and opacity for five long years in order to boost profits in a low interest rate environment. The strain arose ini-tially in the sub-prime mortgage segment in 2007, but propagated inexorably (Figure 4.1 shows the volatility of systemic asset classes across time).

A difficult balancing act of deleveraging exposures without sinking markets started in the summer of 2007, with senior bank executives feeling increas-ingly fidgety. When one of Wall Street's most illustrious investment banks, Bear Sterns, was narrowly rescued from default in July 2008 (although inves-tors lost their equities), the gravity of the situation became palpable.

Trading floors and boardrooms were filled with rumours about the next casualty and whether insurance companies were hiding what started to be dubbed 'toxic assets' in their balance sheets. The IMF estimated the total losses from these exposures at US$600 billion, putting in doubt the solvency of many systemic banks. Counterparty risk, even in the interbank money mar-ket, which until then had been the most secure marketplace, became a major source of apprehension. In the first week of September 2008, the US Treasury

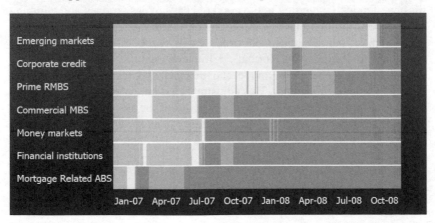

Figure 4.1   The contagion effect in the global financial markets. Darker areas depict higher volatility.

Source: IMF.

Secretary Paulson announced the nationalization of Freddie Mac and Fannie Mae, two quasi-private entities which guaranteed half of the outstanding mortgages and that had built up a degree of leverage unjustified by their function, thanks in no small part to political influence acquired through lavish campaign contributions. Liquidity that had ballooned within the shadow banking system evaporated, forcing a fire sale of the valuable assets left on the balance sheets and a write-down of collateral.[5]

The following weekend the climax was reached with the sudden collapse of Lehman Brothers, a bank founded 150 years earlier, which left US$600 billion of liabilities. All estimates of impending losses quickly shot upwards. The same day Merrill Lynch was put on the block and sold for US$50 billion to Bank of America. A few days later AIG, one of the largest insurers in the world, was on the brink of insolvency and was rescued by an emergency injection of US$85 billion from the public coffers. Then it was the turn of Washington Mutual, Wachovia and Citigroup. Goldman Sachs and Morgan Stanley, the last investment banks surviving, turned into commercial banks, accepting Federal Reserve supervision. Between the end of September and October the repercussions were felt in Europe where Benelux governments had to buy 49% of Fortis, Germany had to rescue Hypo Real Estate and Dexia received a government loan of €6 billion. In mid-October the entire financial system of Iceland collapsed and with it the rest of the economy.

The downward spiral was interrupted only when an emergency plan totalling US$700 billion, conceived by US Secretary of Treasury Paulson, to deal with toxic assets was approved and put in place and the UK government nationalized several banks with an intervention equivalent to €460 billion. By the end of December 2008 the total write-down worldwide due to toxic assets amounted to US$1 trillion according to Bloomberg data.

The world will deal with the aftermath of this crisis for several years. The illusion of quickly reverting to the good old days of easy money and climbing stock indices through massive injections of public money are giving way to the awareness that the adjustment process will be a bumpy ride, which some have come to call the 'New Normal'.[6] Ultimately, stability will not be restored until deleveraging runs its course and the financial institutions drastically change their modus operandi. This adjustment has barely started; actually, bad habits seem to have been restored in key nodes of the system thanks to political complacency and an entrenched reluctance to tackle vexed questions such as pervasive financial regulation. The revamp will take years, however, and

---

[5] The credit freeze spread its contagion globally. With risk aversion at the zenith, shares and bonds in emerging markets were dumped irrespective of their creditworthiness. Banks all over the world were unable to manage their liquidity in any meaningful way and had to halt or ruthlessly curtail their lending. This was felt particularly in those emerging markets where the banking sector relied on external funds to cover the gap between deposits and loans. Covering even a mild gap with the market frozen became a challenge and therefore credit expansion was drastically reduced.

[6] El Erian (2009) has contributed to the popularity of this allocution.

in the meantime the banking systems in the United States and Europe, as well as in other sizeable economies such as Japan and Russia, will not be able to sustain growth in the real economy.

4.2 THE COMPLEX QUALITATIVE NATURE OF RISK: UNCERTAINTY, CHAOS, BLACK SWANS AND FAT TAILS

We have harked back to the phases of the financial crises to stress that its effects are far from over and that the emergency measures taken to reduce its effects have created additional imbalances. In particular, with private debt shifted onto the government balance sheet, fiscal crises in the US, Eurozone and Japan have taken centre stage and constitute the next round of emergencies for policy makers.

The current financial crisis has been unusual in its order of magnitude and its geographical spread, but not in its underlying causes if historical experience is any guide. Together with large chunks of the international banking sector, in late 2008 the notion that unregulated markets are inherently stable and financial market professionals can manage risk better if they are left free to take decisions unfettered by authorities' intrusion sunk. In reality financial markets without checks and balances imposed from the outside are inherently unstable for a number of reasons, primarily: (a) asymmetric rewards for success and failure, (b) a marked tendency to herd behaviour, (c) ineptitude to monitor at the same time all sources of risk, (d) over-reliance on short memory and recent experience and (e) absence of checks and balances in decision making.

A few good years inevitably spark overconfidence and complacency. As a result, paradoxically, virulent financial crises almost always follow periods of buoyant growth, almost never periods of stagnation or slow growth.

Capitalism is all about risk. Growth, progress, new ventures, technological advances and implementation of new discoveries all involve a degree of uncertainty. Risk does materialize no matter how many precautions one adopts, so a capitalist system is inherently subject to instability, cycles, crises and disruptions. This does not imply that it is 'wrong'. It implies that risk management is at the core of capitalism and the cornerstone of free markets. **Widespread incompetence in risk management is more dangerous** for free markets than any collectivist ideology. Those investing for future generations in a world increasingly intricate and cracking at the seams need to internalize risk management as second nature.

There exist various forms of risk. The qualitative complexity of what we colloquially call risk is extremely varied and, despite considerable research effort, still poorly understood. Among financial professionals, at least until the Lehman bankruptcy in 2008, the prevailing misconception that risk was accurately measurable through statistical analyses performed on a set of historical data. Dissenting voices were mostly marginalized outside academia or restricted circles of hedge funds.

This faith was strengthened by the development of what seemed ever more sophisticated econometric techniques and asset pricing models. The availability of massive databases of financial time series on which to test the predictive properties of these models seemed to add soundness to these methodologies. The misconception is now shattered. Current mathematical knowledge does not allow the precise measurement of the tangle of complex interactions which give rise to the phenomena collectively dubbed 'risk'. Models are useful in conceptualizing and summarizing intricate phenomena, but the maze of inter-relations among agents, their expectations, their information, their strategic behaviour and the effect of policy actions escape quantification even based on the most sophisticated scientific knowledge currently available. Actually it is doubtful that such knowledge will ever be reached outside the realm of science fiction novels and movies.

The economist who outlined a modern theory of risk was Frank Knight. In his PhD dissertation published in 1921 'Risk, Uncertainty and Profit', he distinguished between 'risk' and 'uncertainty'. The first refers to an event whose occurrence is governed by a law of probability which can therefore be calculated mathematically, and any negative outcome can be insured against. 'Uncertainty', by contrast, refers to an event whose probability is unknown because, for example, it is rare (an earthquake followed by a tsunami), or because it has never occurred in the past (9/11) or because its consequences are unimaginable (the Lehman default or an asteroid hitting a large urban area). Financial professionals have developed tools to deal with certain forms of risk (not all) as defined by Knight, but obviously uncertainty in the Knightian sense cannot be addressed or analysed through quantitative methods in any meaningful way. It can only be treated very imperfectly through some qualitative framework.

Knight did not have financial markets in mind when he wrote his dissertation, but the level of entrepreneurial profit in perfect competition, so his views did not influence financial practitioners in his time. Quantitative methods made their debut on Wall Street in the 1960s with the discovery that asset price returns resembled a random walk.[7] As early as 1961 Benoit Mandelbrot, a mathematician who later became famous as the 'father' of fractals, pointed out that the notion of risk has qualitative connotations that are difficult to treat rigorously because 'the variety of natural and social phenomena is infinite, while the mathematical techniques capable of capturing them are very few'.[8] Mandelbrot's notion of risk does not coincide with Knight's; rather he made a distinction between 'benign risk' and 'wild risk'. Loosely speaking, the first is

---

[7] Actually Luis Bachelier at the end of the nineteenth century had already developed the idea and applied what came to be known later as Brownian motion to the study of agricultural prices.

[8] Mandelbrot (1997b) part II.

the kind of risk associated with the Gaussian paradigm, i.e. asset returns fluctuate around a mean while large, persistent deviations are sporadic. The second is the risk deriving from large, rare and erratic jumps and/or the persistence of deviations from the mean.[9] As this second form of risk cannot be treated within the realm of standard statistical models it has been largely ignored in the mainstream literature. Occasionally, especially after major market disruptions, it receives attention under various colourful denominations, for example Chaos Theory became popular after Black Friday in 1987, and Black Swans[10] became an all-encompassing explanation of the market meltdown in 2008. Fat tails and extreme events are now part of everyday discourse on trading floors. However, very little has changed in the risk management models (apart from some less trenchant assurances) because fundamental mathematical advances in this field have not occurred. And even if they did, the most sophisticated models, by definition, cannot help to see through the fog of Knightian uncertainty which surrounds and will always surround us.

Across history, events that have spread havoc in financial markets originated either from catastrophic events or the random conjunction of several factors (the perfect storm effect), which induced a reversal of unduly optimistic expectations after several years of continuous growth. Regulations should be aimed at setting buffers for unpredictable circumstances, but more crucially also at limiting the accrual of risk during expansionary phases. Risks are taken up during good times and materialize during negative conjunctures. In contrast, as we shall see in the next section, regulations tend to exacerbate cyclical variations and erode the defence against severe shocks.

4.3 BANKING REGULATION, HERD BEHAVIOUR AND CONTAGION

Markets are the result of complex interactions among agents with conflicting objectives and interests which need to be regulated by independent public agencies, with pervasive powers, sufficient resources and no ulterior motives or conflict of interests. Markets can rarely adopt a reliable charter of self-regulation. Too often private entities in charge of establishing or enforcing rules tend to perform these functions to their own benefit and to the others' detriment. To be credible, rules must be enforced by independent referees not subject to the temptation of becoming players themselves.

Financial regulations inevitably design a set of incentives with profound consequences. Often they are crafted to address a problem only to create an unforeseen one. The financial regulation framework that was enshrined in the

---

[9] Mandelbrot, with reference to the Biblical characters, called these two effects the Noah and Joseph effects.
[10] The definition came from the book *The Black Swan* written by Nicholas Taleb in 2007 and extended in 2010 to incorporate the events after the Lehman downfall.

New Capital Accord, the so-called Basel 2,[11] was signed in 2004, revised in 2006 and implemented in Europe at the beginning of 2008 (in the US it had not yet been introduced during the financial crisis).

Basel 2 was designed to improve the use of capital by banks and induce better risk management by establishing a link between risk exposure and capital. However, several snags became rapidly apparent. Here we consider the main four.

1 **The conflict between micro and macro level**. Prudential criteria focus on the solvency of single institutions, mandating that they restore capital after they suffer losses. But if a shock hits the entire financial system or the economy, a collective adjustment triggers a chain reaction by large market participants that must raise capital or dispose of assets at the same time. The net result is an exacerbation of the downturn, a fire sale of securities and a credit crunch. In other words, Basel 2 hinged on the mistaken presumption that preserving the solvency and the stability of each financial institution makes the whole system safe. On the contrary, failing to distinguish between macroeconomic and microeconomic stability destabilizes the finance sector through contagion.[12] Markets need both optimists and pessimists, but prudential regulations designed to cope with microeconomic issues forces pessimists to tail optimists and vice versa, so the financial system is bound to swing wildly from one excess to the other.

2 **Reliance on quantitative models**. Basel 2 allowed banks to run an internal risk management system. This in practice meant that the banks were left free to determine the appropriate capital adequacy (with only a cursory control) because in many cases regulators lacked the expertise to verify carefully the properties of the models, especially those set up by large banks. Furthermore a number of institutions adopted models built by a handful of quantitative analysts which therefore produced similar directional indications across markets and geographies. Specifically, the adoption of Value at Risk (VaR) methodology was a major blunder because it generates unreliable and often misleading measures of risk (see Box 4.4).

---

[11] Basel, Switzerland, is the location of the Bank for International Settlements, the institution in charge of the defining the international accord on banking supervision. Information on Basel 2 and the more recent changes to the Capital Accord following the financial crisis can be found at the website of the BIS, http://www.bis.org/bcbs/index.htm.

[12] The notion that the financial sector can exacerbate normal business cycles fluctuation is not novel. It was most famously underscored by Irving Fisher (1933), who observed that in downturns financial institutions reduce credit. More modern contributions pioneered by Minsky (1977) and Kindleberger (1978) pointed to the specular phenomenon in upturn which is spurred by overoptimistic expectations and the role of collateral. With regards to how the latest financial crisis can be seen as a 'Minski moment', see various contributions by G. Magnus, Senior Economic Advisor at UBS Investment Bank. His first article entitled 'What This Minski Moment Means' appeared for the first time in the *Financial Times* on 22 August 2007. More contributions and articles can be downloaded free from http://georgemagnus.com/home.

3 **Reliance on market prices.** Prices that we observe on the markets reflect the asset valuation of the marginal demander and the marginal supplier. Does it reflect a robust assessment? Is it a 'correct' assessment? Certainly prices reflect information and the analysis thereof made by some buyers and some sellers. But demand and supply curves in reality are not smooth and continuous as depicted in textbooks: they might be jagged, discontinuous and, above all, unstable (see Box 4.1). Events that induce a change in valuation occur frequently, mistakes are common and volatility might snap, causing prices to swing wildly.[13] Goodhart and Persaud (2008) argued that:

> The crash of 2007–08 has laid bare the poverty of the current regulatory philosophy. At the heart of the present approach are estimates of risk and value that use current and past market prices. This convergence of market measures of risk and regulatory capital looks sophisticated and makes life easier for banks. But it is puzzling why market measures of a bank's risk should be at the centre of financial regulation. The reason why we have bank regulation is that every now and then markets fail and the resulting crashes have widespread and devastating effect. Yet regulators have used market prices to build their defences against market failure. Unsurprisingly, this has proved as much help as the Maginot line. If market prices were good at predicting crashes, they would not happen.[14]

In other words prudential regulations should ensure the solidity of the system (or at least its survival) in case markets become dysfunctional.[15]

4 **Reliance on ratings agencies.** With prudential criteria hinging on ratings issued by a handful of (supposedly) specialized agencies, banks forsake risk assessment (de facto relinquishing their main social function), and pursued uncontrolled increase in leverage spurred by an incentive to invest in complex securities rated AAA (often as a result of a conflict of interest). For unsophisticated banks (i.e. those without an internal risk system) Basel 2

---

[13] Regulators could require systemically important institutions to complement pricing models with internally developed capabilities to exercise judgment in case of market failures, something analogous to what the Federal Reserve did when it engineered the bailout of LTCM. And this is indeed what is currently happening with the so-called resolution plans being finalized by the largest banks at the request of regulators. On progress so far see BIS (2011b).

[14] Charles Goodhart and Avinash Persaud, How to Avoid the Next Crash, *Financial Times*, 30 January 2008.

[15] It is important to stress that until not long ago capital adequacy ratios could be very low, even 3% for Tier 1 without ever giving rise to problems as long as banks stuck to commercial loans, overdrafts and mortgages. Bankruptcies or the financial stress of clients were manageable because sudden swings were rare. The need to introduce high capital adequacy ratios arose when banks and systemic financial intermediaries started to rely on and be exposed to market securities.

Box 4.1 Price and valuation

Any asset has a different value for the buyer and the seller. When they agree on a price and complete a purchase transaction it means that the value for the seller is below the agreed price and vice versa for the buyer.

This simple truth apparently escaped the regulators for whom price and value are identical. The value for the seller and the buyer is different for a number of reasons. The owner of a successful restaurant who wants to expand his business because he cannot accommodate all the clients, values the retail space next door much more than somebody from out of town who want to open, say, a furniture store. A struggling company with a well-known brand is worth much more to someone who could exploit that brand than to someone who would only be able to strip its physical assets.

In other words observable market prices are not necessarily an accurate assessment of value. It is true that in a liquid market the current price provides a measure of what can be raised through a quick sale, but this is relevant information if the seller is a marginal agent. If all agents are forced to sell, this measure is meaningless.

A buyer tries to determine the maximum he is prepared to pay for an asset or a company, while a seller's aim is to ascertain the minimum he is willing to accept. Both values change over time depending on a set of circumstances. It also depends on comparisons with other assets. For example, if one thinks that the future prospects of IBM are brighter than those of Apple (although not necessarily negative), or vice versa, the price they are willing to pay is affected.

In short, a firm's value results from the sum of its assets values which vary depending on the use the buyer can make or the benefits he can extract. Obviously this reasoning cannot be applied to securities such as government bonds or FX derivatives, but the point is that the function of financial markets is to intermediate between buyers and sellers or investors and savers. Financial institutions create the market which is an imperfect mechanism, subject to failure. If markets always worked properly and never failed there would be little need for regulations and no need for capital adequacy ratios. Hence prudential regulations must set a safety net to pull in case of disruptive events or widespread panic which neglects market signals and hinges on some other valuation criterion.

---

assigned to each rating a weight to calculate the riskiness of a security in the capital.[16] Ratings agencies therefore became the cornerstone of global financial stability. When they started assigning triple A to risky structured

---

[16] For example, 100% government bonds rated triple A would be used in the calculation of Tier 1 capital, roughly corresponding to equities.

Box 4.2 Handle with care

Models, however sophisticated, cannot help various real-life situations.

1 In a sharp downturn the interrelationships and the dynamics among asset prices are too complex and variegated.
2 Any phenomenon induced by financial innovation, such as derivatives, cannot be judged through the lenses of estimated parameters which reflect past history.
3 A loss of confidence that forces the bankruptcy of a large financial intermediary triggers events which are rapid and unpredictable in extent.
4 Correlations and other measures of dependence can change in sign abruptly over a few feverish market sessions for long enough to push a financial intermediary into bankruptcy, but not long enough to be recorded, say, in monthly data. Estimations depend on the quality of data used and the length of the sample period.
5 Counterparty risks, aggregate liquidity risks, interconnection risk, reversal of expectations and a few other phenomena which have marred the financial system spectacularly in the crisis of 2008–2009 (but also other crises, unfortunately forgotten, such as the LTCM demise or several emerging market crises in the 1990s) cannot be modelled in any meaningful way and certainly cannot be predicted with any degree of accuracy (Rattaggi, 2010).

The unusual severity of the 2008 crisis played a crucial role in the dramatic build-up of leverage and the concentration of aggregate risk in systemic financial institutions beyond any reasonable level and outside internal or external control. Leverage is essentially induced by distorted perceptions of correlations and over-reliance on the effectiveness of hedging.

---

products, there was no one in charge of 'rating the raters' and the point of no return was fast approached. The downfall of banks was caused by the leverage built through the tranches of structured asset-backed securities much more vulnerable to shocks than their rating would indicate.

To summarize, Basel 2 linking banks' regulatory capital (i.e. the buffer against losses) and the risk of assets is inherently pro-cyclical so it induces herd behaviour.[17] Rigid limits on minimum bank capital that ignore macroeconomic

---

[17] Herd behaviour, is a 'collective' behaviour adopted by many uncoordinated individuals who choose to replicate the actions of a certain group. It is inherent in human nature having been documented in cognitive psychology and is emphasized in the body of economics literature known as behavioural finance. It might arise from perfectly rational motives (like when someone tries

conditions exacerbate economic fluctuations because asset prices tend to be positively correlated with the business cycle: during booms the value of bank capital and collateral used to guarantee loans (particularly real estate) increases. Hence it is easier for households and firms to obtain loans and banks are more inclined to lend. Credit growth boosts investment and consumption, so without a brake the spiral continues until a shock knocks down the house of cards. At that point the mechanism works in reverse, forcing an offload of assets and a credit squeeze.[18]

Stated differently, risk-based capital requirements are a main vehicle through which contagion spreads across all segments of the financial sector, because the price of risk, determined by investors' risk aversion, is countercyclical: it decreases during upswings and increases during downswings (see Adrian and Shin, 2010). This contagion effect cannot be stopped through monetary policy alone, because a change of, say, 1% in short-term interest rates is not enough to offset the effects of a double digit movement in share prices or a similar variation over the expected return on investments.

4.4 THE EVOLUTION OF THE REGULATORY FRAMEWORK

In the aftermath of the Great Crisis, policy makers around the world while doling out hundreds of billions of dollars, pledged to take draconian measures to avoid a repetition of the meltdown. A new, more global regulatory framework was supposed to be designed and implemented swiftly after some degree of stabilization in financial markets had been regained. In reality nothing drastic has been undertaken and progress in this area has been painfully slow, often bumping against a wall of resistance erected by those whose interests are threatened by more stringent rules.

The debate and the decision making process which is shaping the new financial architecture will have a tremendous impact on the performance of SWFs and even more so for FWFs. Nevertheless the implications are still not fully grasped by senior decision makers in emerging markets. Inexplicably they are not fully taking part in the high-level discussions and have contributed no strong views on the agenda and the priorities. Essentially they seem to be awaiting decisions from developed countries. Nevertheless, SWFs and FWFs protecting their long-term investments face a fight on three main fronts:

---

to infer the quality of a restaurant from the number of people dining there) or from imitation of people supposedly having better information or more sophisticated analytical capability.

[18] This danger imbued in Basel 2 was brought to the attention of the BIS by Danielsson *et al.* (2001), but was largely ignored.

Box 4.3 The failure of self-regulation

Poor risk management practices by banks and insurances along with distorted incentive structures for executive compensation, shortcomings in disclosure, fundamental faults in the practice of the originate-to-distribute model and a tick-box approach to regulatory checks, were some of the poisonous ingredients that led to the financial crisis.

But there is a common thread that connects the series of financial scandals of this century: the fallacy of self-regulation. Private entities have incentives to abuse their positions as referees or de facto regulators. During the dotcom bubble it was the financial analysts in investment banks; with the corporate governance crises – Enron, Worldcom, Parmalat and related episodes – the auditing firms were the culprits; the sub-prime crisis was facilitated by the rating agencies assigning triple A to complex products.

Both the EU and the US are moving towards regulating credit rating agencies and extending the regulatory net to encompass investment and other financial intermediaries. Until September 2006 rating agencies were essentially deregulated and afterwards the only requirement was an obligation to register with the Federal Reserve. Given the oligopolistic structure of the ratings market, the regulatory framework currently in place hinges on self-regulation in the form of the Fundamentals of a Code of Conduct for Credit Rating Agencies issued by the International Organization of Securities Commissions (IOSCO).

---

1 curbs on unfettered risk taking by intermediaries through a binding limit to leverage (especially in systemic institutions);
2 circuit breakers in the form of cyclically adjusted capital requirements to reduce GDP volatility, stem contagion and limit herd behaviour;
3 bounds to entities deemed too big to fail, or too interconnected to fail, possibly through tighter capital requirements for larger institutions.

The practical implementation of these principles encompasses several areas and probably will proceed in conjunction with the implementation of Basel 3, which in its present form is utterly inadequate to tackle the vexed questions that the crisis has laid bare. A new effective approach should be much bolder than the patchwork of half-baked initiatives and strongly emphasize, among other things:

- rigorous stress-testing, particularly in downturns for strengthening capital treatment of complex securities;

- substantial reduction of the scope of OTC markets, by transferring transactions, especially of widely traded derivatives, in organized markets with proper supervision, clearing, settlement and market making;
- more pervasive powers to request timely information and investigate extensively dubious practices through subpoena of documents or phone tapping;
- clarity in accounting rules including off balance sheet items;
- stronger corporate governance by Board of Directors, e.g. through the inclusion of debt holders representatives, with frequent and pervasive examination of risk exposure by key desks.

This last issue has arisen frequently since the demise of Barings: the ever-increasing complexity of large and complex financial institutions has emasculated the role of governance from existing shareholders and non-executive board members. For these entities, the traditional board model (suitable for other industries) – characterized by infrequent meetings and rather stable external conditions – is obviously inadequate. The bottom line is that board members are out of touch with the swiftness and strategies by which the risk profiles of these institutions can be altered by sophisticated (or reckless) traders and securities desks. A possible mechanism for improving the boards' oversight may be a requirement to assign a board seat to a regulator and one or more prominent subordinated debt holders or others with an interest (and the competence) to rein in reckless risk practices.

Aside from these points much remains to be done to bring all institutions (banks, insurances, funds and alternative investment vehicles) under one regulatory umbrella and prohibit significant off balance sheet operations by any sort of institution. The domain of the regulators cannot be limited otherwise there will always be an incentive to use shadowy areas for shadowy deals and practices. Unfortunately on this issue the reform has proceeded in a rather elliptical way. The provisions in the Dodd-Frank Bill did little to rein in off balance sheets positions which remain largely unregulated. The law recognized the systemic risk caused by the shadow banking system and devised some tools to attenuate its effects through closer oversight and wide security margins. But in practice it contains a lengthy set of instructions to regulators to investigate various areas and only afterwards write binding rules with broad discretion, a likely target for politicians, lobbyists and pressure groups. Specifically the Law set in place a council of regulators, the Financial Stability Oversight Council, with power to identify and manage systemic risks. This body has the power to recommend significant changes in regulation, deemed necessary to ensure financial stability, but how it will use it is hard to divine.

Lastly we should remember that financial regulations affect not only the economic cycle and the intensity of crises, but also cost and availability of capital. According to some estimates discussed in the next chapter, banks will need to raise a substantial amount of capital in the next few years (McKinsey

Global Institute, 2010). As a result bank financing will be more expensive and alternatives to bank financing will be more palatable for companies, especially unlisted ones.

SWFs and FWFs, as we pointed out in Chapter 3, will be the major supplier of long-term capital and therefore their returns will depend on capital scarcity which determines its cost. This issue is interwoven with the reversal of the so-called savings glut which is likely to unravel as the world population ages and the infrastructure investment in the high growth economies intensify. We will touch upon these phenomena in the Chapter 7.

4.5 SKETCHES OF RISK MANAGEMENT FOR SWFs

Over the next few years a more uncertain landscape will prevail with tremendous challenges coming from the public debt sustainability in the US, the restructuring of the European Union fiscal policy, the demographic decline in mature economies, the inflationary pressure in emerging markets, the redrawing of geopolitical maps (North Africa is only the latest hotspot) and the reformatting of the monetary and financial architecture. The objective of an asset manager is to identify an acceptable level of risk (i.e. tolerance for losses and mistakes, which are inevitable) and then devise strategies, within those parameters, to optimize returns over the investment horizon. Ultimately risk management is human judgment guided by a set of imperfect (to different degrees) quantitative tools and constantly updated qualitative assessment. Quantitative tools are useful to highlight the relationships between different assets and their dependence on macroeconomic dynamics, but they must not be considered an auto-pilot system. Asset valuations are probability distributions, not exact calculations. The foremost point to stress is that these probability distributions are and will always be influenced by the business cycle, which remains the fundamental driver of market and systemic risk. The fluctuations in macroeconomic conditions are conditioned by technological progress, policy choices, demographics, reversal of expectations, and disruptions of various natures (defaults, accidents, wars or natural catastrophes). Current scientific knowledge and past experience might, in the best circumstances, attenuate the negative effects of these fluctuations on enterprises' profits, solidity of financial institutions, and portfolio returns, but forecasting tools and hedging techniques to avoid them altogether do not exist and never will.

SWFs and other asset managers who do not constantly monitor the macroeconomic environment are destined to bear severe losses or at best to underperform. But having formed expectations on the macroeconomic outlook is not enough, because the link between macroeconomic fluctuations and asset prices is innately unstable. Models that aim to estimate the parameters of such a relationship are not reliable, nor are models that rely on past data to estimate a probability distribution of returns and correlations to provide a measure of risk (see Box 4.4). Furthermore it is hard to grasp the broader consequences of infrequent macroeconomic disruptions.

Until recently SWFs were not renowned for their risk management culture. Exceptions include Singapore's GIC which has provided in its Annual Report

---

Box 4.4 The Value at Risk deception

One of the most notable failures on the road to financial meltdown was the so-called Value at Risk (VaR) methodology. After recommendations by the Basel 2 Committee on banking supervision in 2004, VaR models become one of the most critical inputs in risk assessment by banks, investors, asset managers and also regulators. Their results were taken as an accurate representation of reality and not as a mere statistical technique yielding a range of values based upon arbitrary (or ad hoc) underlying assumptions. This widespread appeal was due in no small part to its deceitful simplicity, i.e. an assessment methodology which summarises the total portfolio risk into a single number, the maximum loss over a certain period of time. Behind the more or less advanced techniques used to calculate the result stood the notion that:

1 the real world can be meaningfully modelled through a multivariate normal (or elliptical) joint distribution of asset returns;
2 asset returns in different periods are independently and identically distributed;
3 the relationships among asset prices are linear; and
4 financial time series are stationary.

Beyond the technical jargon, this meant that the effectiveness of portfolio diversification is grossly overestimated, that the probability of a contemporaneous drop in all asset prices is underestimated and therefore severe downside risks are neglected. VaR models are just a subset of risk management tools that rely on unrealistic assumptions; most statistical methods in fact suffer from this kind of fallacy, but the endorsement of VaR by the BIS paved the way to its widespread acceptance.

In fact the Amendment to the Capital Accord to Incorporate Market Risks (Basel Committee on Banking Supervision, 1996) gave three guidelines:

- 'In calculating the VaR, a 99th percentile, one-tailed confidence interval is to be used.'
- 'In calculating VaR, an instantaneous price shock equivalent to a 10 day movement in prices is to be used.'
- 'Banks may use VaR numbers calculated according to shorter holding periods scaled up to ten days by the square root of time.'

> This naive quest to condense extremely complex issues into a simple index or number, produced the pernicious consequence of spreading a false sense of security within financial institutions and freeing Board members (many of whom had scant knowledge of quantitative methods let alone complex financial products) from their main responsibility: question the claims of management, demand alternative scenario stress tests and assess independently the overall exposure. The ultimate effect was to underestimate the frequency and magnitude of negative events and so to make the increase in leverage acceptable.

(GIC, 2011) a detailed account of its risk management approach encompassing not only financial risk but also broader concepts such as process risk and people risk.

Aware of this shortcoming, the IFSWF devoted its May 2010 meeting in Sydney to a discussion of the risk management framework best suited for SWFs.[19] A subcommittee presented its recommendations on best practices and challenges (touching upon crucial topics such as fat tails) summarized in four planks:

- macroinvestment policy design – including strategic asset allocation, currency hedging policy, selection of asset managers, and structuring exposure to alpha – by senior investment decision-makers;
- portfolio construction incorporating innovations in investment risk management, e.g. multi-risk, event-sensitive, and full-scale optimization technologies; regime-dependent risk estimation; and measures of continuous exposure to loss;
- rigorous stress-testing of portfolios using regime-specific risk estimates that reflect a broad distribution of economic and financial scenarios, including systemic shocks;
- careful management of implementation risk and risk-adjusted post-evaluation of investment performances.

While a SWF might have the best intentions and policies, it needs to devise an apt practical implementation. In essence, if one were to take on board these principles, what would be the hurdles that SWFs and FWFs face? And how different would they be from those faced by other financial institutions?

We have argued that SWFs enjoy a unique position among asset managers: their mandate emphasizes returns over an extended horizon, they are not much

---

[19] Some of the presentations discussed at the IFSWF's meeting in Sydney and some additional information concerning the work of this institution can be downloaded from the IFSWF website at http://www.ifswf.org.

leveraged, they rarely face sudden redemptions, and hence they do not need to be over-concerned about liquidity risk or crippling margin calls.[20] Stable endowment and long-term focus do not imply, as some are inclined to think, that they can be more complacent on risk management or that they can be less rigorous in their risk assessment.[21] It means that they need to assign a different set of weights to various sources of risks than mainstream asset managers. For example they need to be less concerned about cash flow and pay more attention to long-term inflation and demographic trends both globally and in the countries where they invest. On the other hand, we will stress that they require a risk management framework poles apart from the concepts prevailing among most asset managers.

When asked, virtually all asset managers claim to be focusing on the long term. What this really means, however, is never completely clear and even for SWFs the practical implications are hazy. After all, the long term is a sequence of short terms.

So, while a long-term investment strategy is one that, in theory, neglects short-term volatility or occasional short-lived disturbances, there is no way to be sure whether a phenomenon is temporary or permanent and consequently how short the short term is.

In specific cases, such as farmland, which every once in a while suffers from drought, one can be sure that there will be light at the end of the tunnel. Therefore it is a matter of enduring the effects of occasional, possibly prolonged, adversity.

In general, however, assessing the duration of economic shocks or their cyclical nature is fraught with uncertainty. One example being those SWFs that acquired large stakes in Western banks before the Lehman demise. They reckoned that the predicaments were of a temporary nature, and although the banks' capital was dented, their profitability would quickly rebound. So they

---

[20] Most financial professionals would envy such a position. However, in reality the degrees of freedom are tighter as the board of SWFs, like any supervisory body or shareholder, would not be pleased to see recurrent quarterly losses and would fail to appreciate the argument that in the long run everything will be fine.

[21] GIC in its Annual Report (GIC, 2011) describes its long-term investment philosophy under the heading 'Looking at performance and risk over different time periods':

20-Year Return: As a long-term investor, GIC's performance should be measured over a suitably long time horizon. GIC invests across many asset classes, including illiquid asset classes such as real estate and private equity, and adopts strategies that are consistent with our long-term time horizon. A 20-year period is appropriate as it spans several business cycles and hence encompasses a number of market peaks and troughs. Thus our investment horizon of 20 years is matched by the 20-year annualized real rate of return metric, which is the key focus for GIC. The use of the real rate assures us that the international purchasing power of the reserves is maintained.

5-Year and 10-Year Returns: The 5-year and 10-year rates of return reflect an intermediate measure of GIC's longer term performance because they provide a better representation of the variation in returns over the market cycle.

felt it was a rare occasion to snatch stakes in lucrative businesses, momentarily impaired by unusual circumstances. With hindsight, that proved somewhat inaccurate.

In financial institutions risk measures are typically calculated for a one-day to a two-week horizon from time series of asset prices. For longer time periods (say one year and beyond) little research exists and in practice it does not help much because the links between macroeconomic fluctuations and asset prices variations are muddled. Furthermore SWFs have a large exposure in non-listed companies, for which the asset valuation is largely subjective. A long-term investor should follow three steps:

1 forming an opinion on the drivers of trend growth;
2 defining strategies to take advantage of them;
3 analysing the risk to which these drivers are subject.

This kind of approach echoes the so-called factor-based allocation strategy (see Monk, 2011), which tries to detect investment themes rather than asset classes in order to diversify risk. For example, CalPERS from July 2011 adheres to an asset allocation based not on the usual classification into equity, fixed income, real estate, etc., but on 'factors' such as income (15.9% of the portfolio); growth (63.1%); real (13.0%); inflation-linked (4.0%); and liquidity (4.0%).

The approach illustrated in Chapter 3, hinging on the main drivers of long-term growth (which is somewhat analogous), must be complemented by an appropriate risk management methodology. First one needs to ascertain how vulnerable the various drivers are to unpredictable shocks and whether these shocks are independent, which means whether these drivers are subject to the same influences (especially in bad times when all asset prices tend to drop) and to the same extent.

Let's start from demographics. This factor is stable for several years, hence sources of revenues such as payments on project financing for infrastructure (toll roads, airports, hospitals) or utilities which are linked to population growth, are relatively unaffected by cyclical fluctuations. Likewise investments in technologies such as innovative energy sources or green technology also are resilient to short-term economic fluctuations (energy saving ventures might actually be countercyclical), but are nevertheless subject to the uncertainties surrounding the adoption and spread of new technologies.

Turning to macroeconomic factors, fiscal stability can be unsettled suddenly, as in Spain and Ireland, by a reckless private sector, especially banks and real estate developers. On the other hand, export sectors sustained by a solid comparative advantage, thanks to wage differential, technology prowess, logistics or favourable location, maintain their resilience even though it might go through cyclical downturns. Another long-term driver is the expansion of international trade and the integration of supply chains among distant geographical locations which boost productivity. The Great Recession has highlighted that this driver can be hit severely by major hiccups, but its quick rebound in 2009 underlines that the trend still points upwards.

At the other end of the risk spectrum are investments that aim to take advantage of a return to normalcy in war-stricken countries. This driver is largely independent of global macroeconomic conditions, but needless to say, the success of investments in places like Iraq or Ivory Coast is a bet that spans at least 5–10 years. Few dare to invest in such places but to sceptics it suffices to mention that Lebanon has been one of the best performing economies throughout the Great Recession and that the Iraqi stock market was a stellar performer in 2010–2011.

These examples highlight that factor-based investments are subject to risks not necessarily measurable through some conventional concept of volatility. If one decides to ride the demographic wave or bet on the ascent of the middle class in populous Asian countries, a backward looking calculation of correlations or concepts such as 'alpha' and 'beta' and VaR (or whatever acronym marketing of botched ideas might have produced) are utterly useless. It would be wiser to focus on risks such as:

1 political disruptions or backlash against reforms;
2 food and energy shortage;
3 inflation due to bottlenecks in infrastructure and housing;
4 availability of human resources.

Some of these risks can be hedged, for example political risk can be insured through MIGA, a World Bank agency created for this purpose or private insurers. Food and commodity risks can be attenuated by purchases of futures and options on commodities. Others cannot be diversified away or hedged at reasonable cost.

Analogously if the decision to stake his funds on the super-cycle is made, two main uncertainties have to be faced:

1 technological advances that reduce the need for certain commodities (e.g. advances in superconductivity would affect copper consumption);
2 long-term elasticity, e.g. substitution with other materials or reduction in consumption.

Certainly the most difficult strategies for risk management are those that pursue technological advances. Here the only meaningful approach is a diversification into several projects. Betting on new technologies requires a huge tolerance for failure, because in the best circumstances only half of the projects survive and even fewer thrive. Initial success might later encounter unpredictable hurdles of a regulatory and economic nature. For example, the supersonic airplane Concorde, a technological jewel but extremely fuel intensive, came on the market right before the first oil shock; furthermore the Concorde was de facto economically killed by the refusal of the US authorities to allow it to land at New York JFK airport with the excuse of 'noise pollution'.

One of the quandaries ensuing from the globalization is the synchronization of the economic cycle across main economic areas and the rapid spread of contagion across distant geographies. In practical terms geographical diversification is less effective than, say, 20 years ago. The decoupling of China and India from mature economies is a too recent phenomenon to be relied on with a certain degree of confidence. Hopefully the new generation of financial regulations will reduce the contagion effects as we advocated earlier and the Great Synchronization will recede, but for the time being it is a reality that has to be dealt with.

A related issue is the variation in the size of assets markets and in their geographical distribution. Stated in plain words, the sizes of markets for each asset class and across countries change drastically and liquidity conditions will vary accordingly. Table 4.1, for example, shows the relative weights of various geographical areas in the capitalization of world stock markets.

Brazil, Russia, India and China saw their share increase almost ninefold over 10 years, the rest of emerging markets saw their share double, while the US recorded a drop of almost 20 percentage points.

There are no ready-made recipes to address the manifold challenges and even if there were they would need to be constantly verified and adapted to a changing environment. As a first step it is always wise to devise a forward looking set of indicators combining macro and financial data.

Second, for SWFs that invest primarily in non-listed companies or illiquid assets, it would be advisable to tackle 'valuation uncertainty' by using a battery of pricing models, stress test them and compare the results periodically.

In this regard we feel it is important to underscore an issue too often downplayed or flatly ignored. Accounting rules ignore the fact that asset valuations are a probability distribution and not a precise universally agreed number. The accounting community and professional organizations stubbornly insists that balance sheets must present a single number on the bottom line, not a range which would confuse shareholders and investors.

We disagree. In our opinion trust in accounting rules and market evaluation is not strengthened; for example, if the stock market capitalization is lower than book values and vice versa. Whatever the rights or wrongs in this dispute, it is advisable to keep in mind that assets and liabilities reflect simply average valuations with a variance subject to great uncertainty. It would be a decisive step towards clarity if uncertain valuations, for example of intangible assets and non-traded securities, were assigned a range.

Table 4.1 World stock market capitalization by geographic areas

	1999	2000	2001	2002	2003	2004	2005	2006	2007	2008	2009	2010 (E)
World market cap	100%	100%	100%	100%	100%	100%	100%	100%	100%	100%	100%	100%
United States	46%	47%	50%	47%	45%	43%	39%	36%	31%	33%	31%	31%
Rest of developed	46%	45%	41%	42%	44%	44%	44%	44%	41%	41%	41%	39%
Emerging markets	8%	8%	9%	11%	12%	13%	16%	20%	28%	26%	28%	30%
BRIC	2%	3%	3%	3%	4%	4%	6%	9%	17%	15%	17%	17%
Rest of emerging	6%	5%	6%	7%	7%	9%	11%	10%	11%	11%	11%	12%
of which GCC	0.3%	0.3%	0.4%	0.9%	0.9%	1.3%	2.5%	1.3%	1.7%	2%	1%	1%

Source: Standard & Poor's.

4.6 AN UNCONVENTIONAL DIMENSION OF RISK MANAGEMENT: SHAREHOLDERS VS STAKEHOLDERS

Risk management goes beyond devising strategies that take into account the dynamics of asset prices. One critical dimension, especially for those SWFs and FWFs that invest in equities, involves corporate governance. SWFs must make headway from purely passive investors into more active shareholders taking an interest in the companies where they hold a stake.

The management of many SWFs – as we highlighted in the Introduction by citing the interview to *Handelsblatt* by Sheikh Ahmed Bin Zayed – insist that they are merely passive investors. It is hard to say whether this attitude came in response to the charges of undue influence periodically levelled against SWFs or is actually part of their mandate. In either case it is the wrong attitude. Passive investors are the modern equivalent of absentee landowners. It was a typical figure in the European aristocracy who delegated the management of their possession to trustees. With time the landlords found themselves impoverished while the trustees prospered.

We feel that corporate governance tenets have not been adequately incorporated into investment decisions. The financial crisis has compelled all investors, not only the SWFs, to take up responsibilities too often blindly relinquished to management. Investors, as a group, largely failed to recognize that good corporate governance is crucial to safeguarding their long-term interests as shareowners in contrast to being simply shareholders. This hands-off approach led to suboptimal performances, hence the renewed emphasis on stricter governance principles and a timely flow of information. Creating value is not merely the result of investing wisely in financial resources, but a holistic mix of several elements. SWFs should contribute to force best practices and accurate reporting in the companies where they acquire a stake, especially those not listed. Indeed, in the epicentres of the financial crisis, the US and UK, the new corporate governance framework places much responsibility on the shoulders of investors for monitoring the governance practices in the companies they invest in. In the UK for example, best practice is emerging through the issuance of a Stewardship Code that applies to shareholders, rather than to companies. A similar code is under development in South Africa and at EU level.

It is already becoming common for SWFs to request a seat on the board and perform a more active role. Board members must ask unpleasant questions, have direct access to every position in the organigram, open the books, inquire into bank relationships, monitor conflict of interests, ascertain that effective risk management is in place, and protect whistle-blowers. In fact opaque management practices, mutual back scratching and cosy relationships are the most serious threats to equity investments.

Finally it must not be forgotten that corporate strategies are successful within a certain context. When circumstances change, strategies must adapt and management must be forced to change or retire. So it is important to understand what drives the profit generation and how vulnerable it is to a relapse. A team that has produced positive results is rarely induced to critically assess its modus operandi. It must be forced to by an external controller.

5

SWFs in the Geopolitics of the Twenty-first Century

The process of ever-closer economic integration across the world which is synthetically referred to as 'globalization' is propelled by momentous forces: demographics, financial liberalization, advances in computer science, diffusion of telecommunications and revolution in logistics. An analogy can be drawn with an equally momentous phase of globalization at the end of the nineteenth century when the telegraph, the railroads and the steamships transformed international commercial and financial relations, paving the way for the integration of the Western Hemisphere into the world economy dominated by Europe and its colonial empires.

The current wave of globalization – set in motion by the fall of the Berlin Wall, the Single Market in the EU, regional trade agreements (NAFTA, Mercosur, Asean Free Trade Pact) and the advent of China as a manufacturing powerhouse – became an irresistible, earth-shattering crescendo after the creation of the WTO on 1 January 1995 under the Marrakech Agreement (which superseded the General Agreement on Tariffs and Trade, GATT) at the completion of the so-called Uruguay Round of negotiation. Custom tariffs were slashed drastically across the board through a multilateral framework applying to all major exporters and importers. More importantly, the international legal framework on import and export rules became clearer and subject to the judgment of an independent international court rather than national policies, ad hoc interpretations, unilateral whims and gruelling negotiations. When China joined the WTO in December 2001 (under a 900-page long Protocol of Accession which required 15 years of negotiations almost as complex as the Uruguay Round itself), world trade received an additional impetus.

The innovations in telecommunications and freight transport (primarily containerization) – combined with the overhaul of a decayed political landscape in Latin America, Eastern Europe and the Far East at the end of the twentieth century – intensified interactions between far-off locations, redesigning the economic geography in favour of populous countries such as China and India and spreading the advances to places such as Korea, Taiwan, Brazil, Vietnam, Poland, Turkey and Russia. This shift has now rendered meaningless classifications such as developed and developing countries. Mature and high-growth economies would be a more apt characterization, while new linkages among adjacent areas are replacing the outdated economic relationships between North and South.

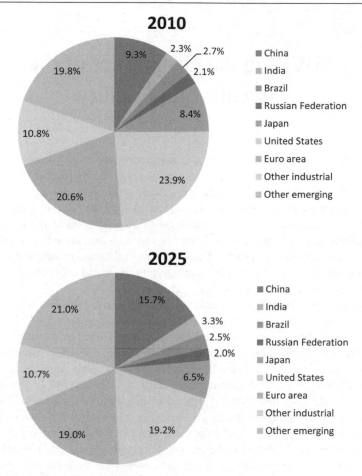

Figure 5.1   The relative weight of main economic areas.

Source: World Bank – Global Development Horizons 2011. Reproduced by permission of the World Bank.

The ascent of the 'high growth economies' has already shaken up the balance of global economic power. In 2010, the combined output of the developing economies accounted for 38% of world GDP (at market exchange rates): on reasonable assumptions it could exceed the developed world's share within the current decade.[1]

Within emerging markets the case of China is even more striking: in Figure 5.1, which reports the data from the World Bank's Global Development Horizons 2011, we see that on current trends the weight of China in the global

---

[1] When measured at purchasing power parity (PPP), emerging economies overtook the developed world in 2008.

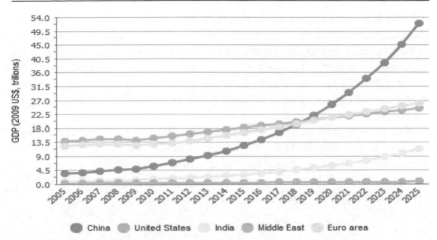

Figure 5.2   Simulation of relative growth of major economic areas.

Source: Authors' simulation on World Bank database at http://go.worldbank.org/EDHFXJKW10

output is projected to grow from 7% in 2005 to 16% in 2025. But if we change the underlying assumptions, increasing the projected inflation and the appreciation rate (5% and 3%, respectively), China will overtake the US and the euro area to become the largest economy before the end of this decade (Figure 5.2) and by 2025 could be double the size of the US economy at Purchasing Power Parity (PPP) rates. Obviously these forecasts reflect the mechanical projection of a trend, so they should be considered as a sketchily plausible scenario rather than a foregone outcome; nevertheless it is a measure of the potential entrenched in the awakening of Asia.

This economic miracle is sometimes downplayed as a mere consequence of a demographic effect destined to subside: China and India being the most populous countries in the world, obviously their GDP weights considerably more in global output. As we stressed in Chapter 1, however, it is not tautological that populous countries prosper and prosper more than proportionally compared to others with less exuberant demographics. Many might recall that until recently a large population was associated more with penury, famine, epidemics, early mortality, etc. So while demographics are a primary force, the virtuous circle needs numerous engines.

According to *The Economist*,[2] by 2010 the share of emerging economies has almost equalled or surpassed that of advanced economies in several areas, revealing the new facets of the world economy. For instance, emerging economies already account for 60% of steel, copper and oil consumption, 50% of world exports and 50% of inflows of foreign direct investment.

---

[2] Economic Focus: Why the Tail Wags the Dog, *The Economist*, 6 August 2011.

These economic figures reveal the upshot from the first wave of globalization which stemmed from the disruption, dislocation and relocation of physical capital – particularly in the manufacturing sector – from advanced economies to emerging markets. The next phase of globalization could be driven by human capital, urbanization and education, reinforced by the rise of emerging markets' corporates and more efficient financial institutions of which SWFs might represent the spearhead.

With fertility rates still well above 2.2, the Middle East, the Indian subcontinent and especially Africa will enjoy the benefits of an expanding labour force; and the massive internal migration will feed a powerful process of urbanization that will have the most profound effects on their future economic dynamics (Figures 5.3 and 5.4).

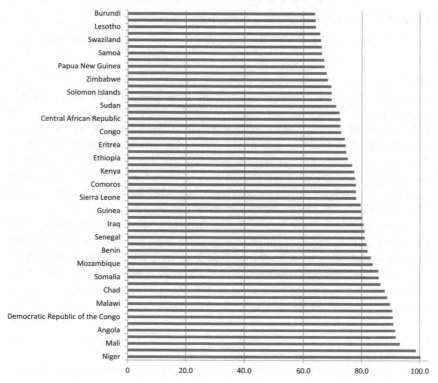

Figure 5.3   Countries with largest child dependency ratio (ratio of population of age 0–14 to population of age 15–64). Inflation: China 5%, US 1.5%, India 6%, Euro area 2%, Middle East 3%. Appreciation against US$: China 3%, India 2%, Euro Area 0%, Middle East 0%.

Source: United Nations, Population Division.

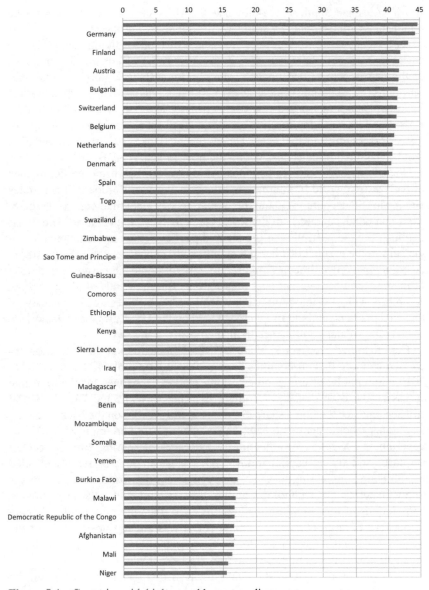

Figure 5.4 Countries with highest and lowest median age.

Source: United Nations, Population Division.

Cities are an environment where productivity improvements and network economies display their full effects. Gradually the synergies within the urban environment and openness to the outside world foster a powerful process of upward mobility: between 1990 and 2005, for example, in the Middle East,

North Africa and South Asia[3] (known as the MENASA region), the size of the middle class almost doubled, from 360 million to 620 million.

As a result, if we look at some measures of modern living standards, the emerging markets' share has already surpassed that of advanced economies or the gap is being filled up very quickly, for instance: mobile phone subscriptions (82%), motor vehicle sales (52%), fixed investments (50%), world's imports (47%) and world's retail sales (46%). The rise of the urban middle class – and its consumption growth – is a trend set to continue: in India, for instance, according to the Asian Development Bank, 70% of the population will be classified middle class within the next 15 years (ADB, 2011).

One of the main features of globalization, so far, has been the dominance of the Western world in international finance. Western Europe, United States and Japan still account for about three-quarters of global financial assets (cash, stock and bonds) and 65% of the world stock market capitalization. The dollar dominates in the portfolios of private and public investors and the creation of the euro in the early 2000s has not significantly dented its dominant position; emerging markets currencies are used mostly for domestic purposes and none of them is used for international transactions. But the winds of globalization, combined with the international financial turmoil, widespread volatility of financial markets, and the fiscal crisis faced by the US, Europe and Japan, are eroding the Western dominance in finance.

The emerging economies' share of world stock market capitalization increased by more than three times during 2000–2010 (Table 4.1) and in 2009–2010 initial public offerings on emerging market exchanges for the first time surpassed those on developed country exchanges. While the Western world still accounts for the lion's share of private sector wealth, on the back of generally higher income per head, emerging economies hold an impressive 81% of government FX reserves, reflecting two decades of soaring current account surpluses and strong capital inflows. This huge amount of state-controlled wealth is now increasingly being deployed across the world to secure access to raw materials and technology, and to open up markets for the fast-growing corporations of the emerging markets. In 2010, the emerging markets' share of outward Foreign Direct Investment (FDI) was already nearly 30% of the world's total and almost a quarter of Fortune 500 largest firms in terms of revenues now come from these countries (in 1995 it was a mere 4%).

SWFs play a key role in the deployment of this wealth by providing the financial backbone for major corporate deals with corporations both in advanced economies and other emerging markets.

The shifting of international finance towards emerging markets is also challenging the international currency system centred on a single currency. Most of the FX reserves controlled by emerging markets are currently invested primarily in assets denominated in US dollars, the 'world's currency', and to a

---

[3] In this classification, South Asia includes India, Pakistan, Sri Lanka and Bangladesh.

lesser extent in euro, yen and a few other minor currencies. But after more than half a century of undisputed dominance of the greenback, its appeal seems to be gradually weakening as the US economy struggles to resume its pre-crisis growth pace and prepares for a brutal fiscal consolidation. The recent loss of the AAA status of US sovereign debt might have coincided with the beginning of a reduction of the absolute dominance in reserve management as the world moves towards a regime where other currencies – including those of the largest emerging economies such as the Chinese yuan, the Brazilian real or the Indian rupee – are also set to play an important role (Eichengreen, 2011). By diversifying FX reserves largely invested into US dollars, SWFs play an important role in reducing the international role of the dollar and paving the way for a multicurrency arrangement which could see the dawn when the yuan becomes fully convertible (see Chapter 7).

The only economic measure where advanced economies maintain an unchallenged leadership over emerging markets is debt: they are responsible for 83% of the global outstanding government debt. This massive burden will not only reduce their growth potential over the next few years as these economies will be forced to raise taxes and redefine the functions assigned to the public sector; it will also determine a crowding-out of private investments. Together with the new financial regulations requiring the European and US banks to substantially increase their capital, after several years of ample availability of funds and historically low interest rates, the global economy might be entering a period of capital scarcity that will result in a 'war for capital' where emerging markets seem to have the upper hand thanks to low debt, huge accumulated wealth and higher investment returns (McKinsey Global Institute, 2011).

5.1 THE SHIFT TO THE EAST OF THE GLOBAL ECONOMY: THE NEW SILK ROUTE

There are several statistics that can be invoked to illustrate the rebalancing of the world economy towards the East. A compelling one is depicted in Figure 5.5 which shows the per capita GDP of several emerging countries as a percentage of US per capita GDP. We have used the database which the IMF World Economic Outlook updated in 2011. China's GDP per head calculated at Purchasing Power Parity (PPP) jumped from 2% of the US level in 1980, when Deng Xiaoping's reforms began to produce some effects, to almost two-thirds in 2011. The only other economy that comes close is Korea, increasing from slightly less than 20% to over 60%. India's per capita GDP has merely doubled to 7.4% in comparison to the US; Brazil's has actually come down from 28% to 24%. When calculated as a share of world GDP the latter two economies have actually diverged (Figure 5.6). They were roughly similar in the early 1990s, while in 2011 India's share was almost double.

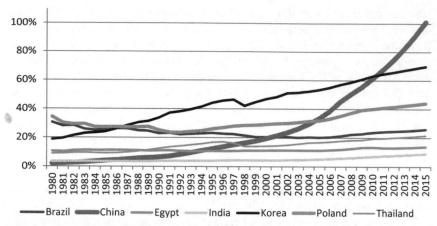

Figure 5.5   Per capita GDP (in purchasing power parity) as a percentage of US per capita GDP.

Source: IMF WEO Database.

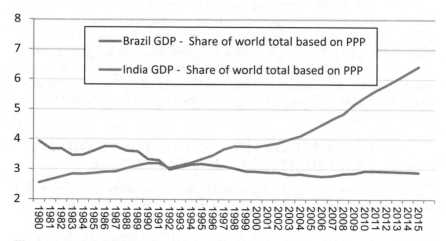

Figure 5.6   Relative size of emerging economies.

Source: IMF WEO Database.

In essence, Asia is the continent emerging as the winner, so far, of the globalization game. Seen from a secular perspective, the awakening of China and India constitutes the reversion to a balance of power among main economic areas that prevailed before the nineteenth century and that was perturbed by the great expansion of European empires reaching its apogee at the turn of the twentieth century, as depicted in Table 5.1.

Table 5.1   Share of world GDP

	1870	1913	1950	1973	1998	2009	2015 (f)
China	17.3%	8.9%	4.5%	4.6%	11.5%	12.6%	17.0%
Germany	6.4%	8.8%	5.0%	5.9%	4.3%	4.0%	3.4%
France	6.5%	5.3%	4.1%	4.3%	3.4%	3.0%	2.6%
Italy	3.8%	3.5%	3.1%	3.6%	3.0%	2.5%	2.1%
Japan	2.3%	2.7%	3.0%	7.7%	7.7%	6.0%	5.1%
UK	9.1%	8.3%	6.5%	4.2%	3.3%	3.1%	2.7%
USA	8.9%	19.1%	27.3%	22.0%	21.9%	20.4%	18.4%
India	12.3%	7.5%	4.2%	3.1%	5.0%	5.1%	6.3%
Former USSR	7.6%	8.6%	9.6%	9.4%	3.4%	4.3%	4.3%

Source: Maddison (2005) and IMF WEO Database for 2009 and 2015.

History exerts a powerful influence on trade patterns, for example the main land routes in Europe still trace the Roman communication network, while the Strait of Malacca has for centuries been one of the lifelines of world trade. However, novel transport technology or the addition of transport infrastructure may lead to a deep alteration of existing networks. The revolution in transport systems brought about by container shipping, jumbo aircrafts and the adoption of IT in transport management has wrecked established equilibria and forged a new spatial structure of transport routes worldwide. The emergence of Asia and China, and of the Gulf on the back of soaring Asian energy demand, can be interpreted as the reassertion of the Silk Route patterns after two centuries of Atlantic predominance.

The Silk Route 2000 years ago was a network of interlinked trade routes across the Afro-Eurasian landmass connecting East, South and Western Asia with the Mediterranean world as well as part of North and East Africa. The sea routes extended from the Red Sea to East Africa, India, China and South East Asia., Along these routes at that time, spices, teas, precious stones, jewels and of course silk were exchanged across continents via sea or land. The Silk Route remained a major trade gateway for many more centuries; its decline started in the course of the fifteenth century but accelerated with the rise of Europe earlier and the Americas later, resulting in a shift of the centre of gravity of the world towards the West. The last two centuries of Atlantic predominance was largely sustained by cheap hydrocarbons as the major source of energy which, incidentally, maintained the oil producing Middle East in the economic orbit of the West.

The Silk Routes (the one via land through Central Asia and the sea route through the Strait of Malacca and Arabia) are experiencing a revival as the backbone of a multipolar world embracing Asia and the Middle East. The New Silk Route is a strategic tapestry whose 'threads are hydrocarbons, petrodollars, consumer products and technologies, military ties, labour migration and even religion' (Magnus and Castelli, 2006). The strategic interplay is mutually beneficial for two reasons:

1 emerging Asia gains access to a stable supply of energy and capital;
2 the Gulf can rely on the supply of cheap goods, high-return investment opportunities and immigrants needed to sustain its growth.

Since 2006, China has overtaken the US as the world's largest exporter to the Middle East and, according to some estimates, by 2020 total trade flows between China and the Middle East could reach US$500 billion. China already imports about 50% of its oil from the GCC and this share will rise to 70% by 2015. The soaring trade volumes along the New Silk Route have already moved the gravitational centre of world trade: according to HSBC, of the top 10 container seaports in the world, one is in Europe, one in Dubai and eight are in Asia (20 years ago not a single Chinese port figured in the top 10).

The New Silk Route is a conduit not only for goods and commodities: capital, labour and know-how are also flowing in both directions. Mega-projects proliferate: in the energy sector, oil refineries in Guandong, Shandong and Fujian have been carried out by Saudi Aramco and Kuwait Petroleum Corporation in cooperation with Chinese Sinopec; in logistics, the co-development of a container port in Tianjin, China, is promoted by Dubai Ports World; phosphate projects in Northern Saudi Arabia and a production facility in Jazan Economic City, Saudi Arabia, are run by Chinalco, the Chinese state-controlled aluminium manufacturer.

SWFs are active players in these investment flows into Asia, with a stronger focus on portfolio investments: for instance, ADIA invested in the Indian blue chips Infosys Technologies and Shapoorji; Mubadala invested US$7 billion in the Malaysian Sarawak Corridor project; KIA invested in Chinese ICBC; QIA in the JSM Indochina Property Fund (China & India), Raffles Medical (Singapore) and Agricultural Bank of China. Political cooperation between emerging Asia and the Middle East, despite still lagging in the economic and financial arenas, is also on the rise. The Shanghai Cooperation Organization, created 10 years ago to deal with border and security issues, has actually emerged as an economic cooperation forum between China, Russia and other Central Asian countries with an increasingly strategic focus on the energy sector. Other Asian countries, including Pakistan, Afghanistan, Iran and India already participate in the summits of the organization and could become full members in the next few years. Political relationships between China and the GCC are being cemented with bilateral agreements in various sectors including oil, gas and mining. The bilateral relationship between Saudi Arabia and China is actually growing faster than ever: in 2006 Saudi King Abdullah, on his first overseas travel after ascending to the throne, did not travel to the US, historically the Saudi's strongest ally, but to Beijing, the first Saudi King to visit China (which incidentally might have, by some estimates, the largest Muslim population in the world). This political cooperation has translated into a spate of Free Trade Agreements between the GCC and various Asian countries including China, Japan, Pakistan, Thailand, Singapore, Korea and India (some already finalized

while others are under negotiation). The increasing political cooperation between the Gulf and Asia also involves the activities of SWFs: for instance,
KIA was granted the status of Qualified Foreign Investment Institution (QFII)
to trade in Chinese currency on the Shanghai Stock Exchange.

While the old Silk Routes were a trade network linking Asia and Europe via
the Indian continent, the Middle East and a narrow corridor in Central Asia,
the new Silk Routes also involve Africa and Latin America. Increased protectionism and hostility from the West induces Chinese authorities to strengthen
economic ties with other Asian countries and emerging markets. The patterns
already involve trade relationships with Africa, Central Asia (Kazakhstan) and
Latin America to secure food supplies and natural resources; infrastructure
investment around the world, especially those necessary to move commodities
to ports and other transport nodes.

This activism has attracted a lot of attention and criticism being depicted
as a form of neocolonialism or a callous design to extend political influence,
leveraging financial clout in poor countries. These arguments are reminiscent
of the qualms over undue influence levelled in the West against SWFs before
the Great Recession. Is Chinese economic activism part of murky geopolitical
ambitions or merely the only reasonable diversification strategy for a country
heavily exposed to the US government debt and US dollar-denominated financial assets? The next section will try to offer a perspective.

5.2 THE LAW OF UNINTENDED CONSEQUENCES? CHINA'S INFLUENCE THROUGH FINANCIAL MUSCLE

When the share of an economy in the world GDP increases considerably in
a relatively short time the perturbation is felt at various levels. China's fast
rising sway in global capital markets is a point in case, but it extends in general
to all emerging economies that are becoming an increasingly important source
of foreign capital. According to the McKinsey Global Institute in 2010 total
outflows from emerging markets amounted to US$922 billion, 30% more than
inflows. With over US$400 billion, China accounts for nearly half of the total
– by far the largest emerging economy in terms of foreign investments. The
majority of China's foreign investments consist of the acquisition of FX reserves by the central bank and financial investments by SWFs; but with US$44
billion of foreign direct investments, Chinese companies are pursuing to acquire raw materials and land, build up technical and commercial expertise, and
gain access to foreign markets.

All this activism smacks of political aims, but when one looks at finer granularity, reality is less sinister and more prosaic. The rise of China's Foreign Direct Investments (FDI) has a long way to run if history is any guidance. Britain
accounted for 45% of the world's FDI in 1914, the last epoch of tumultuous

globalization; after the US took the baton of the largest economy as well as the financial market, its share of FDIs reached 50% in 1967. Today mainland China, plus Hong Kong and Macau, has a paltry 6%. Listed Chinese firms, which are largely state-controlled, are already some of the world's biggest, and account for over 10% of global stock market value. But they are still mainly domestic outfits held back sometimes by outdated legislation, insular mentality and political constraints. If the Chinese capital markets integrate more closely into world finance, there will be an inevitable tendency for Chinese entities to spread their presence in foreign economies[4] and hopefully a mirroring process by foreign companies into China.

Most Chinese outbound investors are active in manufacturing sectors, spanning an increasingly diversified range. Textile and machinery and equipment sectors figure most prominently within manufacturing, reflecting China's strong export performance in these industries. The investments made by Chinese enterprises mainly aim to improve access to overseas markets with Asia the main destination, followed by Europe and North America, while only a few respondents have overseas investments in other regions. In terms of future investment plans, African destinations are likely to become more important.

High-profile deals often involve odd situations and peculiar outcomes, partly because of cultural differences and partly because of amateurish approach. *The Economist* interviewed, anonymously, executives in 11 Western companies who dealt with Chinese counterparts either because their companies had been acquired by or because they had sold stakes to Chinese firms, or because they had been negotiating operations worth more than US$1 billion. Despite awe at China's ambition and at the technical skill of the counterparts, they were less positive about the ability of Chinese managers to run an international business or make sense of a complex organization. At the end of the day, behind the facade of bold multinationals, state-backed firms are still embroiled in opaque practices and decision making is more geared towards political issues than towards efficiency.[5]

---

[4] According to a Survey of Chinese investors (conducted by China Council for Promotion of International Trade in cooperation with the European Commission and UNCTAD), in terms of investment scale, the proportion of Chinese enterprises having made overseas investments is 25%, especially among SMEs; 61% of responding firms indicated that their overseas investments remained below US$1 million, while more than 80% of investments are below US$5 million. Very few companies have been capable of making large-scale overseas investments in excess of US$100 million.

[5] According to the report by *The Economist*, the substance of the negotiation often has two parts: marathon sessions at an investment bank's offices, often in London, and visits by target firms' executives to mainland China or Hong Kong. Apparently the lines of authority within Chinese firms are unsystematic, with an internal power structure which is a mystery to outsiders, even the few Westerners who sit on the boards of big state-backed companies. Some are convinced that there exists a parallel hierarchy of Communist Party officials. The most senior party man in a firm, the general secretary, is not necessarily the most senior executive.

Wherever the truth might lie, the point is that China cannot be considered as a monolith. Often, several Chinese firms pursue the same deal. Green lights given to an acquisition might suddenly turn red for inscrutable reasons. Negotiation can be chaotic and progress difficult to assess. In essence to imagine that Chinese authorities, SWFs, banks and companies march in synchronicity to pursue a common, superior objective is at best simplistic. This being said, the sheer size of Chinese activities worldwide has reached a scale that stands out and that will have historic repercussions whether intended or not.

One sector where China appears more determined to pursue a superior strategic goal, over and above short term financial convenience, is access to energy sources. In Chapter 3 we looked at the geographical and sector distribution of SWFs' direct investments and we found evidence of a growing involvement by Chinese (and other Asian) SWFs in the energy sector. However we did not delve much into whether this investment behaviour reflects motivations that go beyond purely financial returns. After all, natural resources are an obvious diversification play for any asset manager. Now we return to this issue by specifically analysing the case of CIC and its wide-ranging forays into the energy sector.

Chinese authorities insist that their emphasis on the energy sector is underpinned by a purely financial rationale: energy commodities constitute a solid hedge against inflation and moreover – as underlined in previous chapters – the commodity sector was hugely profitable during 2000–2010 and might be on the rising phase of a super-cycle. Furthermore, it is hardly a mystery that the Chinese economic miracle is heavily dependent on the availability of raw materials, but more crucially the 'factory of the world' is oriented towards energy-intensive industries. Having turned into a net energy importer in the early 1990s, for China external energy supplies are vital, especially since its industrial plants are far from a paradigm of efficiency. The 'strategic' role of CIC in this area might therefore become relevant.

According to an interesting paper applying a 'network mapping' methodology to SWFs' investments, until 2010 almost 100% of non-financial sector direct investments by CIC were in the extractive and energy sectors (Haberly, 2011). CIC's investments in the energy sectors are very concentrated (15–20% stakes), often making CIC the largest shareholder; there is a high degree of direct and indirect overlap between CIC's investments and those of Chinese state-owned enterprises; the firms in which CIC invests tend to be strongly oriented towards the Chinese market and the Chinese investment is often associated with promises of better market access to mainland China and lucrative contracts with Chinese state firms.

Chinese investments in the energy sector are often facilitated by political dialogue and increased cooperation with the recipient country. A good example of such an attitude is that of energy-rich Canada, where CIC has become very active in the past few years, culminating in the establishment of a CIC representative office in Toronto in early 2011. For most of the previous decade,

Canada was pretty cold about Chinese investments in its energy sector and the bilateral ties between the two countries remained limited. In 2009, the government of Canada changed political course, probably as a result of the global crisis that rendered Chinese capital attractive, and official relations suddenly improved as witnessed by the first ever visit of a Chinese head of state to Canada in 2009. The strengthening of the bilateral relationship translated into a surge of Chinese investments in the Canadian energy and mining sectors: between July 2009 and May 2010 China invested more than US$10 billion, of which about US$3 billion was invested by CIC and the rest by state-controlled oil companies like Petrochina and Sinopec. The purchase of ConocoPhillips Co.'s 9% stake in Syncrude Group by Sinopec worth US$4.6 billion is by far the largest Chinese ownership stake in an active, oil-producing venture in Alberta's energy sector and provides China with access to Syncrude's potential 5.1 billion barrel oil reserves (CIC, 2010).

As argued by Haberly (2011) 'the resource acquisition strategy, apparently being pursued by CIC in conjunction with Chinese state extractive firms, constitutes a significant departure from the strategies of previous rising industrial powers' like the United States and Japan. While earlier strategies directly targeted overseas resource deposits – witness policies pursued by the US in the Middle East in the post-war period – the Chinese strategy is largely aimed at foreign resources companies by establishing far-reaching global partnerships reinforced through direct investments in parent companies and their subsidiaries. Similar strategies to the one for Canada are also being pursued by China in Australia (e.g. CIC's investment in Fortescue, Australia's third largest producer of iron ore), the US (e.g. CNOOC's investment in the Texas oil and gas operations of Chesapeake Energy) and in France (where, as mentioned earlier, CIC joined forces with GDF Suez). The investment policies in the energy sector by CIC, in conjunction with other state-controlled enterprises, clearly fit within the 'go-out' policy of the Chinese authorities.

While before the global crisis Chinese authorities might have been reluctant to explicitly disclose the purpose of their foreign investment policy, fearing Western political backlash, in its aftermath most recipient countries have become more 'open' to Chinese investments. Recently, officials and advisers to the People's Bank of China talk more openly about diversifying FX reserves towards strategic aims: for instance, Xia Bin, an academic adviser to the Chinese central bank recently stated at a public forum that 'the Chinese government is certainly worried about (the safety) of its FX reserves [...]. China should reduce the portion of financial assets in its reserves and increase the portion of non-financial assets and use them to buy overseas energy, resources and equity instead of buying euro debt'.[6] Chinese government think tanks furnish intellectual ammunition to strategically oriented SWFs by arguing that the 'China government should establish the strategy funds as part of the national energy

---

[6] China Needs to Diversify FX Reserves – Central Bank Adviser, *Reuters*, 23 August 2011.

strategy to hedge the risk in order to improve the national welfare' (Miao and Liyan, 2011). Essentially the investment behaviour of CIC in the energy and mining sectors is consistent with such policy orientation.

China is a latecomer in the global natural resource market so almost all valuable primary energy sources are already engaged by Western conglomerates. This explains why China typically pays a price for natural resources that might appear hefty by the standards of Western companies. The truth is that China needs to invest its foreign reserves and faces a dilemma: to buy natural resources at inflated prices or to buy US debt at prices that are possibly even more inflated.

In other words, the value of the US T-bills is to some extent an illusion that China contributes to maintain with its purchases. Therefore even if China pays a premium for the investments in natural resources it is still a better use of funds than holding low yield assets denominated in a debased currency. The Chinese policy in the international energy sector is being emulated by other Asian countries. India is currently working on the establishment of a US$10 billion SWF funded from FX reserves to acquire natural assets such as oil, coal and gas abroad.

At any rate, China's strategy seems to have matured lately, and deals are undergoing a more rigorous risk/return assessment. Moreover, changes may be on the cards and China might show more willingness to work with the World Bank and IMF if these institutions display a greater understanding of the Chinese viewpoint, as we will see in the next section devoted to the activities of SWFs in Africa.

5.3 SWFs INVESTING IN THE LESS DEVELOPED ECONOMIES: AFRICA AS THE LAST INVESTMENT FRONTIER

According to the World Bank, the combined resource flows from non-OECD emerging economies[7] to infrastructure projects in Africa are now comparable to traditional official development assistance from OECD countries or to capital from private investors. The largest non-OCED financiers include China, India and the Gulf States; China is the largest contributor to infrastructure projects in sub-Saharan Africa (Foster *et al.*, 2008). Emerging economies' and particularly Chinese investments in Africa have attracted a lot of policy makers' and media attention (with the usual dose of criticism).

Among the biggest recipients of Chinese infrastructure investments in Africa are some large oil exporters such as Nigeria and Angola, and often the financing terms are based on a repayment scheme linked to natural resource

---

[7] The OECD includes only very few emerging economies; Chile, Mexico, Poland, Korea, Czech Republic and Turkey. None of the BRIC (Brazil, India, Russia and China) are members of the OECD.

exports (the so-called 'Angola mode'). The criticism is often based on the fact that the Chinese investment arm for such investments, the Chinese Export-Import bank, applies conditions (for instance environmental standards) that are less binding for the recipient countries than those adopted by OECD official development assistance. Furthermore, China does not have any limitation in dealing with countries that are excluded from official development assistance on political grounds (e.g. Sudan or Myanmar).

Inevitably the arrival of new players in the circles of international development assistance traditionally dominated by advanced economies raises diplomatic eyebrows.

Nevertheless this new role of China and other non-OCED emerging economies should be viewed in the context of the growing south–south trade linkages. The strategic focus of China in the Africa infrastructure sector – particularly power generation and transports – reflects the competitive advantage gained by China in the construction industry, which fits in the existing Africa infrastructure gap. On the other hand, Africa is already a natural resource exporter and an enhancement of its infrastructures is crucial for further developing this potential. In this light, the growing links between China, India and Africa are simply a manifestation of the Ricardian comparative advantage theory at work. The criticism against China also seems unjustified when seen in the context of the total investments made by international companies in Africa. Chinese direct investments in the African oil sector – US\$10 billion according to the World Bank – still represent a tiny share of total international investments (US\$168 billion); in fact, most African oil exports are still directed towards OECD countries compared with only 16% to China.

Chinese and other emerging markets' investment activism in Africa is somewhat different from that of mature economies because it aims to establish long-term strategic partnerships. The China-Africa Development Fund (CADF) is one of eight initiatives announced by the Chinese government at the 2006 Beijing Summit to build a new Sino-African Partnership (Monitor Group, 2011). CADF has already committed US\$3 billion and invests alongside Chinese ventures seeking to enter African markets. Its investments – despite a concentration in the commodity sector – are diversified across other sectors including manufacturing and services. Istithmar, the Dubai-based SWF, and Qatar Diar were also active across the African real estate and tourism markets, while the Libyan LIA has launched various investment projects through its subsidiaries, the Libya-Africa Portfolio and the Libyan Arab African Investment company.

Last but not least, after the commodity boom the SWFs fever also has spread in Africa. Nigeria, Mozambique, Ghana, Angola, Tanzania and other African countries – including non-commodity-exporting countries like Mauritius – already have or are in the process of establishing SWFs that will facilitate investments from non-African SWFs as they assist in the identification and management of investment opportunities.

The investments carried out by foreign and domestic entities in Africa favour private equity, which is indeed booming. Private equity has a deeper impact than official development assistance because it creates and nurtures local ventures. SWFs are among the very few investors that can afford to accept the embedded risk in frontier economies.

5.4 THE NEW FINANCIAL GEOGRAPHY: THE EMERGING MULTIPOLAR FINANCIAL ARCHITECTURE

This shift of the economic barycentre towards the East has obviously led to a reshaping of the financial geography. With the Asian emerging economies enjoying a quick rebound from the crisis (unlike the mature economies), this process is bound to intensify, but the speed at which it develops depends on many factors, foremost the capability of setting in place a legal and institutional framework which is business friendly, well regulated and non-discriminatory.

The financial system can be described as a complex network that connects a number of nodes, of various dimensions. Until recently, at the centre of this web stood Wall Street and the City of London, the hubs through which the major operations tended to be arranged or triangulated, where innovations would be developed, and where wealth would be concentrated and deployed.

A handful of other key centres, e.g. Tokyo, Frankfurt, Hong Kong, Chicago and Zurich, home to sizeable institutions (Nomura, UBS, Deutsche Bank), would play a weighty role, occasionally rivalling the major ones. Centres with a regional or sector relevance, such as Munich, Sao Paolo, Toronto, San Francisco, Paris, and Shanghai would find a role in the outer zone of the network.

Any major financial operation taking place anywhere in the world would involve at least one of the two key nodes, possibly both, and if necessary one of the regional spokes. This arrangement is increasingly anachronistic for three main reasons.

1 London and New York became the main financial centres because the economies they were serving were major exporters of capital; now they are capital importers.
2 The two major nodes (and some of the minor ones) are clogged by toxic assets whose elimination will involve a long and painful process, with no assurance of success.
3 The concentration of risks in two locations with the same loose regulatory framework is an intolerable threat to world stability which needs to be defused.

According to the McKinsey Global Institute (2011), in 1999 the largest cross-border ties were between the US, Western Europe, and to a lesser extent

Japan. In particular, the US was dominant as its entities were partner to 50% of all outstanding international financial positions. A decade later, the web of cross-border investments had grown more complex: the US' share of total cross-border investments had shrunk to 32%, reflecting the surge in Western European cross-border investment following the introduction of the euro and – more importantly – the growth in the size and complexity of linkages with emerging markets.

Emerging markets have not only become major counterparts of Western Europe and the US but the linkages have also acquired prominence among different emerging market regions. Before the crisis, these south–south linkages were growing twice as fast as those with mature economies and this pace of growth will gradually resume. With the emergence of a multipolar world, the financial architecture is therefore evolving into a spiderweb system with numerous interconnected international financial centres across the globe that have the capital market depth and regulatory sophistication to absorb excess capital from their own regions, as well as from elsewhere. In 2000, of the US$208 billion of global initial public offerings (IPO), those carried out in the stock exchanges of London, New York and other advanced economies accounted for more than 90%. Companies in emerging markets, striving to raise capital from investors, were forced to list on the most established stock markets. In 2010, of the US$280 billion of global IPO, those carried out in advanced economies' stock markets fell to around 40%. The stock markets of Hong Kong, Shenzhen and Shanghai accounted for US$125 billion, rivalling New York and London for new listings and increasingly attracting corporations from advanced economies as shown by the listings of Glencore and Prada in Hong Kong.

The financial crisis has undoubtedly contributed to the acceleration of the reshaping of the financial geography. In the advanced economies, the shattered trust in financial institutions will weigh on any attempt to recover. Moreover the crisis has laid bare the moral hazard embedded in many entities too big to fail, all operating mainly in two or three main centres, which heightens financial fragility and threatens the stability of the world economy.

For these reasons the current 'hub and spike' system needs to be replaced quickly by a network of financial centres, a web of interrelation that would make it more flexible, efficient and resilient. In other words, if an Indian investor wishes to invest in a Brazilian company, they will be able to bypass New York and arrange the operation directly in Mumbai, or maybe in Dubai, drawing expertise and human resources from more than one location if necessary. It is conceivable that even in the 'web' system not all nodes will be equal, some will be specialized in certain areas, others will enjoy economies of scale in professional competencies and knowledge. But essentially, while each financial centre will play a useful function, none of them must be indispensable for the stability of the global system. The funds from which the financial institutions can rebuild their capital, for example, will originate in those countries which have amassed large current account surpluses and large reserves (with the exception of Japan, which has never engineered a solid recovery from its own 1990s bubble burst). These countries are located in the periphery of the global financial system, but with the main hubs effectively remaining dysfunctional for several years to come, they will naturally forge closer and more direct links. Investors, funds, banks and companies in China and Hong Kong, the Far East, the Middle East, the Indian subcontinent and to a lesser Eastern Europe and Latin America will find it more convenient to deal directly with each other. This decentralization will translate into a shift of influence towards the centres where institutions are solid, the regulatory framework proves to be effective, and the real economy is capable of growing and creating value, not merely paper assets.

An aspect that has so far remained in the background, however, is the role of SWFs or FWFs in shaping or at least influencing the shape of the new financial architecture. SWFs have the political clout, the financial means and the interest to create the linkages among peripheral financial centres and to build the capabilities for conducting business outside New York or London. A trend is already discernible. Sizeable deals between emerging markets that until recently would have been arranged through a major financial centre, now take place through direct links. China, with its huge current account surplus and accumulated net foreign assets, is at the forefront of this new wave, but other areas, including the GCC are increasingly stepping outside their traditional narrow perimeter.

A consortium of SWFs poured US$1.8 billion in fresh capital into BTG Pactual, the independent Brazilian investment bank. The deal was 'a sign of a new financial order', according to Pactual chief Andre Esteves, and represented the SWFs' first big step into Brazil in particular and Latin America in general. The investment – by nine funds, including Singapore's GIC, China's CIC and the Abu Dhabi Investment Council – marked the biggest ever SWF commitment in Brazil. Its new resources according to Esteves 'will underpin an attempt to take Pactual beyond Brazilian borders'. Likely areas of expansion include Mexico, Colombia, Chile and Peru.

5.5 THE DOMINANCE OF THE US$ IN GLOBAL FINANCIAL MARKETS: SWFs AS US$ DIVERSIFIERS

According to a recent survey of central bank reserve managers controlling more than US$8000 billion (UBS, 2011), the US$ will lose its status as the global reserve currency and will be replaced by a portfolio of currencies within the next 25 years. In the analogous surveys carried out in previous years, the majority of central bank reserve managers always stated that the dollar would retain its reserve currency status. The views expressed by central bankers are shared by a recent World Bank report arguing that the shift to a multicurrency international monetary system centred around the US dollar, the euro, and the renminbi (RMB) could happen in the next 15 years (World Bank, 2011).

This shift is primarily driven by the fact the US is less dominant than 50 years ago. After the Second World War, the US accounted for half of the combined output of the Great Powers (advanced economies of the time including Japan and the Soviet Union), it was the largest importer and exporter in the world, and the leading source of foreign capital. Thus, it made sense that the bulk of international trade and international financial business was carried out in dollars. Today, the US is no longer the dominant economy, reflecting the catching-up of other mature economies including Europe and Japan and, in part due to the recent upsurge of Brazil, Russia, India and China (the BRIC; Table 5.1).

The US is no longer the largest exporter in the world (China and Germany compete for the top spot) and it only accounts for less than 20% of foreign direct investments. It is mostly a vestige of the past that despite the erosion of its dominant economic position and huge public debt, the US dollar is still the 'world's currency'. According to the IMF, in 2009 the US$ accounted for around 62% of global FXs reserves, down from over 70% in 2000 but still well above the share of the second most important reserve currency, the euro (27.5%). Various factors contribute – among others the still strong political and military prominence of the US in the world – but primarily the advantage of incumbency: because the majority of countries transact in dollars, no individual country can really move away from the dollar (Eichengreen, 2011). The financial crisis with its epicentre in the US and the fiscal challenge that ensued (exacerbated by the downgrade of US debt by Standard & Poor's) has weakened the incumbent advantage and, crucially, has reinforced the sense of urgency in emerging markets to diversify their FX reserves.

According to estimates, 65% of the Chinese FX reserves are currently invested in dollar-denominated assets, making China the largest holder of the US paper – mostly US Treasuries – in the world. Chinese authorities were staunchly reluctant to open their capital markets and make the RMB internationally traded. Recently, though, this attitude has changed and China has embarked on a gradual process of liberalization and internalization of the RMB based on three prongs:

1   increase the use of the RMB to settle cross-border trades;
2   make the RMB an investment vehicle;
3   make the RMB an international reserve currency (World Bank, 2011).

Since 2009, China started a RMB cross-border settlement programme allowing more of China's cross-border trade to be settled in RMB; since its launch, the value of Chinese merchandise trade settled in RMB has grown very fast and by the first quarter of 2011 it reached RMB360 billion (US$55 billion), representing around 7% of the total Chinese trade (up from 3% in 2010). As companies are allowed to trade in RMB, they accumulate RMB deposits that are predominantly held in Hong Kong where most of these transactions are settled; as a result, Hong Kong is gradually establishing itself as the primary offshore RMB financial centre. According to the Royal Bank of Scotland, Hong Kong deposits reached RMB450 billion by March 2011 and Chinese officials estimate that they will double to RMB900 billion by the end of the year. This growing pool of offshore liquidity held in Hong Kong increases demand for RMB investment vehicles and the Chinese authorities are responding by developing an offshore RMB bond market (stage 2).

Since the first ever issuance of a RMB bond in Hong Kong by the China Development Bank in July 2007, there has been a gradual increase in the issuance of so-called Dim-Sum bonds. Issuers include not only Chinese banks taking advantage of low funding costs in the RMB offshore market but also multinational corporates such as Volkswagen, Unilever and Caterpillar, and – more importantly for the prospect of the RMB as a future reserve currency – the Chinese government. By March 2011, the outstanding value of Dim-Sum bonds reached RMB80 billion, still tiny by international standards but on a notable upswing. The timing for stage 3 – make the RMB an international reserve currency – remains uncertain as its implementation requires a liberalization of the RMB capital account. Some timid steps were undertaken during 2011 – for instance the lifting of some restrictions on RMB overseas direct investments by Chinese enterprises in January and on RMB foreign direct investment on a case-by-case basis in June – but more substantial freedom on investment in onshore markets, liberalization of cross-border borrowing– lending and lifting of restrictions on portfolio investment flows are needed. According to Deutsche Bank, this might happen within the next five years, faster than previous 'guesstimates' of 12–20 years, as the political moon in China has shifted under the fear of impending mayhem in the US. Why is it so important for China to establish the RMB as an international currency? And what is the role of SWFs in such a scenario?

As the largest holder of US Treasuries in the hands of official foreign owners, China currently faces the dilemma of how to reduce its exposure to the greenback without suffering losses on its huge sovereign accumulated wealth. Should it decide to reduce its holding of US Treasuries at a rapid pace, their prices would sink and China would suffer heavy losses. The alternative of gradually diversifying into euro – an ongoing trend among large holders of FX reserves in the past few years – has become less attractive following the predicaments of the euro area, and other currencies do not provide enough liquidity given the size of the Chinese reserves. Furthermore, as most countries around the world trade in dollars, China needs to hold a substantial amount of its reserves in dollar-denominated assets, however reluctantly.

Would it be different if the RMB were used in international transactions? Yes. China would not need to hold huge amount of reserves denominated in foreign currencies as it could print its own money in the amounts needed to support the balance of payments or to subsidize its domestic production. But with the internalization of the RMB still faraway, SWFs are becoming the vehicle to reduce the dollar exposure. By shifting part of the reserves to CIC in 2007 – and by eventually shifting more in the future to CIC or the new SWFs created by the Chinese government[8] – China intends to build a hedge against US inflation which looms as a tempting solution to the current fiscal crisis, being the path of political least resistance.

5.6 SWFs AND THE NEW REGULATORY ENVIRONMENT FOR FINANCIAL INSTITUTIONS: THE UPCOMING 'WAR FOR CAPITAL'

Following the 2007–2008 financial crisis, under the impulse of the G20 and the Financial Stability Board, a new regulatory framework for banks and other financial institutions started being developed. The various regulatory initiatives under implementation, ranging from the regulation of over-the-counter derivatives trading to the so-called too-big-to-fail conundrum (i.e. the threat posed by systemically relevant financial institutions to global financial stability), will lead to a substantial increase in capital requirements for banks. The new capital adequacy under Basel 3 will be phased in during the current decade and come fully into force by 2019. By then financial institutions will have to raise a substantial amount of capital (in addition to that already raised during the crisis to cover the losses on toxic assets and on sovereign debt).

A report by McKinsey Global Institute (2010) estimates that by 2019 the European banking system will need approximately €1.1 trillion of additional Tier 1 capital (i.e. equities or quasi-equities which are more expensive to fund). The smaller US banking sector will need 'only' €600 billion of additional Tier 1 capital. Closing this gap will have a massive impact on profitability: *ceteris paribus*, the full implementation of Basel 3 would reduce return on equity for the average bank by 4% in Europe and by 3% in the US. In short, bank financing will be more expensive, banks will be reluctant to lend and alternatives to bank financing will be more palatable for companies, especially non-listed ones.

The impact of the new capital requirements is already being felt across the financial sector as banks gradually reduce cross-border lending and bring their capital back home. During the financial crisis of 2008–2009, all types of cross-border capital flows declined sharply, but the largest decrease in absolute terms was in cross-border bank lending. In 2010, cross-border bank lending resumed but it was still nearly US$4 trillion below the peak touched in 2007 and it

---

[8] China in late 2011 announced the creation of another SWF, in addition to the CIC, with the specific task of pursuing exclusively foreign acquisitions. According to media reports, US$300 billion of FX reserves could be shifted to the newly created SWF, targeting equity investments in Europe and the US.

does not seem likely that it will resume to the pre-crisis level any time soon (McKinsey Global Institute, 2011). Several financial institutions are shifting resources to their domestic markets by pulling out of non-core markets, in particular emerging markets, as regulators demand more capital being allocated in the parent country to avoid any future bailout by the government.

SWFs and FWFs, as we pointed out in Chapter 2, will be major supplier of long-term capital and therefore their returns will depend on capital scarcity which determines its cost. This issue is interwoven with the reversal of the so-called savings glut which is likely to unravel as the world population ages and the infrastructure investment in the high-growth economies intensify.

6

The Politics of SWFs Engagement

We remarked in Chapter 1 that financial markets are viewed by policy makers, economists and the general public in mature economies as the preserve of private entities and investors. Governments' participation – apart from the regulatory functions – is limited to the issuance of public debt (through financial intermediaries) and occasionally the sale of state-owned companies. In essence, when governments access financial markets they are on the sell side. There are exceptions – e.g. publicly owned banks or the Post Offices which run a retail bank arm, as in Japan and in Italy – but after a wave of privatizations in the 1990s they became much rarer. The direct role of the government in those economies has long been on the wane.

The public sector's primary interface with markets is the central bank which routinely conducts operations through money and foreign currency markets, but in the pursuit of monetary policy objectives, not returns or profits. Central bank reserves, as stressed in Chapter 3, are invested in liquid high-grade securities to ensure that domestic economic agents have access to the foreign currency needed for their business, travel or investments. Central banks in the West do not engage in active asset management, but merely maintain a cache of financial ammunitions to fight the consequences of external or domestic shocks.

Most companies fully owned or controlled by the state in advanced economies had been privatized, and the successful integration of the ex-centrally planned economies in the capitalist world in the 1990s had completed the process. It is therefore not surprising that in the main OECD countries, government-owned foreign entities raise anxiety when they make acquisitions in financial markets. Globalization itself initially has been a process mostly driven by competition among private corporations expanding internationally and mostly by private investors allocating financial capital across borders. The role of governments was supposedly confined to guaranteeing that the key rules of the game – notably trade liberalization and the free movement of capital – remained firmly in place and were not abused.

The crisis in 2007–2008 called into question the expansion of the private sector globally and the continuing reduction of the role of governments in economic and financial affairs. The *Financial Times* published a supplement on 'The Future of Capitalism' in 2009 which voiced rather scathing critiques of the mess caused by investment bankers and rather pessimistic assessments on future prospects of freewheeling markets.

The Great Recession marked an abrupt and unexpected return of governments in economic affairs in most advanced economies whose financial

markets almost melted down (Bremmer, 2010). After the de facto nationalization of large chunks of the international financial system and the blank cheques
written by governments to 'strategic' industries such as the automotive, the
furore against state-sponsored investments lost much of its fuel. The warnings
over the danger supposedly emanating from government influence over SWFs
sounded preposterous. And as to transparency, the measures carried out by
Western authorities left much to be desired. The public was essentially kept
behind a confusing curtain of smoke while bankrupt bankers and managers
were scrambling for public money.

From a historical perspective, governments and state-controlled corporations have often played an important role in the allocation of capital across
productive sectors, regions and different social groups. The most extreme cases
were the centrally planned economies. But also in many non-centrally planned
economies, particularly in Europe in the years of rapid capital accumulation
following the Second World War, the state played an important role in sectors
considered 'strategic' by either allocating public capital at favourable conditions (i.e. subsidies) or through the establishment of state-controlled corporations. In this respect, one may say that government intervention in economic
affairs has been experienced, with different intensity, across regions, in several
countries (Yergin and Stanislaw, 1998). What makes today's 'state-capitalism'
in countries such as China or Saudi Arabia worrisome is the role they might
exert in the era of globalization. In most Western countries, the involvement
of governments in economic affairs was limited to domestic issues with scant
(visible) international implications, possibly with the exception of a few industries with geopolitical implications such as energy. In countries from where
most SWFs and FWFs originate, the government's role has a distinctive international dimension as most funds are invested abroad and in many cases – for
instance the Gulf-based economies – SWFs are a key pillar of wealth creation
and redistribution. In these economies, the government owns the underground
wealth, is in control of its commercial exploitation through state-controlled
corporations and is in charge of redistributing its rent domestically. The same
can be said for several non-commodity-exporting countries where either the
state owns and directly controls a large part of the economic system through
state-controlled corporations (e.g. China) or where the economic interests of
the ruling elite and those of the country as a whole coincide (e.g. Singapore). It
would be surprising if in these countries the government did not play a pervasive role in the control of how the national surplus is invested internationally.

6.1 NATIONAL RESPONSES TO THE GROWING ROLE OF SWFs

The initial Western political response to the increasing activities of SWFs
and other state-controlled corporations in global markets has taken place at

national level through a review of regulations on foreign investments. Typically a regulatory reaction was triggered by a specific event under mounting
public opinion pressure; often though it was simply a sense of urgency to react
to the growing role of state-controlled investment vehicles in global markets.
Two examples of a policy response dictated by specific 'threat to national interests' are those of the US and Australia, following bids for strategic stakes
in some corporations by Arab and Chinese state-controlled institutions. In the
US, the event was actually not an investment carried out by a SWF but the attempt in 2005 by Dubai Port World, a partly state-owned company based in the
United Arab Emirates (UAE), subsequently listed on the stock exchange of the
Dubai International Financial Center, to take over the management of some
US ports as part of its purchase of UK-based port operator P&O. As a result of
the political controversy surrounding Dubai Ports (described in the Introduction) – with President Bush strongly supporting the deal fearing that a block
could send the wrong signal to foreign investors and Congress against it – in
2007 the US revised the Foreign Investment and National Security Act, raising
the scope of the reviews carried out by the Committee on Foreign Investments
in the US (CFIUS). The bill expanded the conditions under which CFIUS
must conduct a full 45-day investigation by including two circumstances: first,
transactions involving the acquisition of critical infrastructure; second, acquisitions by a foreign government or any entity controlled by or acting on behalf
of a foreign government. Since the 2007 reform, the number of CFIUS's reviews doubled and instances of so-called 'mitigation agreements' and withdrawals of foreign investments have also risen dramatically The expansion of
the scope and powers of CFIUS did not stop US politicians from lobbying for
more regulation. Following China's US$3 billion passive investment in the
private equity group Blackstone in May 2007, Democrat Senator Jim Webb
sent a letter to the Treasury Secretary Henry Paulson expressing his fear that
the investment would provide the Chinese government with an 'opportunity
for undue influence' in sensitive deals.

In Australia, the trigger was the acquisition in 2008 of a 9% stake in mining giant Rio Tinto by a Chinese state-controlled mining company Chinalco,
in a move to block a planned takeover by BHP, Australia's biggest company.
Following the aggressive Chinese move, the Australian Treasury issued an
additional set of principles for state-backed foreign investments, according
to which the Foreign Investment Review Board must consider whether the
prospective investors operate independently of their respective governments.
As in the case of Dubai Port World in the US, these measures were introduced
following a bid by a state-controlled corporation rather than a SWF. The Australian rules, however, extend to intermediaries such as private equity funds,
where state-controlled entities might have a stake.

In other countries, policy reactions came in response to a threat which had
not materialized but was perceived as imminent. For example, in Germany a
new law to protect national interests suddenly rose to the top of the government

agenda during 2008 and led to the revision of its Foreign Trade Act. A new inter-ministerial Committee resembling the US's CFIUS was established with the power to block acquisitions by non-EU state-backed investment funds in German companies on the grounds of 'public security' or because of involving 'strategic infrastructure'. The threshold for the scrutiny was fixed at 25% and the Commission was given the power to cancel an investment up to three months after it had occurred. The legislation does not affect investors from Germany's 26 partners in the EU as well as those from Iceland, Norway, Switzerland and Liechtenstein. When the text of the law was adopted by the German cabinet, the Minister of the Economy at the time, Michael Glos, said the legislation would be applied 'with maximum restraint,' noting that it was rare for foreign investors to take a stake of more than 25% in German businesses (Kern, 2010).

In addition to the US, Australia and Germany, other countries passed specific regulations targeting investments by foreign state-controlled investment vehicles or corporations. For instance, in May 2008 the Russian Duma passed the new Federal Law on Foreign Investments in companies having strategic implications for State Security and Defence.[1] The law restricted conditions for foreign investment in Russia, establishing an approval process for foreign investments in strategic sectors specified in terms of 42 activities ranging from weapons and military equipment to natural monopolies, and introduced a threshold requiring an approval tailored for each activity. Rather than passing tighter legislation on foreign investments, France opted for setting up its own SWF to shield strategic industries from takeovers by foreign 'predators'. In October 2008, French President Nicolas Sarkozy announced the setting up of the first SWF à la française: a fund managed by the Caisse De Depôts et Consignations (CDC), a public financial institution already in charge of performing financial missions of public interests and at the time with approximately €200 billion under management[2]. The Italian authorities were also considering something similar in response to a takeover by Lactalis, a French dairy company of Parmalat, a similar company which had been rescued from bankruptcy after a massive fraud conducted by its former owner, Callisto Tanzi. For France, the decision to establish a SWF did not emanate from the potential threat represented by hostile investment funds from emerging markets, but rather represented the willingness to re-engage in domestic industrial policy.

What immediately became clear during this period was that every country – reflecting its institutional, regulatory and political structure – had its own view on how to regulate SWFs' investments. This reflects the lack of any significant effort to address the issue of cross-border investments at international level. Whilst the WTO had already established itself as the international forum for dealing with controversies between countries in the area of free trade, there is

---

[1] Law No. 57-FZ, signed by the President on 29 April and effective from 7 May 2008.
[2] Un Fondo Sovrano per la Francia, *Il Sole 24 Ore*, 17 October 2008.

no corresponding international forum when it comes to foreign investments. With the exception of some work already carried by the OECD in the context of a project called 'Freedom of Investments, National Security and Strategic Industries', international principles on cross-border investments are yet to be agreed.[3]

The growing concern over the detrimental effects of individual countries' ad hoc measures against SWFs and other state-controlled vehicles on the free movement of capital, in autumn 2007, led the G7 finance ministers to request the OECD and the IMF to develop guidelines guaranteeing an international, level playing field.

6.2 INTERNATIONAL RESPONSE TO THE GROWING ROLE OF SWFs

The shift of the political debate surrounding SWFs from the national to the international level during 2007 followed an initiative by the US government. Already in June 2007, in official remarks in relation to the concerns following the political controversy surrounding Dubai Ports World and Blackstone, Clay Lowery, the US Treasury's Undersecretary for International Affairs, suggested the development of international best practices for SWFs and called for international negotiations. At the same time he called upon the IMF and the World Bank to form a joint task force to work on the issue. Even though both countries with SWFs and investment recipient countries are members of these international organizations, Lowery added that: 'The IMF has the requisite expertise on wider systemic and macroeconomic subjects, such as the link to fiscal policy'. In reality, assigning this task to a supranational organization where national political fingerprints would be less detectable seemed the best way to avoid the possibility that individual countries could end up holding back the free movement of capital waving the excuse of national security.

Following the G7 in October 2007, several initiatives by individual or groups of countries, often in consultation with selected SWFs, were launched to provide support and political momentum to the initiative carried out by the IMF. In February 2008, the European Commission issued a Communication on SWFs where it rejected extra regulation at national level, invoked the respect for the EU treaty on the free circulation of capital and expressed full support to the international policy response being elaborated by the OECD/IMF

---

[3] The Freedom of Investment process, an intergovernmental forum hosted since 2006 by the OECD Investment Committee, brings together some 50 governments from around the world to exchange information and experiences on investment policies at regular roundtables. Here, governments develop guidance for open, transparent and non-discriminatory investment policies. However, this initiative is not binding for governments and is in no way comparable to the role played by the WTO in ensuring free trade at global level.

(European Commission, 2008). While recognizing the positive contribution by SWFs in the stabilization of the financial markets, the Commission assured that it would not enact legislation targeting funds that had invested in sensitive industries, though it reserved the right to do so if 'voluntary' means failed to achieve transparency.

The Commission's rationale for stepping in an area where it had not had much past involvement was the need to define a common approach to avoid unilateral action by EU member states that could distort the bloc's internal market. The European Commission proposed a 'code' for SWFs, setting out five principles, including:

1   commitment to an open investment environment both in the EU and elsewhere;
2   support of multilateral work, in international organizations such as the IMF and OECD;
3   use of existing instruments at EU and member state level;
4   respect of EC Treaty obligations and international commitments, for example in the context of WTO;
5   proportionality and transparency.

In terms of the European contribution to the global work on a common framework for SWF investments, the EU put emphasis on 'greater clarity and insight into the governance of SWFs' and 'greater transparency in their activities and investments'.

With regards to increased transparency, the EU specifically mentioned 'annual disclosure of investment position and asset allocation (…), disclosure of the use of leverage and currency composition, size and sources of an entity's resources and disclosure of the home country regulation and oversight governing the SWF'. The President of the European Commission Manuel Barroso seemed to be quite specific in what he meant by asserting 'The Norwegian sovereign wealth fund is exemplary in terms of transparency, governance and accountability', thereby setting a benchmark against which to judge other SWFs. The quite liberal position expressed by the European Commission was endorsed by the European Heads of States without any significant reservation the following month.

In early April 2008, the OECD released its first report on 'SWFs and Recipient Country Policies' in response to the request of the G7 in late 2007. The report was the result of the work carried out by the 30 OECD members, 14 non-member countries participating in the project, and consultations with SWFs. The aim of the report was to develop a guidance for countries receiving investments from SWFs based on the work already carried out by the OECD in the context of the already mentioned project 'Freedom of Investments, National Security and Strategic Industries'. The OECD's four key principles – transparency, predictability, proportionality and accountability – should guide governments when designing and implementing inward investment restrictions to assuage national security concerns. Crucially, among the principles listed by the OECD, reciprocity is not included. This was one of the issues where the controversy between the liberal approach (championed by the UK) and the more protectionist one (defended by France) was most likely to emerge. The OECD report also stressed 'peer review' over these commitments to guarantee a widespread application of the principles.

However, the initiative kicked-off by the IMF became the most important international effort concerning the finalization of a voluntary set of generally accepted principles and practices for SWFs. In April 2008, following the IMF and World Bank Spring Meetings, the International Working Group of SWFs (IWG) was officially established with the mandate of finalizing the Generally Accepted Principles and Practices for SWFs (GAPP). The IWG, co-chaired by Jamie Caruana, director of the IMF's Monetary and Capital Markets Department, and Hamad al Sawaidi, from the Abu Dhabi Finance Department, included representatives from the most important SWFs, their respective sponsor countries and largest recipients, including the European Union, the UK, the US and Japan. The political momentum created by the various high-level initiatives undertaken by the US, the European Union and international institutions in the months before and the inclusion of representatives from the largest SWFs paved the way for a successful outcome. By October 2008, the IWG announced the finalization of GAPP, or 'Santiago Principles' as they were called following its third meeting in the Chilean capital. Before looking at these principles in detail, it is enlightening to delve into the role played by SWFs in achieving this compromise.

6.3 SWFs' RESPONSE TO INTERNATIONAL PRESSURE

The political clash surrounding the takeover of P&O by Dubai Ports World in the US was a wake-up call for Middle Eastern SWFs. It was not absolutely the first time that a reaction to foreign acquisition was spurred, so with hindsight it should have been preceded by a public relations campaign. On the contrary it was a public relations failure. Members of the US Congress did not have advanced knowledge of the deal and the CFIUS process was a mystery to both the Congress and the American public.

Since then the largest SWFs have established public relations functions within their organizations, but this was not enough to deal with the international initiative. The initial proposal formulation by the Undersecretary for International Affairs at the US Treasury, Clay Lowery, in June 2007 was heavily criticized by SWFs for being paternalistic and unfair towards them and emerging markets in general. For example, Bader M. Al Sa'ad of the KIA said: 'It is time to call a spade a spade. Recipient countries are placing handcuffs on SWFs in the form of regulations termed, in the best tradition of

George Orwell's "newspeak", code of conduct, principles of operations or best practices.'[4] Other SWF representatives made similar comments, including the Russian Deputy Prime Minister Aleksey Kudrin, who outlined the inconsistency over time of the Western approach to foreign investments and claimed that foreign investments has become a problem only when capital was flowing from emerging markets to industrialized countries. Muhammad S. Al Jasser, head of SAMA, commented that SWFs had not violated any of the best practices they are expected to adopt and concluded that 'sovereign wealth funds are guilty until they are proven innocent'.[5] Chinese authorities also warned Western governments against a protectionist attitude towards sovereign investors, stating that national security could not serve as an excuse for hampering the activities of SWFs.

The negative reaction of SWFs to Lowery's proposals reflected the fact that he had raised politically controversial issues, specifically the current account imbalances between the USA and China, when he underscored that SWFs' money must be considered 'as borrowed funds' rather than wealth *sensu stricto*, since its assets come from sterilized exchange rate intervention. It also reflected the lack of any previous consultation with SWFs and their sponsoring governments despite the growing international debate on adequate representation of emerging markets in the governance of the global economy which preceded the launch of the G20. Furthermore, SWFs are not a homogenous group and do not have any representative body or association to deal collectively with policy issues. So a common policy proposal could not be agreed and negotiated with counterparts: as a result the reaction to the growing international pressure was quite varied. For instance, the Norwegian SWF supported the call for higher transparency and better governance standards as its reporting and transparency framework had been indicated as a model in the political debate. However, this model would not work for other funds either because they come from countries with a generally lower level of transparency in government affairs or because they have a different investment style that prevents them from disclosing potentially market-sensitive information on their portfolio (for instance SWFs taking strategic investments in non-listed firms). From this point of view, the establishment of the IMF-sponsored IWG had the important merit of having provided a forum where the negotiation between SWFs and recipient countries could take place on equal terms (Gruenig, 2008).

Following the establishment of the IMF-IWG, SWFs have become less defensive and have used various opportunities to engage into an open dialogue with their Western counterparts. The two most active funds have been ADIA and GIC which, together with representatives of sponsoring governments, met in Washington with US Treasury officials in mid-March 2008 to discuss the issues concerning SWFs, recipient country inward investment regimes and

---

[4] Kuwait Rejects Western Plans for Curbs", *The Guardian*, June 2007.

[5] State Investors Deny Political Motivations, *The Guardian*, 25 January 2008.

efforts to develop best practices. Following the meeting, also attended by Treasury Secretary Henry Paulson and Deputy Secretary Robert M. Kimmit, a joint declaration including some broad policy principles for both SWFs and recipient countries was released. To a large extent, the joint US/UAE/Singapore declaration provided a blueprint for the Santiago Principles that were to be adopted later in the year.

6.4 SANTIAGO PRINCIPLES: RATIONALE, IMPLEMENTATION AND REALITY

Less than six months after receiving the mandate from the G7, in October 2008 the IWG on SWFs presented the agreed international standards for the transparency and conduct of SWFs to the IMF's International Monetary and Financial Committee (IMFC). The Generally Accepted Principles and Practices, or 'Santiago Principles', included 24 voluntary principles covering three key areas:

1 the legal framework, objectives and coordination with macroeconomic policies;
2 the institutional framework and governance structure;
3 the investment and risk management framework (IWG, 2008a).

Given the varied composition of the IWG, the 24 principles were formulated rather generically in an effort to facilitate endorsement across SWF home countries. But the 24 principles should be read in conjunction with the additional information included in Part II called 'Discussion of GAPP-Santiago Principles' that adds explanation and commentary to each principle, including the practical implications of their application. For instance, with regards to the legal framework, the GAPP 1 is quite generic when stating that 'The Legal framework for the SWF should be sound and support its effective operation and the achievement of its stated objectives'. However, the commentary on the GAPP 1 in Part II, specifies three canonical legal structures for SWFs: (a) a separate legal identity with full capacity to act and be governed by a specific constitutional law (e.g. as in Kuwait, Korea, Qatar and the UAE); (b) a state-owned corporation governed by general company law and other SWF-specific laws (e.g. Singapore's Temasek or CIC); (c) a pool of assets without a separate legal identity controlled by either the state or the central bank (e.g. Canada, Norway and Botswana).

The same systematic approach was adopted throughout the 24 principles. In another example, the independence of the operational management, GAPP 9 states that 'The operational management of the SWF should implement the SWFs' strategies in an independent manner and in accordance with clearly defined responsibilities'. The commentary on GAPP 9 is more specific about a key policy issue raised by Western counterparts, when it states that 'To enhance confidence in recipient countries, it is important that managers' individual investment decisions to implement the SWF's defined strategy be protected from undue and direct political interference and influence. As owner, the role of the governments is to determine the broad policy objectives of the SWF, but not to intervene in decisions relating to particular investments'. The commentary on GAPP 9 suggests some mechanisms that can be introduced to reach this goal including vesting responsibility for the SWF's management in a separate entity, providing extensive powers to the CEO and senior managers or contracting out responsibility for making individual investment decisions to external service providers on a fee-for-service basis.

Some commentary and explanations are aimed at reassuring SWFs themselves. For instance, with regards to the politically sensitive issue of the SWFs' operations in host countries, GAPP 15 states that 'SWF operations and activities in host countries should be conducted in compliance with all applicable regulatory and disclosure requirements of the countries in which they operate'. In the commentary to GAPP 15, it is stated very clearly that 'the SWF expects that host countries would not subject the SWF to any requirement, obligation, restriction, or regulatory action exceeding that to which other investors in similar circumstances may be subject'. Similarly, with regard to the disclosure of information on the investment policy, GAPP 18.3 states 'A description of the investment policy of the SWF should be publicly disclosed' but in the commentary it is clearly stated that a qualitative statement on the investment style, or investment themes, the investment objectives, the investment horizon and the strategic asset allocation is enough, thus responding to the concerns of some SWFs reluctant to provide quantitative information on their investments across different asset classes.

The release of the Santiago Principles took place at a crucial juncture for the global economy. Following the bankruptcy of Lehman, in autumn 2008 the international community was becoming increasingly aware of the true magnitude of the financial crisis and the devastating impact on the global economy. In that period, saving the global financial system from a meltdown and avoiding a global depression represented the top priority on the agenda of policy makers and central bankers. The shocking turbulence certainly contributed to the swift finalization of a political agreement between SWFs and recipient countries. With international capital flows in free fall and global investors becoming increasingly risk averse, the US and other Western governments were keen to signal that their economies were welcoming foreign investments, particularly those coming from SWFs, virtually the only investors left with ample liquidity to deploy in the midst of a global financial crisis at the time still perceived mostly as a liquidity problem. Apart from the contingent situation in which they saw the light, is there any real content in the GAPP? And almost three years after the finalization, given its voluntary nature, has there been any concrete progress in terms of SWFs' increased compliance?

When the principles were released, Edwin M. Truman from the Peterson Institute made an assessment of the GAPP against the 33 elements of the Blueprint for Sovereign Wealth Fund Best Practices: out of a maximum score of 100, the GAPP received a score of 74 (Truman, 2008a).

The GAPP scored generally high in terms of required disclosure standard. In fact, 6 of the 24 principles and 4 of the sub-principles deal with public disclosures in a variety of areas including: legal basis and structure, policy purpose, policies and procedures in relation to funding, withdrawal and spending operations, source of SWF funding, governance, and investment policy. According to Truman, though, the GAPP do not score 100 because they leave much to be desired in terms of accountability and transparency, particularly with regard to the general public, reflecting the fact that there are different models of SWFs operating in very diverse institutional contexts. In a book published in autumn 2010 (Truman, 2010), the same Scoreboard adopted to evaluate the GAPP was applied to individual SWFs to assess their compliance and the progress made in the past few years (Table 6.1).

The trend towards more transparency and disclosure started under the impulse of the IMF is unstoppable for several reasons. First, it is part of the trend towards more transparency in the financial service industry – already well under way before the financial crisis.[6] An argument initially put forward by SWFs in rejecting Western demands for more oversight of their activities points to the fact that other financial players such as hedge funds are even less transparent than SWFs and completely unregulated. In the post-financial crisis, this will probably be less true: in addition to banks, all other financial entities will be regulated and more transparency imposed, although it will probably be a matter of a decade rather than a few months.

Second, the largest corporates from emerging markets will increasingly diversify their activities internationally in the next few years, penetrating markets in advanced economies. While reciprocity in the treatment of foreign investments is often mentioned but rarely formally adopted, the demand for more transparency on SWFs' activities by Western countries is likely to be met by emerging markets to reduce the potential backlash against the global activities of their corporations.

Last but not least, SWFs have an interest in reducing any political backlash against their investments in Western countries. As discussed in Chapters 2 and 3, the assets of SWFs are set to double over the next few years and the flow of direct investments into Western listed and unlisted corporations will rise as well. China has already announced the establishment of a new SWF worth

---

[6] For instance, in Europe a new regulation on hedge funds and other alternative funds such as private equity and infrastructure funds – the so-called Alternative Investment Financial Managers Directive (AIFMD) – is currently being implemented. Hedge funds will be required to disclose information about their investments, including details on leverage levels and on the acquisition of strategic stakes in listed corporations. The US is following a similar approach with regard to hedge funds, forcing these entities to register and disclose more information to the regulators.

Table 6.1   The Truman and Santiago scoreboard for SWFs

Sovereign wealth fund	Truman score	Santiago score	Difference
Norway Government Pension Fund – Global	97	96	−1
New Zealand Superannuation Fund (PR)	94	98	4
United States Alaska Permanent Fund	92	96	4
United States Wyoming Permanent Mineral Trust Fund	91	96	5
Ireland National Pensions Reserve Fund (PR)	86	94	8
Timor-Leste Petroleum Fund	85	80	−5
Trinidad and Tobago Heritage and Stabilization Fund	83	82	−1
Australia Future Fund (PR)	80	90	10
United States New Mexico Severance Tax Permanent Fund	80	80	0
Azerbaijan State Oil Fund	76	76	0
Canada Alberta Heritage Savings Trust Fund	74	80	6
Singapore Temasek Holdings	73	82	9
Chile Economic and Social Stabilization Fund	71	70	−1
Hong Kong Exchange Fund	70	74	4
Chile Pension Reserve Fund	68	68	0
United States Alabama Trust Fund	68	76	8
Kazakhstan National Fund	65	67	2
Singapore Government of Singapore Investment Corporation	65	78	13
Kuwait Kuwait Investment Authority	63	71	8
Korea Korea Investment Corporation	60	67	7
UAE (Abu Dhabi) Mubadala Development Company	59	66	7
Abu Dhabi Investment Authority	58	71	13
China China Investment Corporation	57	60	3
Botswana Pula Fund	56	62	6
UAE (Dubai) Dubai International Capital	55	62	7
Russia Reserve Fund and National Wealth Fund	50	52	2
São Tomé and Príncipe National Oil Account	48	58	10
Malaysia Khazanah Nasional	44	48	4
Mexico Oil Income Stabilization Fund	44	42	−2
Kiribati Revenue Equalization Reserve Fund	35	44	9
Vietnam State Capital Investment Corporation	35	4	−27
Bahrain Mumtalakat Holding Company	30	32	2
Algeria Revenue Regulation Fund	29	32	3
Iran Oil Stabilization Fund	29	32	3
Nigeria Excess Crude Account	29	34	5
Venezuela Macroeconomic Stabilization Fund	27	28	1
National Development Fund	27	25	−2
UAE (Abu Dhabi) International Petroleum Investment Company	26	26	0
Oman State General Reserve Fund	23	26	3
Brunei Darussalam Brunei Investment Agency	21	28	7
UAE (Dubai) Investment Company of Dubai	21	22	1
Sudan Oil Revenue Stabilization Account	18	16	−2
Qatar Qatar Investment Authority	15	15	0
UAE (Dubai) Istithmar World	15	16	1

Source: Edwin M. Truman (2011) Sovereign Wealth Funds: Is Asia Different? Peterson Institute, Working Paper 11–12.

US$300bn; no surprise then that CIC has increased its transparency standards and make explicit reference to the Santiago Principles. Also GIC has recently posted on its website a paper outlining how the Singapore-based SWF adheres to the Santiago Principles.

Given the voluntary nature of the Santiago Principles and the lack of any enforcing mechanism, including an institution assessing the adherence of SWFs to the code, following a meeting in Kuwait City in April 2009 the IWG announced the establishment of the International Forum of Sovereign Wealth Funds (IFSWF), a voluntary group that would meet once a year to exchange views on issues of common interest and to facilitate the understanding of the Santiago Principles and SWFs' activities. The mandate of the Forum is to support the four guiding objectives of the Santiago Principles:

1 to help maintain a stable global financial system and free flow of capital and investment;
2 to comply with all applicable regulatory and disclosure requirements in the countries in which they invest;
3 to invest on the basis of economic and financial risk and return-related considerations; and
4 to have in place a transparent and sound governance structure that provides for adequate operational controls, risk management, and accountability (Table 6.2).

David Murray, Chairman of Australia's Future Fund Board of Guardians, was elected by the IWG members to chair the Forum. Jin Liqun, Chairman of the Board of Supervisors, China Investment Corporation, and Bader Mohammad Al-Sa'ad, Managing Director, Kuwait Investment Authority, were elected

Table 6.2 Comparison between OECD and IMF approach

OECD Guidelines	Santiago Principles
1. Recipient countries should not erect protectionist barriers to foreign investment. 2. Recipient countries should not discriminate among investors in similar circumstances. Only legitimate national security concerns are justified. 3. Where national security concerns do arise, investment safeguards should be: – transparent and predictable, – proportional to clearly identified national security risks, and – subject to accountability in their application	1. Legal framework: ensuring regulatory requirements in recipient countries. 2. Appropriate governance for SWFs: transparent and sound governance structures for adequate operational controls. 3. Accountability: public disclosures in a variety of areas, although mindful of SWFs' competitive position. 4. Prudent investment practices: invest only on the basis of economic and risk and return, contribute to stable financial markets.

Source: Rolando Avendaño and Javier Santiso, Sovereign Wealth Funds and Infrastructure: A Perspective for Latin America. Presentation at the CAF-IFC-OECD Seminar on Infrastructure Financing in Latin America.

to be deputy chairs of the Forum. Sub-committees dealing with specific issues were also established to move forward the agenda of the Forum.

Following the Kuwait declaration, the International Forum of SWFs met for the first time in Baku, Azerbaijan in October 2009. The meeting was attended by around 20 SWFs, and representatives of international financial institutions also participated in the meeting. Much of the discussion in the inaugural meeting of the Forum was on the lessons of the financial crisis, particularly the reliance of models in the investment process, and the importance of truly understanding SWF objectives, investment horizons and risk so as to protect the interests of the SWFs stakeholders and the community in general. The rejection of financial protectionism and the support to the Santiago Principles were once again emphasized. The second meeting of the International Forum of SWFs was held in Sydney, Australia in May 2010. In addition to best practices in risk management (reviewed in Chapter 4), and the investment challenges faced by SWFs, a first assessment of the application of the Santiago Principles was carried out. The final statement mentioned the progress made in the application of the principles since their adoption in October 2008. The issuance of annual reports and the increased availability of information on websites of some SWFs were mentioned as the most notable progress. The need for divulging the Santiago Principles to the public was also mentioned as an important area where further progress was needed. Following the third meeting in Beijin, China, on May 2011 Jin Liun from CIC replaced David Murray as the Chairman of the Forum and the Forum members agreed to move towards a permanent Secretariat funded by the members themselves.

All in all the Santiago Principles constitute a useful roadmap to guide the actions of large SWFs when investing in sensitive areas and a common ground to avoid outlandish pretexts to stop foreign acquisitions. But a real test of the framework has yet to come. It will be interesting to see how another spate of 'economic patriotism' will be handled and how the Santiago Principles will be abided by on both sides.

6.5 A DIGRESSION ON PUBLIC VERSUS PRIVATE ROLE IN THE ECONOMY

Historically, the demarcation line between the public and private sphere in the economy is unstable and swings erratically in response to circumstances. At the beginning of this chapter we remarked that in mature economies financial markets are widely viewed as a preserve of individuals, firms and private institutions in general, so that any interference by a publicly owned entity would be seen as an undue interference at odds with well-established laws, norms and practices.

But how accurate is this presumption? Before the sub-prime crisis turned into a financial disaster, requiring bailouts of key international banks and industries, this claim could have been justified. Afterwards it sounded quite hollow as it became clear that private liabilities can be transformed into public liabilities at the stroke of a pen and often even without the hassle of a vote by Parliament. 'No taxation without representation' became 'Nationalization without representation'.

Invoking Keynesian policies suddenly became fashionable and massive government intervention suddenly acquired a respectable aura even on the pages of the *Financial Times*. Articles, essays and blogs on the demise of capitalism or at least on robust corrections to its shortcomings proliferated.

But even in normal circumstances governments do exert an influence on markets. We have mentioned repeatedly public pension funds. But every country also has development agencies that provide support to domestic companies plus various kinds of grants and subsidies, often in the form of preferential interest rates. Then there is a host of international institutions. The most famous is the International Bank for Reconstruction and Development, best known as the World Bank, which borrows in international markets taking advantage of its triple A rating and then funds all sorts of infrastructure in member countries that cannot access international markets. One could argue that this intervention is justified because the World Bank focuses on infrastructure and deals primarily with governments, filling a vacuum in financial markets that are not willing to give credit to poor countries. But the World Bank Group includes the International Financial Corporation (IFC) which has a mandate to operate like a private sector entity to foster market developments and to yield returns in line with private operations, without charging concessional rates.

The World Bank is just the largest of this kind of lending institution. There are numerous regional banks modelled after the World Bank that attract much less attention, but whose role is of paramount importance in many countries. The older ones are the Inter-American Development Bank, the Asian Development Bank, the African Development Bank and, after the demise of the Soviet bloc, a European Bank for Reconstruction and Development was founded to operate in Eastern Europe and in the former Soviet Union. On the wings of the peace process between Israeli and Palestinians in the early 1990s, a Middle East Development Bank was created, but it never went beyond an embryonic stage.

Then there is the European Investment Bank, which finances infrastructure in the member countries of the European Union, again taking advantage of its triple A ratings. Furthermore there exist a host of national entities and funds for all kinds of enterprises, often with the mandate to finance new ventures, young entrepreneurs, women, etc. Even the US has institutions such as the Tennessee Valley Authority and various state agencies that try to attract business with incentive schemes.

Several countries have, even before the Lehman default, exerted a tight grip on banks. The case of the German Landesbanken has been a point of contention between the German government and the European Commission for years, because of the implicit subsidy on interest rates it enjoys thanks to its government guarantees. A large number of Italian banks are still controlled by 'Foundations' – the vestiges of an era when all the major banks and most local banks were state owned – whose Boards are appointed by local authorities. They are supposed to be at arm's length from management, but in reality their influence is pervasive.

Then there are the Post Services which in several countries also own a bank arm. Most famously the privatization of the Japanese Post Bank has long been a thorny political issue and has led to the resignation of a few governments over the years. The Italian Post runs a bank which has increased its offer of services over the years and issues debt in competition with the Treasury.

We can add to the list of public institutions with a pervasive role the French Caisse of Depôt and Conseignation, the KfW in Germany, the Cassa Depositi e Prestiti in Italy, and analogous institutions in Spain, Austria and Portugal which are supposed to finance infrastructure, but in a few cases use public funds to support (domestic) companies.

There are a few industries where state ownership has a venerable tradition: for example, defence, aviation, shipbuilding, energy or railways, and in general the public utility sector (with the exception of the Anglosphere) is usually dominated by state-owned enterprises such as France's Electricité De France, but also semi-public like Enel.

Indeed, the conflict between the two competing models – state capitalism and free market capitalism – could not be more evident than in the global struggle to secure and control access to energy. Governments already own the majority of the world's energy reserves and Western oil companies have already been pushed out from the most promising markets. Chinese foreign policy is increasingly driven by its fast rising energy needs and state-controlled corporations, and investment vehicles are aware of this priority. In the aftermath of the crisis, there is even less restraint on the use of government influence: if the market can no longer be relied on, the state will intervene. This reversal of attitudes risks exciting protectionist tendencies as governments extend their reach to other areas. In the post-crisis 'New Normal', market forces tend to be mortified when the outcome of competition runs against 'national' interest.

The clash between national interests and economic liberalism is illustrated in a cable released by Wikileaks from the US ambassador in Thailand: 'Our ability to manage a counterstrategy to China's charm offensive is complicated by the fact that, unlike the Chinese, most of the US–Thai trade and investment relationship is based on decisions made by private US firms and not by the US government'. The sudden turn in advanced economies over the involvement of governments in economic matters is probably a temporary phenomenon closely related to the risk of a further escalation in the crisis. In the US, the UK and other countries, the governments have made clear that they are willing to withdraw from the capital of banks (and the automobile sector in the US) following injections of public funds during the financial crisis. Some continental European countries – notably France and Italy – have never really fallen in love with economic and financial liberalism, and following the crisis, the support for government involvement has definitely increased. For instance, following the example of France, the government in Italy has mulled over the establishment of a SWF-like entity to defend national champions from hostile foreign takeovers.

Where this process will lead is still uncertain. A return to the role of the State in economic affairs as in the 1960s and the 1970s does not seem likely, particularly in the light of fiscal restructuring in most advanced economies. Given the poor state of public finances, a new wave of privatization actually seems likely, as already communicated – for instance – by Spain and Greece.

Nevertheless, the textbook description of a private sector rigidly separated from the public sphere which concentrates only on regulations and policy is a gross oversimplification. In reality the role of the government always remains pervasive, but takes different forms depending on the *zeitgeist* or the political mood of the electorate. Sometimes public intervention is exerted discretely behind the scenes through moral suasion or veiled threats to private actors. In other cases it is more blatant as the influence is exerted directly through the ownership or the control of key enterprises and financial institutions under various guises.

The mood swings, often in response to economic hardship. In periods of boom, the government is loathed and is blamed for anything that the crowd does not like. When a crisis bites, then the government is invoked as the saviour and the indispensable counterweight to fat cats' greed, financers' excesses, moral hazard, bankers' incompetence, intolerable income disparities and a long list of grievances. Rising tensions between free market economics in the Western world and state capitalism in many emerging markets also threaten the free movement of capital across countries, a key pillar of globalization.

As a final remark, one can also notice that sometimes the interests of a private corporation handing out generous campaign contributions are more closely safeguarded by elected officials than the interest of an investment fund which manages the wealth for future generations, but from which politicians cannot gain any direct personal benefit.

7
Wrapping Up

Writing about SWFs eschewing polemics against foreign ownership of 'strategic' assets, diatribes over the sinister influence of shadowy institutions, or tirades against the 'locust' irrupting into the harmonious Western economies, requires a comprehensive look at the forces that, unleashed by the globalization, are reshaping the economic and, as a consequence, the financial geography in the twenty-first century.

Often parochial views, held by those still living in the twentieth century, tend to ignore the sway of mega-trends that are bound to forge the twenty-first. Indeed, the stance against SWFs or FWFs hinges mostly on economic neo-patriotism rather than on incidences of regulatory failure, risk build-up, unfair competition, manipulative pressure on national authorities or undue weight in corporate decisions.

In this book we have endeavoured to put the emergence of SWFs within the broader context of the new economic reality rising above the political diatribes that emerged before the financial crisis. We stressed the underlying factors that have caused a momentous growth in the number and magnitude of SWFs and FWFs, propelling them onto the global stage. We have tried to disentangle specious arguments, tinged with populist overtones, from the genuine worries about the soundness of financial markets and the imbalances in the world economy. Above all, we have stressed that clogging the financial channels between mature and emerging markets will have serious consequences for a world entangled in the most severe and prolonged crisis since 1929.

The cornerstone of our argument underlines the fact that a country with persistent current account surpluses can:

1 fund current expenditures (conceivably even a direct distribution to the population);
2 build physical infrastructure;
3 improve public goods (defence, justice, statistical data compilation);
4 extend the provision of public services such as health, education or research;
5 accumulate funds for precautionary reasons or for transfer to future generations.

In emerging markets and commodity exporters a sizeable portion of the current account surplus ends up in the reserves of the central bank. The rise of the SWFs stems from the disposition to diversify the investments of these reserves initiated during 2000–2010 (Rybinski and Krynska, 2010). In the 1980s and

1990s, preparedness in reacting to shocks was the overriding objective of foreign exchange reserves management. As the amount of reserves increased, returns became an issue and central banks started diversifying across asset classes and currencies. Similarly SWFs, which were already investing in a range of riskier and less liquid asset classes, further expanded their investment universe.

This process has reached such a scale that the revenues from financial investments of the SWFs in some countries have become as important as commodity revenues. Take as an example the UAE: if the estimates of the AUM by ADIA are roughly accurate, let us say in the order of US$600–700 billion, a return on its portfolio in the order of 7–8% would be on par with oil export revenues assuming oil prices at US$80 per barrel. A similar conclusion can be reached for Norway and possibly a few other smaller countries whose resources have been almost exhausted. It is also worth mentioning that not all the wealth accumulated from commodity export is managed by SWFs and other official entities. Often it is dispersed in a myriad of smaller channels not easy to detect, such as subsidiaries or 'family offices'.

What is the optimal investment strategy for a government-owned fund? This is one of the recurrent questions explicitly or implicitly asked by those who fret about the hidden agenda of SWFs. Easy questions rarely lend themselves to easy answers. It depends on what objectives are deemed optimal and what constraints the 'optimizer' faces. The optimal investment strategies of government-owned funds can be analysed through several dimensions.

SWFs that manage the revenues from a commodity or a set of commodities, whose prices are highly correlated, like hydrocarbons, must adopt a different approach from those that manage the proceeds of current account surpluses by countries with a rather well-diversified economy.

In particular, a small country exposed to the fluctuations of its main commodity export and whose population's livelihood is highly dependent on the price of this commodity should maintain a rather liquid position and forgo investments in long gestation projects.

Seen through these lenses it is evident that the behaviour of SWFs and FWFs is not much different from that of a private fund entrusted with analogous tasks. Until the end of the twentieth century a few SWFs held notable resources, but as a group their weight in financial markets was minimal and remains tiny if compared to other major classes of assets managers. In the years of the irrational exuberance of the stock markets and the dotcom euphoria, the SWFs and the FWFs played a marginal role in the financial markets and maintained a relatively low profile. But the shift of the economic centre of gravity and the emergence of a multipolar economy let new actors on the main stage, of which the SWFs are a mere subset.

The sector distribution of SWFs' assets before, during and after the acute phase of the global financial crisis shows how their investment behaviour is guided primarily by economic and financial events, not by ulterior political motives. SWFs hold a remarkably diversified investment portfolio, including real estate, financial services, energy, commodities, retail and leisure, and construction. Investments in sensitive industries such as defence or even technology are rare.

7.1 TOWARDS A MULTIPOLAR WORLD

The ascent of the SWFs stems from a process reshaping the global economy, linked primarily to the population growth in Asia, but amplified by the effect of economic reforms in China during the 1980s and 1990s. What we colloquially call 'globalization' originated from closer economic integration fostered by trade liberalization after the launch of the WTO, technology transfer, advances in communication technology and free capital movement.

The process has been so pervasive that the old classification into developed and developing economies sounds utterly old-fashioned, reflecting a reality which was prevalent until the 1990s. But even the classification of developed economies and emerging economies starts to be out of touch with reality, because a number of emerging economies have, in fact, emerged and overtaken some of those classified as developed, which in turn are sinking (Greece is just a case in point) like South America in the 1970s. So it would be more apt to talk about mature and high-growth economies.

The expanding role of SWFs reflects this secular inversion in the distribution of global wealth from mature economies, primarily the US and Europe, to countries such as China, India and Brazil which enjoy favourable demographics, and to those with sizeable natural resources such as the UAE, Norway, Australia and Russia.

The surge in capital flows that we have witnessed over the past 25 years is the fundamental propeller of this rebalancing because it has transformed the sign of the demographic variable in the equation of economic development. Fast population growth was always associated with a vicious circle of too many mouths to feed, subsistence agriculture, abysmal education levels, low savings and insufficient investment growth to lift productivity. Liberalization of capital movements gave rise to an investment surge in countries with limited domestic resources, and shallow domestic capital markets. The phenomenon first involved the so-called Asian Tigers, but it mounted as China progressively dismantled the Maoist centrally planned economy. With the fall of the Soviet Bloc the process gained additional momentum at a time when South America was also shedding decades of military autocracy and underachievement. The reforms of the semi-socialist, autarchic Indian economy in the mid-1990s, albeit circumscribed and inadequate, had nevertheless injected some dynamism into a country where, due to its sheer size, small changes produce a large impact. As all these pieces fell into place, the demographic wave that has swept the world for three decades ceased to be a liability and became an asset. In short, the perpetuation of underdevelopment due to overpopulation was shattered by the liberalization of capital flows combined with more market-oriented policies.

From the inception of the twenty-first century, the accession of China to the WTO, its consolidation as the factory of the world, the emergence of a sizeable middle class in Asia and Latin America, and the development of infrastructure also triggered an upsurge in commodity prices. The secular shift in the economic centre of gravity underwent acceleration during the Great Recession, when emerging markets became the engine of global growth, while mature economies were forced to deleverage and bring their living standards in line with their means after a decade of debt-financed growth.

Against this background the shift of SWF direct investment into emerging markets seems to be a long-term phenomenon. The surge of investments into Western banks in 2007–2008 interrupted this trend, reflecting a temporary opportunistic behaviour. The strategic focus of SWFs on emerging markets largely reflects the shifting barycentre of the global economy: as these economies upgrade their physical and human capital, their share of the global economy is destined to surge and projects in energy, commodity and infrastructure will constitute a powerful magnet for long-term investors such as SWFs.

7.2 GOVERNMENTS' ACTIVISM IN ECONOMIC AND FINANCIAL AFFAIRS

The structural imbalances in the global economy with countries maintaining a structural current account surplus and others maintaining a mirroring structural deficit has, in many instances, benefitted government-owned entities for two reasons. In countries endowed with natural resources the revenues accrue to the public coffers. In other countries, where the current account surpluses come from a broad export base, capital markets are often too limited, the monetary authority maintains a fixed peg and therefore it offsets the appreciation pressure by printing money. In both cases capital inflows end up in the central bank reserves and beyond a certain amount are often transferred to SWFs.

In other words, an increasing portion of capital flows is channelled through SWFs or other state-owned entities, because in many countries with large revenues from commodities exports and a few which have accumulated a large stock of foreign assets, the state retains a pervasive role and unfettered control over large swathes of the economy (Russia, China, GCC).[1] This contrasts with the private-sector, market-oriented framework prevalent in mature economies.[2]

---

[1] In Chapter 2 we have provided a rough estimate of the future growth of the SWFs' assets if the world economy does not experience major disruptions over the next few years.

[2] In many countries the borderline between the public and private sector is blurred and therefore is not helpful in evaluating the actions of asset managers. Actually, public entities might pursue aggressive return maximization while private ones might be more attentive to social objectives.

The activism of government-controlled institutions shot to the top of the international political agenda after decades in which, following an intense ideological and political battle, the public hand in Western countries, Latin America and especially Eastern Europe had retrenched.

The label 'Sovereign Wealth Fund' has come to denote a wide array of financial vehicles, whose common feature is the public ownership, but whose purposes, investment strategies and modus operandi vary widely. For example, as the IMF observed, 'SWFs with a stabilization objective would put more emphasis on liquidity and have a shorter-term investment horizon than SWFs with a saving objective, where liquidity needs are low'.

The political backlash, the concerns over the motives driving the strategies of SWFs and FWFs, and the calls for restraining them under various pretexts probably arose from the astonishment at the reappearance of powerful foreign public institutions in financial markets from where the domestic public hand had been painstakingly removed.

Accordingly, the issues raised in recipient countries pertain to the fundamental traits that have defined the economic systems of mature economies and that might collide with the approach followed by China, Korea, Singapore, Vietnam and Qatar (to name just a few) in their development strategy where the dividing line between the private and public economic sphere is blurred. The themes raised involve sensitive areas and legitimate concerns such as government manipulation of private markets, transparency of financial institutions, supervision of market transactions and the grip of bureaucrats on economic levers. But often the accusations selectively voiced when Western companies[3] with powerful connections see their interests affected by foreign takeover or investments in competitors are a screen for more prosaic and less noble interests.

7.3 BARBARIAN AT THE GATES OR WELCOME PARTNERS?

A key message conveyed in this book is that the characteristics of each SWF and in general of state-owned entities and their mandate are so diverse that it would be pointless to impose restrictions on their activities and acquisitions. In any case, such restrictions would be easy to circumvent by setting up an investment vehicle in, say, Luxembourg, therefore operating as an EU-based entity. In short, influence and ownership can always be concealed behind the screen of a complex corporate structure.

We feel that the controversy over greater disclosure of the activities of SWFs is a thin veneer for protectionist and, at times, paranoid arguments. Sound governance, timely reporting of deals and transparency are principles

---

[3] It is interesting to notice that in Japan virulent reactions to SWFs' acquisitions have so far been rare.

that promote better management and ultimately better returns in the long run. It is in the interest of the SWFs to abide to these principles, because openness, transparency and accountability are the best preventive cure against mediocrity, complacency and corruption, while improving decision making in any organization (and SWFs are no exception). If, in addition, openness could assuage fears over the operations of SWFs, all the better.

However the solicitations for disclosure over strategies and intentions seem either pointless or naive: strategies are just vague statements of intentions, unless they are tied to a measurable and observable benchmark. For example, if an asset manager declares that his strategy consists of targeting the S&P500, then any deviation from the stated objectives can be easily detected. But if an asset manager says that he is targeting growth companies in South America, or total returns in East Europe, how can a deviation be detected? How could one argue that the strategy has not been pursued?

These simple objections, after the 'Barbarians at the gates' reactions in the US, have helped to reduce the hysteria, as part of a turnaround in attitudes after the Lehman bankruptcy, which we have pointedly documented in this book. A foremost example is the testimony to the US Congress by Edwin Truman, a Senior Fellow at the Peterson Institute for International Economics (Truman, 2008b) where he developed a coherent argument based on six points.

1 Sovereign Wealth Funds are here to stay and likely to grow in their relative importance in the international financial system as financial globalization continues.
2 The US economy is thoroughly intertwined with the global financial system on both the asset and liability side of our balance sheet through both the private and public sectors. We are a major player in the SWF game. It follows that advocates of formally regulating SWFs should be careful what they wish for. Any regulations or other restrictions that are applied to foreign SWFs properly should be applied to our SWFs and would be applied to them by other countries.
3 The most promising approach to dealing with the SWF phenomenon is via 'reciprocal responsibility'. Countries with SWFs should embrace a voluntary international standard of best practice along the lines of my scoreboard outlined below [see Chapter 6]. Countries receiving SWF investments should strengthen the openness of their financial systems. At present more progress is being made by countries making SWF investments than by recipient countries. The financial turmoil that would result from an outbreak of financial protectionism would make recent events feel like a mere squall.
4 It is fundamentally impossible to distinguish Sovereign Wealth Funds by their degree of political motivation in their investment decisions. They are governmental entities, and governments are political.
5 SWFs do not pose a significant new threat to US economic and financial interests. As long as we put in place and maintain sound economic and

financial policies, we control our own destiny. We have adequate mechanisms to address any potential national security concerns posed by SWFs or other forms of foreign government investment in this country. At this point they appear to be minimal.

6 I am a bit uneasy about the possibility that some funds may exercise 'undue influence' in connection with foreign governmental investments in our financial institutions. I hope our existing processes can deal with the more heavily regulated portion of our financial system. Improvements in the accountability of large hedge funds and private equity firms, which I favor, could help elsewhere.

These six points mark a departure from the rhetoric on malevolent and shadowy entities and finally offer a platform that fits extremely well with the Santiago Principles and other multilateral initiatives, for example by the OECD. The cooperative framework can assuage the points of contention and the IMF IFSWF is the umbrella under which all the SWFs that have accepted the Santiago Principles can discuss practical implementation. Countries with sizeable SWFs should take the responsibility to influence the process that is shaping the new financial architecture to promote their views and insert their needs in the list of priorities.

An area where more activism could be warranted is the implementation of the reciprocity principle. SWFs or other publicly owned entities from countries whose economies and financial markets are not fully open to foreign investors might face a tough challenge in their claim not to be treated differently by recipient countries. Investment openness and freedom to acquire ownership (or a controlling stake) should be reciprocal.

7.4 THE END OF THE SAVINGS GLUTS AND THE COMING ERA OF CAPITAL SCARCITY

We repeatedly stressed that SWFs and FWFs receive funding essentially from the foreign currency reserves of the central bank. The difference between reserve management and a global portfolio consists of two elements: currency allocation and liquidity. A central bank needs to maintain the bulk of its reserves in three or four currencies (some add gold ingots) with a preponderance of low-risk liquid short-maturity sovereign bonds. SWFs and FWFs face no such constraints and therefore allocate their portfolio according to their risk-return preferences across global assets, currency exposure and liquidity characteristics. This process diverts a sizeable chunk of international capital flows from mature economies (to which reserve management is skewed) to high-growth economies with repercussions that at present are not fully grasped. FWFs especially must display a tendency to be overweight in high-growth economies in order to pursue their mandate and are likely to assign less importance to liquidity, which is a characteristic of developed financial markets. Indeed they are encouraged by their Boards to act as private equity funds, i.e. supplying liquidity in capital-starved economies and investing in so-called hard assets.

As populations age in the West, Japan and in the not-so-distant future even in China, more savings will have to be invested in bonds to match pension liabilities. Furthermore the deleveraging of Western financial institutions will dry up the pool of risky capital and reduce the liquidity generated through the swollen shadow banking system.

Actually the regulatory reforms, under the impulse of the G20 and the Financial Stability Board, will have serious repercussions on the availability of financial capital worldwide. In addition to the various regulatory initiatives under implementation covering issues ranging from the regulation of over-the-counter derivatives to the so-called too-big-to-fail (i.e. the threat posed by systemic financial institutions to global financial stability), Basel 3 means a substantial increase in capital requirements for banks.

The new capital adequacy rules will be introduced gradually during the current decade and will come fully into force by 2019. One of the key implications of Basel 3 is that financial institutions will have to raise a substantial amount of capital (in addition to that already raised during the crisis to cover the losses on toxic assets). We recalled a report by McKinsey estimating €1.1 trillion of additional Tier 1 capital, for EU banks and about €600 billion for US banks (McKinsey Global Institute, 2011).

As we pointed out in Chapter 3, the impact, already felt across the financial sector, will make SWFs and FWFs major suppliers of long-term capital and therefore their returns will depend on capital scarcity, which determines its cost. This issue is interwoven with the reversal of the so-called savings glut which is likely to unravel as the world population ages and infrastructure investments in the high-growth economies intensify.

The consequences of Basel 3 will in all likelihood be a restricted access of emerging market companies (perceived as more risky) to Western banks. This could open up interesting opportunities for growth of international banks in emerging markets especially in the GCC, China and India. If the Chinese financial sector reform and the cleaning of NPL proceed steadily, banks from China and other developing nations will emerge internationally, especially if the Shanghai Stock Exchange opens up in earnest to foreign capitals and the Hong Kong Exchange allows listings in renminbi.

7.5 TOWARDS A MULTICURRENCY REGIME

The financial crisis of 2007–2008 and the fiscal crisis of 2010–2011 have eroded the incumbent advantage of the US dollar as an international currency and have reinforced the political willingness of emerging markets to accelerate the diversification of their FX reserves away from the US dollar. In economic terms, the world has already moved to a multipolar regime, with high-growth economies accounting for the bulk of global growth; the dominant role of the US dollar in international finance seems anachronistic and the seeds for a shift to a multipolar currency regime are already sowed. According to some, the internalization of the RMB and its ascent to the status of international reserve currency might happen much faster than currently thought, even before the end of 2020.

As recently noted in an editorial in the *Financial Times*, 'given the assumption that the dollar will depreciate and that the US government will issue far more debt to inflate its way out of its fiscal hole, investors from abroad are likely to seek to purchase more hard assets and fewer financial investments'.[4]

The hegemonic position of an international currency derives primarily from the relative size of its underlying economy, its openness and the size of its financial markets. It is reinforced by the legal system, the military reach of the issuing government and the long-term stability in purchasing power over goods, services and assets that it affords (in other words sound and sustainable macroeconomic and fiscal fundamentals).

The rise of the dollar as the principal international reserve currency was a natural consequence of the US ascendance to the top of world economies combined with the solidity of its political system. However, the transition from the dominance of the British pound to that of the US dollar was rather slow even after the 1870s when the US had become the largest national economy. One can argue that the US dollar dislodged the British pound as the dominant currency only when the gold standard came under strain and was abandoned by Britain in 1931, while the US re-established the dollar peg to gold at \$35 per ounce. In short, the size of the US economy was paramount, but the stability conferred by the backing of gold was the tipping point that led to a dollar-centric system.

How important is the relative size in underpinning the status of a reserve currency? The answer can be put in relation to the insight by the Belgian economist Robert Triffin[5] in the 1960s that a country whose national currency serves as reserve currency must run a current account deficit to supply the global liquidity required for international transactions.

The economy must be large enough to sustain a current account deficit sufficient to finance international transactions, but the deficit cannot be so large as to make the ensuing debt service unsustainable. In other words, any country that issues a reserve currency must be willing to import more than it

---

[4] Earlier in this book, we have noted how SWFs' direct investments are on the rise and this is a trend that will accelerate in the future; CIC is increasingly becoming more similar to a private equity house rather than an asset manager and soon the bulk of its activities will largely consist of the direct acquisition of hard assets in advanced and emerging economies.

[5] See Robert Triffin (1960) *Gold and the Dollar Crisis: The Future of Convertibility*, Yale University Press, New Haven.

exports, but is exposed to the risk that its external debt burden will undermine its stability.[6]

To be accurate, the liquidity could also be provided by a deficit of the private capital flows (and indeed this was the case for the US in the 1960s) or it could be supplied by entities in other countries that issue liabilities denominated in the reserve currency (as happened in the 1970s). But in practice these are exceptions and in fact the bulk of international liquidity over the past two decades has been supplied by a widening current account deficit in the US. Therefore the key issue is whether the US can continue to provide the indispensable volume of assets. The answer can hardly be positive, because the US deficit is clearly unsustainable (and the current US administration is determined to reduce it as a matter of priority), while emerging countries continue to accumulate reserves at a pace close to their (growing) current account surpluses. In plain words, if the US adds further to its external liabilities, the privilege of borrowing internationally in its own currency might be jeopardized.

Some figures might help to illustrate the problem. According to WTO data, in 1948 total world merchandise export (excluding re-export) was US$58 billion; in 1971, at the time of the Bretton Woods demise, total world export had grown to US$354 billion; in 1995 when the trade liberalization started to take off after the launch of the WTO, the figure had reached US$5.2 trillion and in 2008 total exports touched the highest level at US$16 trillion, to drop to US$12.5 trillion in 2009. To this we need to add trade in commercial services which were about US$300 billion in 1980 (when the WTO series starts) to almost US$4 trillion in 2008 and a little more than US$3 trillion in 2009.

The external liabilities of the US, measured as the difference between foreign assets owned by US residents and US assets owned by non-residents went from almost zero in the early 1990s to almost US$4 trillion in 2008 and then declined sharply to just short of US$3 trillion (Figure 1.1 and Table 7.1).

On the other hand, global foreign currency reserves by central banks amounted to US$8.1 trillion by the end of 2009 according to the US Treasury, with China having amassed US$2.4 trillion, enough to cover the short-term debt of the 12 largest reserve-holding emerging markets and still maintain an adequate buffer in case of a crisis.

It is also worth pointing out that other phases of rapid large reserves accumulation (such as at the end of the 1960s and the end of the 1970s) have

---

[6] Actually this point has not been uncontroversial. Kindleberger (1978), in his works on the Great Depression effect, concluded that hegemony is conducive to systemic stability, as a hegemonic power would be able to internalize the externalities of a global public good, such as an international currency. However, Kindleberger's analysis was suitable for a situation in which an economy is dominant. With the emergence of several great economic powers, it is very much in question today. Also it has been pointed out that central bank reserves since 1999 have increased also in euro, yen and Swiss franc, but that none of these economies had a current account deficit. The apparent contradictions can be explained by the fact that the financial sector in these countries issued liabilities in their domestic currencies and invested in dollar denominated assets.

Table 7.1 Components of changes in foreign-owned assets in the US with direct investment at market value, 1989–2010 (US$ millions)

Year	Position beginning	Financial flows (a)	Valuation adjustments		Other changes[2] (d)	Total (a+b+c+d)	Changes in financial derivatives[3]	Position ending
			Price changes (b)	Exchange rate changes[1] (c)				
1989	1,986,887	222,777	137,439	-1,046	37,891	397,061	—	2,383,948
1990	2,383,948	139,357	-72,481	10,787	-18,003	59,660	—	2,443,608
1991	2,443,608	108,222	178,682	-2,464	-14,105	270,335	—	2,713,943
1992	2,713,943	168,349	46,560	-8,078	-22,150	184,681	—	2,898,624
1993	2,898,624	279,759	62,608	-7,181	-20,617	314,569	—	3,213,193
1994	3,213,193	303,174	-109,718	12,873	5,925	212,254	—	3,425,447
1995	3,425,447	435,102	381,972	12,059	-12,454	816,679	—	4,242,126
1996	4,242,126	547,885	231,589	-8,723	-33,733	737,018	—	4,979,144
1997	4,979,144	704,452	548,223	-26,524	-37,943	1,188,208	—	6,167,352
1998	6,167,352	420,794	656,726	11,339	-43,311	1,045,548	—	7,212,900
1999	7,212,900	742,210	472,443	-4,324	-21,283	1,189,046	—	8,401,946
2000	8,401,946	1,038,224	-439,082	-28,023	-35,048	536,071	—	8,938,017
2001	8,938,017	782,870	-489,886	-17,229	11,762	287,517	—	9,225,534
2002	9,225,534	795,161	-783,562	35,228	-56,786	-9,959	—	9,215,575
2003	9,215,575	858,303	775,363	68,781	-312,259	1,390,188	—	10,605,763
2004	10,605,763	1,533,201	278,469	39,532	111,362	1,962,564	—	12,568,327
2005[4]	12,568,327	1,247,347	-66,777	-50,596	1,107,391	2,237,365	—	14,805,692
2006	14,805,692	2,065,169	529,069	44,373	267,433	2,906,044	47,045	17,758,781
2007[r]	17,758,781	2,064,642	243,346	80,144	-54,549	2,333,583	1,308,701	21,401,065
2008[r]	21,401,065	431,406	-2,498,166	-92,130	91,795	-2,067,095	3,479,955	22,813,925
2009[r]	22,813,925	335,793	983,617	85,051	-148,064	1,256,397	-2,601,778	21,468,544
2010[p]	21,468,544	1,245,736	757,200	-12,075	-57,035	1,933,826	176,451	23,578,821

[1] Represents gains or losses on foreign-currency-denominated assets and liabilities due to their revaluation at current exchange rates.

[2] Includes changes in coverage, capital gains and losses of direct investment affiliates, and other adjustments to the value of assets and liabilities.

[3] Represents the total change in the fair values of financial derivatives, first available in 2006. Financial flows and valuation adjustment components of the total change in fair market values of financial derivatives are not separately available.

[4] The 'Other changes' and 'Position ending' for 2005 include new derivatives position data.

Source: US Department of Commerce, Bureau of Economic Analysis.

led to monetary or financial crises because the need to recycle these funds in the economy led to imprudent lending practices by banks (e.g. the sovereign defaults in Latin America in the 1980s).

A solution to the increasing inability of the US to provide the reserve currency could be envisaged along two hypotheses: either another or a few other reserve currencies emerge or a new international unit of account (an international currency) managed by a supranational institution needs to be designed (Saidi and Scacciavillani, 2010).

The former case seemed to be arising with the introduction of the euro, a currency backed by a diversified economy larger than the US, capable of withstanding major shocks. However, the euro area has not been able to match these expectations because it has largely failed to integrate its financial markets, and because the ECB, following the tradition of the Bundesbank, has been cold, even hostile, to the international role of the euro lest it would conflict with its overriding mandate of ensuring price stability. So the euro area does not have deep and broad financial markets and does not supply sufficient liquid and safe assets to satisfy the demand by reserves-accumulating central banks and by the international banking and financial systems. The ascendance of the euro is also constrained by a government bond market fragmented along national lines, unfavourable demographics, and anaemic growth. If one adds the dysfunctional institutional framework after the emasculation of the Stability and Growth Pact, the absence of a lender of last resort (although the current crisis has forced the ECB to act as one by injecting massive liquidity in the banking system and buying government debt in a violation of the Amsterdam Treaty), and a lack of centralized decision making on fiscal policy, it is evident that the appeal of the euro is not widespread. It must also be noted that the currencies of the largest surplus countries in Asia are currently tied to the US dollar while their exporters trade primarily in that currency, so they prefer to hold US dollar-denominated assets.

We need to add that the world's second largest economy issues a currency which is not freely convertible and the Chinese financial markets, including the government debt market, are at present far from deep, liquid or well regulated, and are not accessible by foreign investors. A complete convertibility of the yuan is several years away according to most analysts.[7] In the meantime capital controls and other regulations continue to cause a steady rise in China's foreign currency reserves, at an average monthly rate of US$10 billion. Finally the other major economy, Japan, maintains a large current account surplus so it does not provide substantial international liquidity either and has the second largest stock of foreign currency reserves at over US$1 trillion.

---

[7] There are signs that the Chinese authorities have come to the conclusion that the capital account needs to be liberalized faster than previously envisaged. On 31 December, China's central bank Governor Zhou Xiaochuan in an interview with the magazine *Caixin* (picked up by Koh Gui Quing and Aileen Wang of the news agency Reuters, 'China moving to more convertible yuan') asserted that China 'is not that far from capital account convertibility'.

In conclusion, an orderly transition towards a multicurrency world requires some profound institutional changes in the current international monetary arrangements, in the absence of which the transition risks to be disruptive.

More recently the Chinese authorities and the G20 have renewed the emphasis on the Special Drawing Rights (SDR). A flurry of research and policy papers has reinforced the message[8] with the IMF already developing a framework.[9] The G20 Summit in Toronto supported a general allocation of the IMF's SDR equivalent to $250 billion to boost global liquidity. A general SDR allocation amounting to the equivalent of US$250 billion was made on 28 August 2009. The equivalent of nearly US$100 billion went to emerging markets and developing countries, of which Lower Income Countries received over US$18 billion. To support SDR liquidity, the IMF has substantially expanded the capacity of voluntary arrangements to buy and sell SDR in exchange for currencies in the SDR basket. The G20 also urged a speedy ratification of the Fourth Amendment to the IMF's Charter, first proposed in 1997 to make the allocation of SDRs more equitable. The Fourth Amendment became effective for all members on 10 August 2009. As a result, a special one-off allocation of SDRs, amounting to about US$33 billion, was made on 9 September 2009. On 21 April 2010, the IMF's Executive Board approved measures to facilitate the mobilization of Poverty Reduction and Growth Trust (PRGT) loan contributions, including those from the existing SDR resources. As of 21April 2010, pledges of PRGT loan contributions amounting to SDR 7.6 billion had been made, of which SDR 6.1 billion were to be provided in SDRs by six countries.

7.6 A PROPOSAL TO ALLAY FEARS OVER TRANSPARENCY

Most of the criticism over SWFs has been expressed in terms of transparency. This term is used to designate different concepts often in different contexts to the point of being extremely ambiguous. For example it is unclear what is meant by transparency over the investment 'strategy'. Asserting that a fund adopts a 'conservative' or 'aggressive' strategy is rather vague. Likewise, to hold a 'balanced portfolio' would not dispel fears that the acquisition of a controlling stake in a listed company is motivated by extra-economic motives.

In many areas specific transparency principles are already enforced: for example reporting on holdings of listed companies beyond a certain limit is mandated by stock markets authorities and national regulations. Hence, a SWF

---

[8] See for example Bergsten (2009), the report by the UN Commission presided by Joseph Stiglitz (summarized in Stiglitz, 2009), advocating an expanded SDR.

[9] See the remarks by then IMF Managing Director Strauss-Kahn in Strauss-Kahn (2010), suggesting that the IMF could issue SDRs as an international currency, and Mateos y Lagos *et al*. (2009), who ask whether the size and volatility of today's international capital markets are compatible with the supply of liquidity by a single country.

has to inform the financial supervision authority and stick to the regulations as does any other investor, private, public or institutional.

In order to reassure various constituencies we suggest that a large SWF wishing to display a cooperative attitude could split its asset into different vehicles. Actually some of these vehicles, which would be a separate entity from the original SWF, could be open to private investors. In other words SWFs and FWFs could launch separate funds which would be completely transparent under a regulatory structure that imposes reporting obligations similar to those of other funds open to various classes of investors.

In part this is already taking place. Many SWFs invest in funds and alternative investments (a definition that encompasses hedge funds, private equity funds or real estate funds). They participate under the same conditions as the other partners and therefore do not enjoy any favourable treatment.

But they could go a step further and become themselves a promoter of funds to which they could invite qualified investors. CIC is already operating along these lines – allocating sizeable funds to CITIC, a vehicle based in Hong Kong – which are deployed in various cub funds with an industry or a geographical focus. Limited Partners (LP) in these funds might be institutional investors, other SWFs or banks.

Furthermore one could envisage that investment vehicles be open to individual investors and citizens of the countries where the SWF originates, so they could benefit from the opportunities available to large players.

The involvement of private partners in the capital and the initiatives of SWFs would also strengthen the functional independence of managers from political interference and at the same time encourage better communications and investor relations. At that point acquisitions in sensitive industries or those that could stir nationalistic campaigns could be channelled through the vehicles operating under market-driven principles and standard international transparency rules.

7.7 THE NEW RESPONSIBILITIES ON THE GLOBAL SCENE

Unlike other investment vehicles, SWFs can focus on long-term income growth and/or long-term capital appreciation both in their initial valuation and in the subsequent exit strategies.

Nevertheless the mantra that SWFs are primarily financial investors – meaning that they do not take operational responsibilities – has often contributed to some negligence in the management of their investments. We have argued that absentee landowners are not an example to follow and SWFs would be better off more closely following both the day-to-day operations and the strategic plans of the companies where they invest.

But beyond the microeconomic aspects, they must understand that with prominence come broader responsibilities. Their role as important actors on the global stage requires that they engage in the debate on the new financial architecture. In other words they should not confine themselves to the role of decision takers in the governance of global financial markets, but participate in decision making. They are stakeholders in the soundness and efficiency of capital markets and hence should use their influence.

The SWFs have an interest in the solidity of the global financial markets because they are fully exposed to the shockwaves and as creditors will be called to shoulder heavy losses again in the case of another market plunge. They need to be aware of dysfunctions in banking and financial markets, primarily their tendency to propagate boom and bust. Hence they have a vested interest in defining countercyclical capital adequacy ratios and leverage.

In short, SWFs need to play a role in the design of the new financial regulation framework. More generally it would be in the interest of SWFs to envisage an alternative design of the financial architecture. They could be the backbone of the new linkages among well-regulated peripheral financial centres which would develop into a network capable of by-passing the major financial hubs that have presided over the world in the twentieth century and that at present are entangled in a difficult process of deleveraging and loss pairing.

Such an arrangement would certainly be more robust to crisis and would remove the dangers of contagion from one major financial centre. And if Basel 3 does not evolve into a sound regulatory framework it could be wise for SWFs and their home countries to agree on an alternative approach and demand that financial intermediaries coveting their business comply with it. SWFs have three advantages vis-à-vis other asset managers: they are not very leveraged, they can adopt a longer term strategy, and they do not need to follow the herd behaviour that besets most financial institutions due to ill-designed capital adequacy ratios, ratings and benchmarks. Hence they could be more inclined to follow contrarian strategies and to step in when others are forced to retrench.

Furthermore SWFs can take advantage of their sovereign nature to cut through the swamps of regulatory hurdles, hostility to the private sector, resistance to foreign investors, obstruction to entrepreneurs and other poor business environment features typical of the poorest and worst-managed countries.

The counterpart to more activism and more dynamic investment choices is better risk management. Given the areas where the SWFs enjoy more advantages over other financial players, what kind of risk management tools would be more appropriate? Here the answer is not straightforward, but as global players they should be at the forefront of establishing a more sophisticated risk function and should devote a great deal of resources to monitoring the early signs of turning points.

The crisis has shattered the traditional risk management approach based on VaR and other simplistic data-driven models. The new environment requires a holistic risk-management framework encompassing several scenarios:

specifically they must supplement conventional asset-class diversification, rotation themes and currency exposure with better macroeconomic research and intelligence, setting in place the cost-effective management of tail risks which are likely to become more frequent.

Only with superior analytical tools and human resources dedicated to the navigation of unchartered waters will SWFs be able to disentangle technical and fundamental factors over the long term. The key is not avoiding risk, but understanding the sources and recognizing when it has materialized. This requires spatial outreach, research prowess, adaptability to a fast changing environment, sophisticated vision and unconventional valuation models.

Bibliography

Abu Dhabi Investment Authority (2010) ADIA Review 2009, http://www.adia.ae/En/
News/media_review.aspx (2 February 2012).

Abu Dhabi Investment Authority (2011) ADIA Review 2010, http://www.adia.ae/En/
News/media_review.aspx (2 February 2012).

Adrian, T. and Shin, H. S. (2008) Liquidity, Monetary Policy, and Financial Cycles,
Current Issues in Economics and Finance, **14** (1), January/February.

Adrian, T. and Shin, H. S. (2009) The Shadow Banking System: Implications for Financial Regulation. Federal Reserve Bank of New York Staff Reports, No. 382.

Alaska Permanent Fund (2011) 2010 Annual Report. www.apfc.org (2 February 2012).

Anderlini, J. (2010) China Fund Bond Sale Faces Criticism, *Financial Times*, 24
August.

Asian Development Bank (2011) Asia 2050: Realizing the Asian Century. Asian Development Bank, http://beta.adb.org/publications/asia-2050-realizing-asian-century
(2 February 2012).

Austvik, O. G. (2007) Reflections on Permanent Funds: the Norwegian Pension Fund
Experience, http://www.gordonfn.org/resfiles/Forum_Permanent_Funds_indd.pdf
(2 February 2012).

Avendaño, R. (2010) Sovereign Wealth Fund Investments: Firm-level Impacts, Diversification and Natural Endowments, Paris School of Economics, Paris.

Avendaño, R. and Santiso, J. (2009) Are Sovereign Wealth Funds' Investments Politically Biased? A Comparison with Mutual Funds. Social Science Research Network,
http://ssrn.com/abstract=1525545 (2 February 2012).

Bagattini, G. Y (2001) The Political Economy of Stabilisation Funds: Measuring their
Success in Resource-Dependent Countries, *IDS Working Paper, Volume 2011, No.
356.*

Balding, C. (2008) A Portfolio Analysis of Sovereign Wealth Funds, mimeo, University of California, Irvine. Social Science Research Network, http://ssrn.com/
abstract=1141531 (2 February 2012).

Bank for International Settlements (BIS) (2011a) *Portfolio and Risk Management for
Central Banks and Sovereign Wealth Funds*. Proceedings of the Joint Conference
organized by the ECB and the World Bank in Basel, 2–3 November 2010. BIS
Papers 58.

Bank for International Settlements (BIS) (2011b) Resolution Policies and Framework – Progress So Far. Basel Committee on Banking Supervision.

Barnett, S. and Ossowski, R. (2003) Operational Aspects of Fiscal Policy In Oil-producing Countries, in *Fiscal Policy Formulation and Implementation in Oil-Producing Countries* (eds J. Davis, R. Ossowski and A. Fedelino), International Monetary Fund, Washington, DC. Also issued as *IMF Working Paper No. 02/177.*

Beck, R. and Fidora, M. (2008) The Impact of Sovereign Wealth Funds on Global Financial Markets, *ECB Occasional Paper No. 91.* Available at Social Science Research Network: http://ssrn.com/abstract=1144482 (4 March 2012).

Behrendt, S. (2010) Sovereign Wealth Funds and the Santiago Principles: Where Do They Stand? Carnegie Endowment for International Peace, *Carnegie Papers No. 22, May 2010.*

Behrendt, S. (2011) SWFs and 'Green Growth', in *Braving the New World: Sovereign Wealth Fund Investment in the Uncertain Times of 2010* (eds V. Barbary and B. Bortolotti), Monitor.

Behrendt, S. and Sharp, D. (2011) The Libyan Investment Authority: Sanctions and Post-Conflict Reconstruction, Analysis Sovereign Wealth Funds, GeoEconomica Political Risk Management.

Bergsten, C. F. (2009). *The Long-Term International Economic Position of the United States. Special Report 20*, Peterson Institute for International Economics.

Berkelaar, A. B., Coche, J. and Nyholm, K. (eds) (2010) *Central Bank Reserves and Sovereign Wealth Funds*, Palgrave Macmillan.

Bernstein, S., Lerner, J. and Shoar, A. (2009) The Investment Strategies of SWF. Nota di Lavoro 025.2009, Fondazione Eni Enrico Mattei, Milan, Italy, http://www.feem.it/getpage.aspx?id=1883&sez=Publications&padre=73 (3 February 2012).

Betts, P. and, Nakamoto, M. (2009) China Backs New Champions to Conquer the West, *Financial Times*, June 10.

Bjerkholt, O. (2002) Fiscal Rule Suggestions for Economies with Non-renewable Resources. University of Oslo.

Black, F. and Scholes, M. S. (1973) The Pricing of Options and Corporate Liabilities, *Journal of Political Economy*, **81**, 637–54.

Blanchard, J.-M. F. (2010) Chinese MNCs as China's New Long March: a review and critique of the western literature, *Journal of Chinese Political Science*, **16** (1), 91.

Blanchard, J.-M. F. (2011) China's grand strategy and money muscle: the potentialities and pratfalls of China's Sovereign Wealth Fund and Renminbi Policies, *Chinese Journal of International Politics*, **4**, 31–53.

Bodie Z. and Briere, M. (2011) Sovereign Wealth and Risk Management, *Boston University School of Management Research Paper Series, 2011–8.*

Bracke, T., Bussière, M., Fidora, M. and Straub, R. (2008) A Framework for Assessing Global Imbalances, *ECB Occasional Paper No. 78.*

Bremmer, I. (2010) *The End of the Free Market: Who Wins the War Between States and Corporations?*, Penguin, London.

Brender, A. and Pisani, F. (2010) *Global Imbalances and the Collapse of Globalised Finance*, CEPS Paperback, Centre for European Policy Studies, Brussels.

Brown, A., Papaioannou, M. and Petrova, I. (2010) Macrofinancial Linkages of the Strategic Asset Allocation of Commodity-Based Sovereign Wealth Funds, *IMF Working Paper WP/10/9*, http://www.imf.org/external/pubs/ft/wp/2010/wp1009.pdf (2 February 2012).

Buyuksahin, B. and Harris, J. H. (2009) The Role of Speculators in the Crude Oil Futures Markets, *Working Paper,* US Commodity Futures Trading Commission Commodity.

Caballero, R. and Krishnamurthy, A. (2009) Global Imbalances and Financial Fragility, *American Economic Review Papers and Proceedings*, **99** (2), 584–88.

Canadian International Council (2010) The Dragon Returns: Canada and China's Quest for Energy Security, *China Papers, No. 19.*

Carroll, C. D. and Jeanne, O. (2009) A Tractable Model of Precautionary Reserves, Net Foreign Assets, or Sovereign Wealth Funds, *Peterson Institute Working Paper No. 09–10*, Washington, DC.

Castelli, M. (2008) Sovereign Wealth Funds: Review of Policy and Regulatory Developments, Paper presented at the first UBS Conference on Sovereign Wealth Funds, Abu Dhabi.

Castelli, M. (2010) Sovereign Wealth Funds and Clean Technology: The Masdar Initiative, in *Environmental Alpha, Institutional Investors and Climate Change* (ed. A. A. Cavello), John Wiley & Sons, Hoboken.

Castelli, M. (2011) Sovereign Wealth Funds, in *Investing in 2012*, UBS Global Asset Management Research, November 2011.

Central Bank Trinidad and Tobago (2010) Heritage Stabilization Fund, *Quarterly Report July–September 2010.*

China Investment Corporation (2010) Annual report 2009, http://www.china-inv.cn (2 February 2012).

China Investment Corporation (2011) Annual report 2010, http://www.china-inv.cn (2 February 2012).

Cohen, B. J. (2008) Sovereign Wealth Funds and National Security: The Great Trade-off. Paper presented at the Annual Meeting of the ISA's 50th Annual Convention Exploring the Past, Anticipating the Future, 15 February 2009, New York.

Danielsson, J., Embrechts, P., Goodhart, C., Keating, C., Muennich, F., Renault, O. and Shin, H. S. (2001) An Academic Response to Basel II, *Special Paper No. 130, May*. LSE Financial Markets Group.

Das, U. S., Mazerai, A. and van den Hoorn, H. (eds) (2010) *Economics of Sovereign Wealth Funds Issues for Policymakers*, International Monetary Fund, Washington, DC.

Davis, J. M., Ossowski, R., Daniel, J. and Barnett, S. (2001) Stabilization and Savings Funds for non-renewable Resources: experience and fiscal policy implications, *IMF Occasional Paper No. 205, 2001.*

Dinmore, G. and Segreti, G. (2010) China Launches Investment Drive in Italy, *Financial Times*, 7 October.

Dixon, A. and Monk, A. H. B (2010) Rethinking the Sovereign in Sovereign Wealth Funds, *Transactions of the Institute of British Geographers*, **37** (1), 104–117.

EDHEC-RISK Institute (2010) Asset-liability Management Decisions for Sovereign Wealth Funds, http://www.edhec-risk.com/edhec_publications/all_publications/RISKReview.2010-10-26.3627/attachments/EDHEC_Publication_ALM_Decisions_for_SWF_DB_F.pdf (2 February 2012).

EDHEC-RISK Institute (2011) An Integrated Approach to Sovereign Wealth Risk Management, http://www.edhec-risk.com/edhec_publications/all_publications/RISKReview.2011-07-07.4408/attachments/EDHEC-Risk_Publication_Integrated_Approach_to_Sovereign_Wealth_Risk_Management.pdf (2 February 2012).

Eichengreen, B. (2011) *Exorbitant Privilege, The Rise and Fall of the Dollar*, Oxford University Press.

El-Erian, M. (2008) *When Markets Collide*, McGraw-Hill, New York.

Embrechts, P., Furrer, H., Kaufmann, R. (2009) Different Kinds of Risk, in *Handbook of Financial Time Series* (eds Andersen, Davis, Kreiss, and Mikosch), pp. 729–751, Springer, Berlin.

Enrich, D., Sidel, R. and Craig, S. (2008) How Wall Street Firms Reached out to Asia, *Asian Wall Street Journal*, 17 January, p. 19.

Ernst & Young (2011) *Ernst & Young's 2011 Africa Attractiveness Survey*.

European Commission (2008) A Common European Approach to Sovereign Wealth Funds. Communication from the commission to the European Parliament, the Council, the European Economic and Social Committee and the Committee of the regions, Com (2008) 115, Brussels.

Fama, E. F. and French, K. R. (2003) The Capital Asset Pricing Model: Theory and Evidence, *CRSP Working Paper No. 550*; *Tuck Business School Working Paper No. 03–26*. Social Science Research Network: http://ssrn.com/abstract=440920 or doi:10.2139/ssrn.440920 (2 February 2012)

Fisher, I. (1933) The debt-deflation theory of great depressions, *Econometrica*, **1** (4), 337–57.

Flood, R. and Marion, N. (2002) Holding International Reserves in Era of High Capital Mobility, *IMF Working Paper 02/62*.

Foster, V., Butterfield, W., Chen, C. and Pushak, N. (2008) Building Bridges: China's Growing Role as Infrastructure Financier for Africa, *Trends and Policy Options, Infrastucture*, No. 5.

Franklin, A. and Carletti, E. (2008) Financial System: Shock Absorber or Amplifier?, *BIS Working Papers No. 25, July*.

Friedman, T. L. (2006) *The World is Flat*, 2nd edn. Penguin, London.

Future Fund (2010) Annual Report 2009/10, http://www.futurefund.gov.au (2 February 2012).

Future Fund (2011) Annual Report 2010/11, http://www.futurefund.gov.au (2 February 2012).

Gelb, A. and Grassman, S. (2008) *Confronting the Oil Curse*, World Bank, Washington DC.

GIC (2011) Report on the Management of the Government's Portfolio for the Year 2010/11, Singapore, http://www.gic.com.sg/data/pdf/GIC_Report_2011.pdf (2 February 2012).

Gilson, R. J. and Milhaupt, C. J. (2008) Sovereign Wealth Funds and Corporate Governance: A Minimalist Response to the New Merchantilism, *Rock Center for Corporate Governance Stanford University Working Paper Series No. 26; Stanford University Law and Economics Olin Working Paper No. 355; Columbia University Law and Economics Working Paper No. 328*.

Goldman Sachs Global Economics Group (2007) *BRICs and Beyond*, London: Goldman Sachs.

Goodhart, C. and Persaud, A. (2008) How to Avoid the Next Crash, *Financial Times*, 30 January.

Gordon, L. C. and Monk, A. H. B. (2009) *The Oxford Survey of Sovereign Wealth Funds*, Asset Managers, Centre for Employment, Work and Finance, School of Geography and the Environment, University of Oxford.

Gordon, L. C. and Monk, A. H. B. (2010) Sovereign Wealth Funds: Form and Function in the 21st Century, *Fondazione Enrico Mattei Working Papers, Paper 528*.

Gordon, L. C. and Monk, A. H. B. (2011) Modernity, Institutional Innovation, and the Adoption of Sovereign Wealth Funds in the Gulf States, *Oxford University, School of Geography and the Environment, WPG 11–02*.

Grennes, T. J. (2009) The Volatility of Sovereign Wealth Funds, *Global Economy Journal*, **9** (3), Article 7.

Gruenig, B. (2008) Does the Sovereign Wealth Fund Debate Illustrate Problems of Global Economic Governance in Dealing with Emerging Global Issues?, Dissertation submitted to the London School of economics and Political Science, Master in Global Politics.

Haberly, D. (2011) Strategic Sovereign Wealth Fund Investment and the New Alliance Capitalism: A Network Mapping Investigation, *Environment and Planning, A*, **43** (8) 1833–52.

Hamilton, D. J. (2009) Causes and Consequences of the Oil Shock of 2007–08, *Brookings Papers on Economic Activity*, pp. 215–61.

Hatton, K. and Pistor, K. (2011) Maximizing Autonomy in the Shadow of Great Powers: The Political Economy of Sovereign Wealth Funds, *The Centre for Law and Economic Studies, Columbia University, WP 395*.

Hong Kong Monetary Authority (2011) Annual Report 2010, http://www.hkma.gov.hk (2 February 2012).

Hotelling, H. (1931) The Economics of Exhaustible Resources, *Journal of Political Economy*, **39**, 137–75.

IFSWF (2011) IFSWF Members' Experiences in the Application of the Santiago Principles. Report prepared by IFSWF Sub-Committee 1 and Secretariat in collaboration with the members of the IFSWF.

Ilmanen, A. (2011) *Expected Returns: An Investor's Guide to Harvesting Market Rewards*, John Wiley & Sons, Chichester.

IMF (2007) *Guide on Resource Revenue Transparency*, IMF, Washington DC.

IMF (2008a) IMF Intensifies Work on Sovereign Wealth Funds, *IMF Survey, March 4*, http://www.imf.org/external/pubs/ft/survey/so/2008/POL03408A.htm (2 February 2012).

IMF (2008b) Sovereign Wealth Funds: Current Institutional and Operational Practices, *WP/08/254*.

IMF (2010) *Economics of Sovereign Wealth Funds, Issues for Policy Makers* (eds U. S. Das, A. Mazarei and H. van der Hoorn), International Monetary Fund.

IMF (2011) Investment Objectives of Sovereign Wealth Funds – A Shifting Paradigm, *WP/11/19*.

Irwin, S. H. and Sanders, D. R. (2010) The Impact of Index and Swap Funds on Commodity Futures Markets: Preliminary Results, *OECD Food, Agriculture and Fisheries Working Papers, No. 27*. DOI: 10.1787/5kmd40wl1t5f-en.

IWG (2008a) Sovereign Wealth Funds: Generally Accepted Principles and Practices 'Santiago Principles', http://www.iwg-swf.org/ (3 February 2012).

IWG (2008b) Sovereign Wealth Funds: Current Institutional and Operational Practices. Prepared by the International Working Group of Sovereign Wealth Funds Secretariat in collaboration with the members of the IWG15 September 2008.

Jadresic, E. (2007) The Cost–Benefit Approach to Reserve Adequacy: The Case of Chile, in *Central Bank Reserve Management* (eds A. F. P. Bakker and I. R. Y. van Herpt), Edward Elgar.

Jeanne O. and Ranciere, R. (2006) The Optimal Level of International Reserves for Emerging Market Countries: Formulas and Application, *IMF Working Paper WP/06/229*.

Jen, S. (2007) Sovereign Wealth Funds: What They Are and What's Happening, *World Economics*, **8** (4), 1–7.

Johnson, S. (2007) The Rise of Sovereign Wealth Funds, *Finance and Development*, **44** (3), September.

Jorion, P. (1997) *Value at Risk*, Irwin, Chicago.

Kaldor, N. (1938) The Cobweb Theorem, *Quarterly Journal of Economics*, **52** (2), 255–80.

Kaufmann, R. (2005) *Long-term Risk Management*, Proceedings of the 15th, International AFIR Colloquium, Zurich, Switzerland.

KCIC (2011) The New Silk Road: Asia and the Middle East Rediscover Trade and Investment Opportunities. www.kcic-asia.com/research (3 February 2012).

Keating, A. (2006) *Power, Politics and the Hidden History of Arabian Oil*, Saqi, London, UK and San Francisco, CA.

Kern, S. (2008) SWFs and Foreign Investment Policies – An Update, Deutsche Bank Research, International Topics, Current Issues.

Kern, S. (2010) The Role of SWFs – Towards a New Equilibrium, Edinburgh SWF Dialogue, 15 June 2010.

Khazanah (2011) Annual Review 2010, http://www.khazanah.com.my (3 February 2012).

Kim, W. (2011) Korea Investment Corporation: Its Origin and Evolution, *KDI School of Public Policy and Management, Working Paper 11–06*.

Kindleberger, C. (1978) *Manias, Panics, and Crashes: A History of Financial Crises*, Basic Books, New York.

Knight, F. H. (1921) *Risk, Uncertainty and Profit*, Houghton Mifflin Co., The Riverside Press, Boston, MA and New York, NY. Reprinted by Beard Books, Washington D.C., 2002, http://www.econlib.org/library/Knight/knRUP.html (3 February 2012).

Knight, M. and Scacciavillani, F. (1998) Current Account Deficits: What is Their Relevance for Policy Makers, *IMF Working Paper 98/71*.

Kondratiev, N. D. (1925) *The Major Economic Cycles* (in Russian), Moscow. Translated and published as *The Long Wave Cycle* by Richardson and Snyder, NY, 1984.

Krugman, P. (2008) More on Oil and Speculation, *The New York Times*, 13 May.

Kunzel, P., Lu, Y., Petrova, I. and Pihlman, J. (2011) Investment Objectives of Sovereign Wealth Funds – A Shifting Paradigm, *IMF Working Paper, WP/11/19*, http://www.imf.org/external/pubs/ft/wp/2011/wp1119.pdf (3 February 2012).

Lee, B. and Wang, A. (2011) Reevaluating the Role of Large Public Surpluses and Sovereign Wealth Funds in Asia, *Asian Development Bank Institute Working Papers, No. 287*.

LeRoy, S. F. and Singell, L. D. Jr (1987) Knight on Risk and Uncertainty, *Journal of Political Economy*, **95** (2), 394–406.

Livernois, J. (2009) On the Empirical Significance of the Hotelling Rule, *Review of Environmental Economics and Policy*, **3** (1), 22–41.

Machlup, F. (1966) The Need for Monetary Reserves, *BNL Quarterly Review*, **19**, 175–222.

Maddison, A. (2005) Measuring and Interpreting World Economic Performance 1500–2001, *Review of Income and Wealth*, **51** (1), 1–35.

Magnus, G. (2011) *Uprising, Will Emerging Markets Shape or Shake the World Economy?*, John Wiley & Sons, Chichester.

Magnus, G. and Castelli, M. (2006) Capital Flows and the World Economy: Petrodollars, Asia and the Gulf, UBS Investment Research, November.

Mandelbrot, B. (1982) *The Fractal Geometry of Nature*, Freeman, New York.

Mandelbrot, B. (1997a) *Fractals and Scaling in Finance: Discontinuity, Concentration and Risk*, Springer Verlag, New York.

Mandelbrot, B. (1997b) *Fractales, Hasard et Finance*, Flammarion, Paris, France.

Mateos y Lago, I., Duttagupta, R. and Goyal, R. (2009) The Debate on the International Monetary System, *IMF Staff Position Note, 09/26*, Washington, DC.

McKinsey Global Institute (2007) The New Power Brokers: How Oil, Asia, Hedge Funds, and Private Equity Are Shaping Global Capital Markets. www.mckinsey.com/insights/mgi.aspx (3 February 2012).

McKinsey Global Institute (2010) Farewell to Cheap Capital? The Implications of Long-term Shifts in Global Investment and Saving. www.mckinsey.com/insights/mgi.aspx (3 February 2012).

Mckinsey Global Institute (2011) Mapping Global Capital Markets 2011. www.mckinsey.com/insights/mgi.aspx (3 February 2012).

Mehrpouya, A., Huang, C. and Barnett, T. (2009) An Analysis of Proxy Voting and Engagement Policies and Practices of the Sovereign Wealth Funds, *IRRCi SWF Report prepared by RiskMetrics Group Inc., October*.

Miao, Y. and Liyan, H. (2011) Sovereign Wealth Funds in China: The Perspective of National Energy Strategy, *Energy Procedia*, **5**, 1187–91.

Milken Institute (2011) Structuring Israel's Sovereign Investment Fund, Financing the Nation's Future, *FinANCIAL Innovations LabTM Report*.

Ministry of Finance Chile (2010) Annual Report Sovereign Wealth Funds, http://www.minhda.cl/english/sovereign-wealth-funds/economic-and-social-stabilization-fund.html (2 February 2012).

Minsky, H. (1977) A Theory of Systemic Fragility, in *Financial Crisis: Institutions and Markets in a Fragile Environment* (eds E. I. Altman and A. W. Sametz), John Wiley & Sons, Ltd, New York.

Monk, A. (2011) The Appeal of Factor-Based Allocations, Oxford SWF Project.

Monitor Group (2008) Assessing the Risk: The Behavior of Sovereign Wealth Funds in the Global Economy, http://www.monitor.com/tabid/202/L/en-US/Default.aspx (2 February 2012).

Monitor Group (2011) *Braving the New World: Sovereign Wealth Fund Investment in the Uncertain Times of 2010* (eds V. Barbary and B. Bortolotti), Monitor.

Monitor Group and Fondazione Enrico Mattei (2009a) Sovereign Wealth Fund Investment Behavior: Analysis of Sovereign Wealth Fund Transactions during Q3 2009, http://www.monitor.com/tabid/202/L/en-US/Default.aspx (2 February 2012).

Monitor Group and Fondazione Enrico Mattei (2009b) Weathering the Storm: Sovereign Wealth Funds in the Global Crisis of 2008, http://www.monitor.com/tabid/202/L/en-US/Default.aspx (2 February 2012).

Monitor Group and Fondazione Enrico Mattei (2010a) Sovereign Wealth Fund Investment Behavior, *Semi-annual report January–June 2010*, http://www.monitor.com/tabid/202/L/en-US/Default.aspx (2 February 2012).

Monitor Group and Fondazione Enrico Mattei (2010b) Back on Course: Sovereign Wealth Fund Activity in 2009, http://www.monitor.com/tabid/202/L/en-US/Default.aspx (2 February 2012).

Murrey, D. (2011) SWFs: Myths and Realities, Keynote address at the Global Sovereign Wealth Funds Roundtable, Beijing, 4 May 2011.

New Zealand Superannuation Fund (2011) Annual Report 2010, http://www.nzsuperfund.co.nz (3 February 2012).

Norges Bank Investment Management (2011) Government Pension Fund Global Annual Report 2010, http://www.nbim.no (3 February 2012).

Norwegian Ministry of Finance (2011) The Norwegian Government Pension Fund Global's Adherence with the Santiago Principles, http://www.norges-bank.no (3 February 2012).

Obstfed, M. and Rogoff, K. (1996) The Intertemporal Approach to the Current Account, *NBER Working Papers* 4893, National Bureau of Economic Research.

OECD (2008) Sovereign Wealth Funds and Recipient Country Policies, Report by the OECD investment Committee adopted on 4 April 2008.

OECD (2011) *Pension Fund in Focus*, July 2011, Issue 8.

Ortiz, G. (2007) A Coordinated Strategy for Assets and Liabilities: The Mexican Perspective, in *Sovereign Wealth Management* (eds J. Johnson-Calari and M. Rietveld), Central Banking Publications, London.

Ossowski, R., Villafuerte, M., Medas P. and Thomas, T. (2008) Managing the Oil Revenue Boom: The Role of Fiscal Institutions, *IMF Occasional paper No. 260*, IMF Washington DC.

Park, D. (ed.) (2011) *Sovereign Asset Management for a Post Crisis World*, Central Banking Publications, London.

Petroleum Fund of Timor-Este (2011) Petroleum Fund Quarterly Report – 31 March 2011, http://www.laohamutuk.org/ (3 February 2012).

Posner, R. (2009) *A Failure of Capitalism: The Crisis of '08 and the Descent into Depression*, Harvard University Press, Cambridge, MA.

Prasad, E. S. (2011) Role Reversal in Global Finance, *NBER Working Paper No 17497*.

Prasad, E. S., Rahan, R. G. and Subramanian, A. (2007) Foreign Capital and Economic Growth, *NBER Working Paper 13619*.

Qingxiu, B. (2011) China's Sovereign Wealth Funds: Problem or Panacea?, *Journal of World Investment and Trade*, **11** (5), 849.

Quadrio Curzio, A. and Miceli, V. (2010) *Sovereign Wealth Funds: A Complete Guide to State-Owned Investment Funds*, Harriman, Petersfield, UK.

Quah, D. (2011) The Global Economy's Shifting Centre of Gravity, *Global Policy*, **2** (1), January.

Rachman, G. (2011) *Zero-Sum Future*, Simon & Schuster, New York.

Rattaggi, M. (2010) Crisis and Models: What should we learn?, http://ssrn.com/abstract=1647041

Reinhart, C. M. and Rogoff, K. S. (2009) *This Time is Different: Eight Centuries of Financial Folly*, Princeton University Press

Rose, H. D. and Hanemann, T. (2011) An American Open Door? Maximizing the Benefits of Chinese Foreign Direct Investment. Special Report of the Center on

US-China Relation Asia and the Kissinger Institute on China and the United States, http://asiasociety.org/policy/center-us-china-relations/american-open-door (3 February 2012).

Rozanov, A. (2007) *Sovereign Wealth Funds: Defining Liabilities*, State Street Global Advisors.

Rozanov, A. (2008) The Transparency of Sovereign Wealth Funds, in *The Gulf Region: A New Hub of Global Financial Power* (eds P. Subacchi and J. Nugée), Chatam House, London.

Rybinsky, K. and Krynska, U. (2010) Global Reserve Management, in *Central Bank Reserves & Sovereign Wealth Management* (eds A. B. Berkelaar, J. Coche and K. Nyholm), Palgrave Macmillan.

Saidi, N. and Scacciavillani, F. (2011) SWFs and the Ascent of Emerging Market Economies, in *Sovereign Asset Management for a Post-Crisis World* (ed. D. Park), Central Banking Publications, London.

Saidi, N., Scacciavillani, F. and Prasad, A. (2009) Wealth Effects in the GCC from Energy Commodity Prices, *Economic Note No. 6*, Dubai International Financial Center.

Santiso, J. (2011) SWFs and Latin America in 2010 and 2011, in *Braving the New World*, Monitor.

Scott, H. (Ed.) (2005) *Capital Adequacy beyond Basel: Banking, Securities, and Insurance*, Oxford University Press.

Sekine, E. (2011) The Governance of China Investment Corporation on Its Way to Becoming a Sophisticated Institutional Investor, *Nomura Journal of Capital Markets*, **2** (3), Winter.

Setser, B. and Ziemba, R. (2009) GCC Sovereign Wealth Funds. Reversal of Fortune, *Working Paper, Council for Foreign Relations, Centre for Geoeconomic Studies*.

Standard Chartered (2007) State Capitalism: the Rise of Sovereign Wealth Funds. Report.

Standard Chartered (2010) The Super-cycle Report, https://research.standardchartered.com/researchdocuments/Pages/ResearchArticle.aspx?&R=73895 (3 February 2012).

State Street (2009) Sovereign Wealth Funds Emerging from the Financial Crisis, *Vision*, **IV** (1).

Stiglitz, J. E. (2009) Death Cometh for the Greenback, *The National Interest*, November–December 2009.

Strauss-Kahn, D. (2010) IMF for the 21st Century, Bretton Woods Committee Annual Meeting, Washington DC, 26 February.

Subacchi, P. and Nugée, J. (eds) (2008) *The Gulf Region: A New Hub of Global Financial Power*, Chatam House, London.

Subacchi, P. (2008) GCC Sovereign Wealth Funds: a tale of two continents, in *The Gulf Region: a New Hub of Global Financial Power* (eds P. Subacchi and J. Nugée), Chatam House, London.

Sun, T. and Hesse, H. (2009) Sovereign Wealth Funds and Financial Stability – An Event Study Analysis, *IMF Working Paper, WP/09/239*, http://www.imf.org/external/pubs/ft/wp/2009/wp09239.pdf (3 February 2012).

Szegö, G. (ed.) (2004) *Risk Measures for the 21st Century*, John Wiley & Sons, Ltd, Chichester.

Taleb, N. N. (2010a) *The Black Swan*, 2nd edn, Penguin, New York.

Taleb, N. N. (2010b) Antifragility, Robustness, and Fragility, Inside the 'Black Swan' Domain, http://ssrn.com/abstract=1669317 (3 February 2012).

Tang, K. and Xiong, W. (2010) Index Investing and the Financialization of Commodities, Department of Economics, Princeton University, *Working Paper.*

Temasek (2011) Temasek Review 2010, http://www.temasek.com.sg/ (3 February 2012).

The Economist (2008) Asset-backed Insecurity, 19–25 January, pp. 63–65.

The Economist (2008) How to Spend It, 26 April–1 May, pp. 35–37.

Truman, E. M. (2007) A Scoreboard for Sovereign Wealth Funds. Paper presented at the Conference on China's Exchange Rate Policy, 19 October 2007, at the Peterson Institute for International Economics, Washington, DC.

Truman, E. M. (2008a) A Blueprint for Sovereign Wealth Fund Best Practices, Peterson Institute for International Economics, *PB08–3.*

Truman, E. M. (2008b) Sovereign Wealth Funds: New Challenges from a Changing Landscape. Testimony before the Subcommittee on Domestic and International Monetary Policy, Trade and Technology, Financial Services Committee, US House of Representatives, 10 September.

Truman, E. M. (2010) *Sovereign Wealth Funds, Threat or Salvation?*, Peterson Institute for International Economics.

Truman, E. M. (2011) Sovereign Wealth Funds: is Asia different?, Peter Institute for International Economics, *Working Paper Series, 11–12.*

UBS Global Economics Research (2011) *European Weekly Economic Focus.*

UBS Investment Research (2010) Portfolio for Sovereign Investors: What Does the Past Suggest about the Future? in Q-Series: Global Asset Allocation.

Van der Ploeg, R. and Venables, A. J. (2008) Harnessing Windfall Revenues: Optimal Policies for Resource-Rich Developing Economies, *Oxcarre WP 2008–8.*

Van der Ploeg, R. and Venables, A. J. (2010) Absorbing a Windfall of Foreign Exchange, *Oxcarre WP 2009.*

Venables, A. J. (2009) Resource Rents: When to Spend and How to Save, Paper presented at the International Institute of Public Finance Conference, Cape Town.

Walker, D. (2011) The Agency Challenge and Stewardship Opportunity, Address to the International Forum of Sovereign Wealth Funds in Beijing, 11 May 2011.

Wang, D. and Li, Q. (2011) When Clashes Spur Rules: Domestic Politics of Sovereign Wealth Institutionalization, Paper prepared for the Annual Meeting of the American Political Science Association, September 2011.

World Bank (2008) Report of the Commission on Growth and Development, World Bank, Washington, DC.

World Bank (2010) World Development Indicators Online, World Bank, Washington, DC, http://data.worldbank.org/data-catalog/worlddevelopment-indicators/wdi-2010 (3 February 2012).

World Bank (2011) Global Development Horizons 2011, Multipolarity: The New Global Economy.

World Economic Forum (2011) The Future of Long-term Investing, New York.

Xiaochuan, Z. (2009) Changing Pro-cyclicality for Financial and Economic Stability, Peoples Bank of China, 27 March, http://www.china.org.cn/business/2009-03/27/content_17509029.htm (3 February 2012).

Yergin, D. and Stanislaw, J. (1998) *The Commanding Heights: The Battle between Governments and the Marketplace that is Remaking the Modern World*, Simon & Schuster, New York.

Index